# SPIRIT AND SONG OF THE NEW LITURGY

# SPIRIT AND SONG

# OF THE NEW LITURGY

*by*

**Lucien Deiss, C.S.Sp.**

*Translated by*
*Lyla L. Haggard*
*and*
*Michael L. Mazzarese*

BK - 1939

**WORLD LIBRARY OF SACRED MUSIC**
2145 Central Parkway, Cincinnati, Ohio 45214

First published as *Concile et Chant Nouveau,* Editions du Levain, Paris, 1969.

English translation, copyright © 1970, World Library Publications, Inc. 2145 Central Parkway, Cincinnati, Ohio 45214. All rights reserved.

NIHIL OBSTAT:   Lawrence J. Mick
                     Censor Deputatus

IMPRIMATUR:   Most Rev. Paul F. Leibold
                     Archbishop of Cincinnati

August 4, 1970

ACKNOWLEDGMENTS:

All English translations of Vatican II texts throughout this publication are from *The Documents of Vatican II,* Walter M. Abbott, S.J., ed., © copyright 1966, America Press, New York. All rights reserved.

All citations from the Instructions of the Sacred Congregation of Rites of September 3, 1958, and of March 5, 1967, are taken from the United States Catholic Conference translations.

All scripture quotations are from *The Holy Bible,* English translation © copyright 1952, Confraternity of Christian Doctrine, Washington, D.C. All rights reserved.

Exerpts from the English translation of the General Instruction and Order of Mass, copyright © 1969, International Committee on English in the Liturgy, Inc. All rights reserved. Used with permission.

All musical examples © copyright 1964, 1965, 1970, World Library Publications, Inc., 2145 Central Parkway, Cincinnati, Ohio 45214. All rights reserved. Taken from collections: *Biblical Hymns and Psalms* (Deiss), volumes I and II, and the *People's Mass Book,* 1970 edition.

Library of Congress
Catalog Card Number:   79-143800

# About the Author

Father Lucien Deiss, renowned Scripture scholar and expert in sacred music, is indeed well qualified to comment on the recent liturgical reforms. Following study in Strasbourg, Paris, and Rome, he was named professor of Sacred Scripture at the seminary of Brazzaville (Congo). A specialist in the exegesis of the New Testament, he currently occupies the Chair of Sacred Scripture and Dogmatic Theology at the *Grand Scholasticat des Pères du Saint-Esprit* of Chevilly-Larue (Paris) and participated in the Second Vatican Council in Rome as an appointed liturgical expert. Long involved in liturgical music, Father Deiss was one of the founders of *l'Association Saint Ambroise,* an organization concerned with congregational singing, and is currently liturgical editor of the magazine "Assemblée Nouvelle." Father Deiss, a former student of Dom Suñol in Rome, has been awarded the *Grand Prix de l'Académie du Disque* and the *Prix Madame René Coty* for his recording of Langlais' *Messe Salve Regina.*

His numerous books, articles, and hymn collections indicate the erudition and wide sphere of influence of this French theologian — liturgist — composer. As a result of translations and recordings in English, Spanish, and even Chinese, his works are being read and his hymns are being sung throughout the world.

# EDITOR'S NOTE

*Father Lucien Deiss has long been a friend of the World Library of Sacred Music, and it is with great pride that we present this English edition. For their help and consultation, special appreciation is expressed to Paul W. Welch; Rev. Paschal Varnskuhler, O.F.M.; and Sister Kathleen Dougherty, S.S.M.N.*

*May this translation convey both the great scholarship and the charming personality of this witty Frenchman—who loves to sing the joy of the Lord.*

## RECORDINGS

*English:*
Like Olive Branches
Songs in Celebration
This Is the Day
With Joyful Lips

*Tapes and Cassettes*
The Choir in the New Liturgy
Homilies and Questions
Liturgy and Music

World Library of Sacred Music
Cincinnati, Ohio

*French:*
Acclame Dieu
Chante Ton Seigneur
En Eclats de Joie
Fille de Sion
Je Te Porte, Seigneur
Jour du Seigneur
La Nouvelle Jérusalem
Prières
Seigneur, Notre Joie
Un Seul Seigneur
Messe Salve Regina

Studio SM
Paris, France

*Spanish:*
Hija de Sion
Gloria a Ti, Señor
Un Solo Señor
Pueblo de Reyes

Edicion Berit
Madrid, Spain

# CONTENTS

### Chapter I

## THE "MUNUS MINISTERIALE" OR THE MINISTERIAL FUNCTION OF LITURGICAL SONG

**Chapter II**

# THE PARTICIPANTS IN THE LITURGICAL CELEBRATION

**Chapter III**

# THE DIRECTOR OF THE CONGREGATION

**Chapter IV**

# ACCLAMATIONS AND DIALOGUES

**Chapter V**

# THE RESPONSORIAL PSALM

### Chapter VI

# PROCESSIONAL SONGS

## Chapter VII

# THE LITANIES

## Chapter VIII

# HYMNS

## Chapter IX

# THE CREED

Chapter X

# THE READINGS

Chapter XI

# THE INSTRUMENTS

### Chapter XII

## NOTES ON GREGORIAN CHANT

# FOREWORD

This work is concerned with the liturgical reforms in the field of sacred music as instituted by the Second Vatican Council. The first section treats of what is our prime concern: the ministerial function of singing and music in the liturgy. The second section discusses the roles of those actively engaged in performing the music. Finally, the third and longest section centers its discussion on the various musical forms used in the celebration of the Eucharist, such as:

—acclamations and dialogues;

—the Responsorial Psalm;

—processional hymns at the Entrance, Gospel, Offertory, and Communion;

—the litanies of the Kyrie, General Intercessions, and the Agnus Dei;

—the hymns, which are the Gloria, the hymn based on the Gospel, the hymn of praise and thanksgiving, and the recessional;

—the Profession of Faith in the Credo;

—the readings;

—the use of instruments and a discussion of Gregorian Chant.

It is not the purpose of this work to give a detailed list of all the reforms instituted up till now. Such a list would soon become obsolete. What is more desirable is the presentation of the *principles behind such reforms,* principles which explain the steps already taken and which, to some extent, predict future ones.

Obviously, liturgical reform is not something which can be instituted once and for all, for all generations to come. A "modern" liturgy necessarily limited to one time and one place will soon become just as archaic as that which it replaces. What is new today will be old tomorrow. Let us say, rather, that the liturgy is the "prayer" of the ecclesiastical community, a community which is forever moving toward the Lord and striving for a new fullness by continually searching to deepen its faith, strengthen its love, and solidify its hope in a world that is perpetually in a state of flux.

The Church, the ageless Bride of Christ Jesus (2 Cor. 11:3), has never ceased growing in the beauty of her youth. This is why her prayer, which expresses her dialogue with the Lord, has never stopped conceiving new forms to show her love each new day. A young girl who refuses to change her style of dress or hairdo will very quickly and quite literally become an "old lady"; in refusing to grow up, she will quickly grow old. Likewise, a Church that refuses to wear her new spring robes will quickly become old before her time and her face will be ugly and wrinkled, a face which should be the world's constant reflection of the beauty of Christ himself. For her, then, it must always be springtime, a time of renewal, and her face must always have the grace of a young girl "holy and without blemish." (Eph. 5:27)

Consequently, a revision of the liturgy is always necessary; a reform must always be present. Certainly, the truths God has revealed are eternal; his revelation, as we find it in the Holy Scriptures, is fixed in an immutable form for all ages. But our knowledge of these values remains fragmentary and is progressive. Likewise, the theology which presents this knowledge to the world is evolving and remains subject to various changes. Therefore the Council stated:

> Her (the Church's) purpose has been to adapt the gospel to the grasp of all as well as to the needs of the learned, insofar as such was appropriate. Indeed, this accommodated preaching of the revealed Word ought to remain the law of all evangelization.[1]

Indeed, the liturgical celebration, which expresses the Christian mystery, should also be *adapted to the celebrating community*. Divine truths are received from heaven, but the language and the music used to express them are derived from the community itself. Thus our liturgical dialogue with God utilizes the riches of man's everyday dialogue with his neighbor.

Obviously, too, when studying the principles of reform, we are often led to cite older liturgical documents. This is not merely nostalgia, but the utilization of tradition to help us understand the future. It is the foot-worn path that reveals the direction to be taken. Therefore, the more we strive toward a renewed liturgy, the more we must acquaint ourselves with the past in order to recognize its lines of force.

It should be stated, then, that the liturgical reform of Vatican II does not deny the history of the Church, but is, instead, adapting her liturgy to the present situation. It is not unmindful of her past grandeur, nor does it wish to throw a veil of forgetfulness over her past negligences and weaknesses. Both are remembered. For the face of the Church herself reflects the glory of her past as well as the scars of her negligence. However, what we wish to emphasize is that no liturgical reform is to be a mere criticism of her past, and that we have better things to do than to drench our memory of her failures with tears of remorse. We must construct the present.

Nor, while seeking and discovering new things, do we necessarily *scorn* the old ones; we simply note that they are little, if at all, suited to our own time. Indeed, it is precisely because the past has transmitted certain realizations to us that today we are able to envision our own new reforms!

For the man who peers into the future, a look backward into the past is filled with peace and understanding. Formerly we used to celebrate the Mass in a certain manner; today, however, we celebrate it in a different manner. Formerly we traveled mainly by carriage or wagon; today, however, we travel by airplane. Yet this does not necessarily mean that we are criticizing in any way those people who traveled by carriage or wagon! Likewise, when a young girl of twenty dons her wedding gown, she is not criticizing the pinafore she wore when she was a child of ten. Similarly, when the Church dons her liturgical "gown" of the twentieth century and finds herself adorned with a new beauty, she does not find fault with the gown she used to wear in the past! On the contrary, the Church in every age is made beautiful only by the very splendor of Jesus Christ — a fact which tells us also that modesty and humility must be integral parts of the liturgical reform.

However, we are by no means merely pioneers in the search for the hidden mysteries of the past centuries. Our task is simply to adapt the Church's liturgy to present-day demands. Nor should we think that reform is an end in itself. The purpose of any movement is not change for change's sake, but the attainment of the goal desired. Today the goal of our liturgical reform is to celebrate the solemn mystery of the reality of the Father, through the Son, in the unity of the Spirit. Every reform we institute is to be judged in the light of this transcendent end alone. Therefore it is of prime concern that we change first our hearts and then only, the notes on the page.

Lucien Deiss, C.S.Sp.

On the Feast of Mary, Queen of Heaven
"Mother of my Lord" (Luke 1:43)

*For their help and consultation, special appreciation is expressed to:*

*Paul W. Welch*
*Rev. Paschal Varnskuhler, O. F. M.*
*Sister Kathleen Dougherty, S. S. M. N.*

# CHAPTER I

# The
# "MUNUS MINISTERIALE"

## The Ministerial Function of Liturgical Song

## A. The Question

### 1. AN IMPORTANT QUESTION

From the beginning of Chapter VI of the *Constitution on the Sacred Liturgy,* the chapter devoted to sacred music, the Second Vatican Council was concerned with the question of the ministerial function: " . . . the Roman pontiffs, . . . led by St. Pius X, have explained more precisely the ministerial function *(munus ministeriale)* rendered by sacred music in the service of the Lord."[1]

We see from the very first paragraph of the 1967 Instruction that the Council studied precisely this question:

> Sacred music, in those aspects which concern the liturgical renewal, was carefully considered by the Second Vatican Ecumenical Council. It explained its role in divine services, issued a number of principles and laws on this subject in the Constitution on the Liturgy, and devoted to it an entire chapter of the same constitution.[2]

And in the second paragraph, the Instruction itself is presented as a response to questions touching upon the ministerial function:

> The decisions of the Council have already begun to be put into effect in the recently undertaken liturgical renewal. But

the new norms concerning the arrangement of the sacred rites and the active participation of the faithful have given rise to several problems regarding sacred music and its ministerial role. These problems appear to be able to be solved by ex- pounding more fully certain relevant principles of the Con- stitution on the Liturgy.[3]

This emphasizes the importance the ministerial function enjoys in the current thought of the Church. In fact, it is at the heart of every question raised in relation to liturgical reform and, more precisely, to the problems posed by music.

The expression "ministerial function" is a literal but useful trans- lation of the Latin *munus ministeriale*. The word *munus* denotes duty or function; the adjective *ministeriale* (which has the same root as *munus*) evokes a similar idea of service. In the liturgy, the *munus ministeriale* or the ministerial function of a person or thing is the particular service given to the community in celebration of the liturgy. Thus the ministerial function of the reader is to pro- claim God's word; that of the chalice is to hold the wine for the Eucharist. What, then, is the ministerial function of music, or of particular songs, in the liturgical celebration?

This matter of the ministerial function is much like the simple yet important question a child asks when faced with an unfamiliar object: "What is it for? What does it do?" Liturgically, why have an Entrance Hymn? A Responsorial Psalm? An Agnus Dei?

The ministerial function constantly challenges each song and each rite concerning its reason for existing.

If the microphone in a church doesn't work, of course it is re- placed. When the lector stammers or reads incorrectly he, of course, must be replaced. And when a song or ritual can no longer achieve its purpose, what other conclusion can be drawn? Obviously, it must be replaced with some other song or ritual. In fact, even to ask such a question about ministerial function is to begin a permanent inquiry into the very heart of the liturgy, confronting "head on" every kind of formalism, rubricism, and traditionalism. Not that the ministerial function is opposed to rubrics; rather it accepts only those forms which actually fulfill their intended *purpose*. It does not rise up against tradition, but it will accept only what serves the present-day community.

## 2. A CURRENT QUESTION

The liturgy has always been aware of the ministerial function, even though in different eras it was judged by different criteria. History itself dictates that, in the liturgical celebration, no ritual or song whatsoever may be kept unless it fulfills a well-defined function. It will thus be most deeply rooted in the liturgy only when its ministerial function is perfectly fulfilled. Otherwise, it degenerates into meaningless gestures and is soon swept away by the inexorable tide of history. Such is the hard but sound law of survival. In the liturgy of pre-council times, the problem of ministerial function in its entirety did not arise; it was not spotlighted as it is now.

Why not? Because post-Tridentine liturgy was embedded in an unquestionable immobility which was accepted as hierarchical and soon became tradition. It was plagued with a sterility that caused it to avoid facing the new problems raised by new situations; indeed, it repeatedly gave only old answers to these new problems, coupled with a warning against "modernism." The tidal wave of the Protestant Reformation against Roman rubrics had been so profound and so dangerous that it seemed better to hold on to existing codes at all costs rather than take the risk of drowning in any new experience. The rubrics were not questioned, for the answers were already known. The Council of Trent had affirmed:

> If anyone claims that the rituals received and approved by the Catholic Church in the solemn administration of the sacraments can be held up to ridicule or that they can be omitted at the discretion of the minister without committing sin, or that they can be exchanged for new forms by any parochial pastor, let him be anathema.[4]

The anathema applied even to a bishop who might try to make any kind of changes in the ritual. Thus, going one step further, it was concluded that these rituals could never be changed because they were perfect. As a matter of fact, the format of the Mass has remained unchanged since the time of its promulgation by St. Pius V, on July 14, 1570, a span of four centuries.[5] In addition, the Church has not always escaped the temptation to admire herself in her rubrics and to marvel at the work of her rubricists. At times, she lagged behind in complacency while the world continued to evolve, progress, and change. After reading some of her pre-Council statements, one would think that there was no problem save that of adapting the world to the Church and holding the faithful obedient to its directives. Occasionally it could be justly proud of the fact that a certain uniformity was established which limited extreme individuality among the celebrants.

Since the Motu Proprio, *Tra le Sollecitudini,* of St. Pius X, November 22, 1903, followed by the Holy Week reforms of Pius XII, and culminating in the *Constitution on the Sacred Liturgy* of Vatican II, Christians have learned that the evolution of the liturgy and sacred music need not place one's faith in danger, but can strengthen it, deepen it, and express it more perfectly than before.

The Constitution fearlessly states:

> Holy Scripture, indeed, has bestowed praise upon sacred song,
> and the same may be said of the Fathers of the Church and
> of the Roman pontiffs who in recent times, led by St. Pius X,
> have explained more precisely the ministerial function rendered
> by sacred music in the service of the Lord.[6]

"In recent times . . . more precisely . . . " — do not these words
affirm that there has been an evolution toward a more conscientious look at the ministerial function? This deeper understanding
of the ministerial function of sacred music has not made the Pontiffs its sole beneficiaries; rather, all Catholics will benefit. For a
long time, specialists had been studying and teaching the liturgical
function of music in such a way that the people began to long for
an Introit that would really be an Entrance Song, or for a Kyrie
that would really be a litany of supplication, a Sanctus that would
be the Eucharistic acclamation of people in festive celebration. In
brief, there had arisen in the Church an immense thirst for liturgical authenticity.

Another factor which has effected a more conscientious approach
to the ministerial function was the change from Latin to modern
languages. English places the liturgical texts in the spotlight. This
is a harsh test of truth where no deceit is possible. Texts which
are passable in Latin become beautiful in English; those that are
weak in Latin are revealed to be intolerable in English. Latin had
hidden both the splendors and the weaknesses of the texts. Now
shorn of the halo of mystery with which Latin surrounded the
songs, defrocked of their Gregorian cloak, the texts are presented
to the liturgical community as they really are: marvelous, banal,
or mediocre.

At times, this revelation is brutal. Here, for example, is the Introit
from the Mass *Intret in conspectu tuo* [Ps. 79(78): 10-11], for the
feast of several martyrs:

> Let the prisoners' sighing come before you, O Lord;
> repay our neighbors sevenfold into their bosoms;
> avenge the blood of your saints
> which has been shed.

This text, seen in a modern language and recited aloud in the
liturgical community, can in no way be used as an Entrance Song
for a Eucharistic celebration. It is plainly a song of vengeance, as
mediocre in Latin as it is in the vernacular. For English shouts
aloud what the Latin half whispers in the vacillating tones of
Gregorian chant. Obviously, this text does not fulfill its ministerial
function.

Here is another example, the *Dies Irae* from the Mass of the Dead. We know how the melodic line of this chant can be suppliant, dramatic, or peaceful. But from the very first stanza on, the liturgical community is thrown headlong into this Christian feeling:

A day of wrath that day will be.
It will dissolve the world into glowing ashes,
as David and the Sibyl have testified.[7]

Christian thought does not consider as a "day of wrath" that day when the faithful, in the mystery of their "Pasch," meet their God as a child does his father. Indeed, the word of God recognizes "days of wrath," but only those days when the wrath of God falls exclusively upon the enemies of Israel and those who refuse to be converted.[8] For the just, the eschatological day is a day of light and joy, a day filled with that divine peace so wonderfully sung in the Introit, *Requiem aeternam*. The person who is faithful and who, like Jesus, places his soul in the hands of his Father, finds not the wrath but the love of God. The day of his death is not one of terror, as the first line of the *Dies irae* would have us believe, but a day of triumph as the morning star arises in his heart.[9] As for the Sibyl, whose testimony is invoked along with that of David's, Christians fortunately have not believed in her for some time![10] Thus it is clear that this text, too, could not fulfill the ministerial function attached to it by the rubrics.

## B. Defining the Ministerial Function

The question presented here is this: which criteria are to determine the ministerial function of liturgical music in general and of certain hymns in particular? What are the principles that allow us to understand and judge the liturgical value of a song? In other words, who can define the function of a Kyrie, a Sanctus, or an Agnus Dei? Who can tell us whether this function is being effectively realized?

The ministerial function is defined as:

— On the one hand, the function of the liturgy itself, as it is understood and interpreted by authority according to tradition and its law.

— On the other, the function of the congregation itself which celebrates the mysteries of Christ.

Each of these two references points to the same reality: the people of God celebrating Christ. In fact, the liturgy, according to the teaching of Vatican II, is:

. . . considered as an exercise of the priestly office of Jesus Christ. In the liturgy the sanctification of man is manifested by signs perceptible to the senses, and is effected in a way which is proper to each of these signs; in the liturgy full public worship is performed by the Mystical Body of Jesus Christ, that is, by the Head and His members.[11]

Because the liturgy is the means by which the public worships, it is subject to the authority which holds the legislative power in this area: "Regulation of the sacred liturgy depends solely on the authority of the Church; that is, on the Apostolic See and, as laws may determine, on the bishop."[12]

But it is clear that such decrees are made only for the general welfare of the people. They have no other purpose than the improvement of the liturgical celebration and are meant to be of greater service to the people. The power behind this authority is delegated solely for the improvement of the whole community.

Of course, as history has shown, there can arise a certain tension between those who legislate and those who obey. This happens either when the legislative power is exercised without discretion or without any relevancy to the real situation of the people, or when the people, due to indifference or plain laziness, neglect to regulate their worship according to the accepted norms. Ordinarily, in times of liturgical peace and rubrical tranquility, the governing head and the obeying members — being complements — are continually in dialogue with each other. Together they form the same body; they constitute the same Church of Jesus Christ.

H. Schmidt writes:

> Throughout the Constitution on the holy liturgy, it is the whole Church who speaks, the Mystical Body of Christ, the Head and members; it is Christ himself speaking, he in whom all the members are one.[13]

By defining the ministerial function in terms of the liturgy itself, as understood and interpreted by authority, and in reference to the very congregation involved in the celebration, the ministerial function is forever defined in relation to only one reality: the people of God celebrating Jesus Christ.

## 1. THE FUNCTION OF THE LITURGY ITSELF

The ministerial function is first of all defined in relation to the liturgy itself, as understood and proposed by authority, and according to law and tradition.

The tradition of the Church, i.e., the laws promulgated by competent authority and the directives they give, assigns a special function to each hymn. Therefore, when the Instruction on *Music in the Liturgy* states that the Sanctus is an acclamation to be sung by all the people and that the Responsorial Psalm belongs to the Liturgy

of the Word, the ministerial function of these two songs is defined
in line with both the traditional interpretation and modern enact-
ment.[14]

Elsewhere the Instruction formulates what could be considered
the golden rule of the ministerial function:

> An authentic organization of the liturgical celebration demands
> that the sense and nature of each part and of each chant be
> carefully observed.[15]

To follow this golden rule — which is actually just a rule of
common sense — is to realize the true ministerial function of each
song. Very much like the service performed by a good servant,
each song of the liturgical celebration must fulfill the role assigned
to it by the liturgy according to its laws and traditions.

As this golden rule points out with great acuity, each song must
also be evaluated in the light of the role of music in general. Consider
the role of the music in the Gloria or in the proclamation of the
Gospel. It is not simply a question of "making the liturgy more
beautiful" by adding more music, nor of "making it more simple"
by reducing the music's importance, but rather of "making it more
true." Music should aid each part of the liturgy to fulfill its ministerial function.

Take, for example, the solemn words of the Lord's Supper, which
are the heart of the Eucharistic celebration. The oldest tradition,
as presented in the testimony of Paul,[16] bequeathed us this text in
a hierarchical form, closer to poetry and rhythmic prose than to
the actual wording. From antiquity, then, the oriental liturgies have
justly dreamed of singing this text in very sober and solemn tones.
It is just as valid for the liturgy of the present time to offer this
same possibility. But *what* melody should be used? Obviously, if
these words of the Last Supper were sung in the Palestrinian style,
in four-part harmony, they would be very rich — infinitely richer
than a simple tune of only a few notes. However, Palestrinian music
would not realize the ministerial function of these words. Why?
Because it is the proclamation of the sacrament which is being
fulfilled. Obviously, too, if this piece were sung by a choir of young
girls with angelic voices, the chanting of "This is my Body — this
is the cup of my Blood" could not fulfill its ministerial function
because such a chant is a presidential proclamation to be made
only by the priest, who alone has received sacerdotal consecration.

Of course, this example is quite obvious. But perhaps more
pointed questions should be raised. If the Gloria is a hymn, is it
not necessary to enrich its musical aspect a bit further? If the Profession of Faith is truly a profession of faith, should it be sung
with so many notes? The Kyrie and the Agnus Dei are litanies; how
are they to be treated? In short, the question of ministerial function

forces us to reconsider each hymn in light of the liturgical reforms of Vatican II.

It can be considered filial devotion to Church tradition to think that certain pieces from the traditional repertory fulfill their ministerial function well. However, it is not at all irreverent to feel that some other pieces, even under the best possible circumstances, are inefficacious. The fact is that these pieces were composed in a liturgical atmosphere which was not necessarily the same as that of Vatican II. This holds equally true for both the Gregorian mode and the classical polyphonic repertory. A number of such examples are readily available.

The wonderful melody of the Kyrie from the Mass *Fons bonitatis* is well-known. This ardent supplication, rising toward God with every phrase and coming to rest at his feet, used to be sung on great feast days in almost every seminary. Tradition had thus enriched it with a great esthetic and religious intensity. However, the *Ite missa est* of this Mass uses the very same melody, raising the question: should the Kyrie be said in the same way as "Go in the peace of Christ"? In all honesty, should we really dismiss the liturgical congregation with the same melody as the one used to implore God's mercy? The ministerial function of these two parts is obviously different; should we, therefore, sing the same melody for both? If a certain melody is unique in its beauty, shouldn't it be reserved for one special function only?

Consider the lengthy melody of the Gradual and Tract given in the Roman Gradual for the first Sunday of Lent. It consists of four pages of music for Psalm 91(90)! Can we say that these four pages fulfill their ministerial function when the text of the word of God is completely lost in the meanderings of the melody? Do they effectively "proclaim" this wonderful Psalm 91(90) which is cited in the gospels and which, according to the liturgy, accompanies the Christian community all through Lent even up to the Lord's Passion and Resurrection? How many parishes really sing the whole thing?

Consider any Mass by Palestrina. Notice how the litany of the Kyrie; the hymn, Gloria; the Profession of Faith; the acclamation, Sanctus; as well as the litany of the Agnus Dei are constructed upon the same melodic themes and along the same stylistic pattern. It is evident that Palestrina, whose music rings out like a festive bell from the Kyrie to the Agnus Dei, did not envisage the ministerial function in the same way as Vatican II. Or rather, the ministerial function he assigned to each piece in his Masses was different from that set forth by Vatican II. This takes absolutely nothing away from the glory of him whom Pius XI called the uncontested master of 16th century polyphony.[17] It simply means that we today must use a certain amount of discernment in using his compositions.

It is not enough for a piece of music to be called a "treasure" of sacred music for it automatically to achieve its ministerial function. Each case must be examined individually. If certain pieces, handed down through the centuries, still realize their ministerial function today, they should be kept and joyfully utilized, "taking into consideration pastoral usefulness and the caracter of their own language."[18] But these very same local conditions and this same pastoral usefulness can encourage a community to seek new solutions which better conform to the new laws and requirements of the liturgy.[19] In short, there are no longer universal solutions which apply to every particular situation. There is now only one universal principle — that of the ministerial function, which should be realized in every particular case.

## 2. THE FUNCTION OF THE CELEBRATING COMMUNITY

The liturgical celebration does not exist by itself; it comes alive only when experienced by a living congregation. The ministerial function, then, is more than an outgrowth of laws and liturgical tradition; it is the direct relationship with a particular congregation which is celebrating *hic et nunc*.

The *Constitution on the Sacred Liturgy* of Vatican II marks a decisive step in the history of the active participation of the people. It boldly states:

> By way of promoting active participation, the people should be encouraged to take part by means of acclamations, responses, psalmody, antiphons, and songs, as well as by actions, gestures, and bodily attitudes. And at the proper times all should observe a reverent silence.[20]

The Instruction on *Music in the Liturgy* of March 5, 1967, attempts to apply this decision of the Council without restriction. No previous Roman document has ever been so concerned with the people. None has so persistently taken into account what and how the people are thinking, their desires, or their capabilities.

> In selecting the kind of sacred music to be used, whether it be for the choir or for the people, *the capacities of those who are to sing the music must be taken into account.*[21]

> In order that the faithful may actively participate more willingly and with greater benefit, it is fitting that the format of the celebration and the degrees of participation in it should be varied as much as possible, according to the solemnity of the day *and the nature of the congregation present.*[22]

> The faithful fulfill their liturgical role by making that *full, conscious and active participation.*[23]

One cannot find anything more religious and more joyful in sacred celebrations than a whole *congregation expressing its faith and devotion in song.*[24]

The formulation of the whole people in singing should be seriously and patiently undertaken . . . according to the age, status and way of life of the faithful, and the degree of their religious culture . . . . [25]

Pastors of souls, having taken into consideration pastoral usefulness and the character of their own language, should see whether parts of the heritage of sacred music, written in previous centuries for Latin texts, could also be conveniently used . . . in liturgical celebrations . . . performed in the vernacular.[26]

It is important to stress the newness of these directives. Liturgical music is judged here with respect to the community singing it; its efficacy is measured in this way. Before our time, the rubrics had rarely taken the community itself into consideration; they were more interested in knowing whether the singing conformed, not to the spirit of the people, but to the letter of the law. The entire community of Christians throughout the world, regardless of its desires, had to sing the same Gregorian melodies: for example, the triple Alleluia from the Mass of the Paschal Vigil. The Christians of India were right to protest: "We do not like this melody; it seems very strange to us. We prefer to use the five notes of our pentatonic system. How pretty those five notes are! But the seven notes of your western scale and this Alleluia seem as distasteful to us as would one of our young girls who might dress in American style in shorts or slacks!" The rubrics replied: "That doesn't make any difference! You must sing it anyway — as written!" From the jungles of Africa came this plea: "Please, a little more rhythm for this Alleluia! Rhythm is our joy. That is how we like to sing of the resurrected Christ. But your Alleluia surely resembles a funeral march! And, what's more, we don't even have any books to use!" The rubrics replied: "That doesn't make any difference! You must sing it anyway — as written — even if you don't have any books!" A suburban parish explained: "We can never manage to sing this Alleluia together. Instead of expressing the union of hearts, this song 'turns us off.' Our voices slide over these notes as they would over ice!" The rubrics still responded: "That doesn't make any difference! You must sing it anyway — as written!" Now, however, the Church's new and continual reference to the congregation and its pastorial advantage creates a new situation.

Liturgical music seems to be leaving the paralyzing prison of tradition and stepping into the life of the Christian people. In the past, rubrics said: "Look at the book of Gregorian chant I've given you!" Now they say: "Look to the congregation." Obviously, then, the best music is not necessarily that which is considered best in the rubrics; it is that which is best for a particular congregation.

Certainly, there is still much to be done in this new area. It is not a question of liberating us from the rubrics; rather, the rubrics must help the community. We must not become impatient at the delays we encounter; rather, we should be happy that a start has finally been made.

## C. Ministerial Functions

Liturgical song fulfills its ministerial function by *performing a service* to the liturgy, on the one hand, and to the community celebrating it, on the other. This poses the following question: what are the services liturgical music renders to the community celebrating the liturgy? The Instruction on *Music in the Liturgy* says:

> Liturgical worship is given a more noble form when it is celebrated in song, with the ministers of each degree fulfilling their ministry and the people participating in it.

> Indeed, through this form, prayer is expressed in a more attractive way, the mystery of the liturgy, with its hierarchical and community nature, is more openly shown, the unity of hearts is more profoundly achieved by the union of voices, minds are more easily raised to heavenly things by the beauty of the sacred rites, and the whole celebration more clearly prefigures that heavenly liturgy which is enacted in the holy city of Jerusalem.[27]

This instruction is a synthesis of various statements contained in previous documents. The different "ministries" of song can be classified under the following titles:

— music is an element of solemnity;
— it increases the effectiveness of the texts;
— it enhances the liturgical celebration with beauty;
— it is a unifying element for the congregation.

## 1. MUSIC IS AN ELEMENT OF SOLEMNITY

In the Motu Proprio *Tra le Sollecitudini* of November 22, 1903, St. Pius X states: "Sacred music, being an integral part of the liturgy . . . enhances the beauty and splendor of the ceremonies of the Church."[28]

Some fifty years later, in the encyclical *Musicae Sacrae Disciplina* of December 25, 1955, Pius XII said: "The dignity and lofty purpose of sacred music consist in the fact that its lovely melodies and splendor beautify and embellish the voices of the priest who offers Mass and of the Christian people who praise the Sovereign God."[29]

The *Constitution on the Sacred Liturgy* of Vatican II states that sacred music ". . . enriches sacred rites with heightened solemnity."[30]

The Instruction on *Music in the Liturgy* of March 5, 1967, finally teaches:

> Liturgical worship is given a more noble form when it is celebrated in song, with the ministers of each degree fulfilling their ministry and the people participating in it.[31]

> It should be borne in mind that the true solemnity of liturgical worship depends less on a more ornate form of singing and a more magnificent ceremonial than on its worthy and religious celebration, which takes into account the integrity of the liturgical celebration itself, and the performance of each of its parts according to their own particular nature.[32]

The last Instruction completes and goes beyond the preceding texts by enriching them with a new element. The "noblesse" and solemnity of the liturgical celebration are judged in the light of their true ritualistic function and not simply from the standpoint of a "magnificent pageant." The celebration is "more noble" when each participant — the presiding minister, the reader, the cantor, and the people — participates according to his own function; in this way both the hierarchical character and also the common bond of the liturgical congregation are most clearly manifested.

The progress shown in such a statement can more readily be seen in comparison with pre-conciliar documents. Previously, a celebration was considered solemn if the rubrics for a Solemn Mass were followed, even if the people were not present or did not participate. The Instruction on *Sacred Music and the Sacred Liturgy*, September 3, 1958, defined the solemnity of Mass in an excessively clerical manner, referring only to the music sung by the priest with the help of the "sacred ministers," without any reference whatsoever to the people:

> The Mass is called a "sung Mass" if the priest celebrant actually sings the parts which are to be sung according to the rubrics, otherwise it is a "read Mass." Furthermore, if a sung Mass is celebrated with the assistance of sacred ministers, it is called a *solemn* Mass. If it is celebrated without the sacred ministers, it is called a "Missa cantata."[33]

And so, for example, one could have had a Requiem High Mass even when there was no one to celebrate it except one priest with the responses of a spinster-organist. But, on the other hand, even if there were a thousand of the faithful in dialogue with the priest and singing their assigned parts, the Mass was still considered a Low Mass simply because the priest was reading instead of singing. Vatican II sounded the death knell for such bizarre rubrical practices. For the rubrics must also reflect life as it is lived. They did not create the liturgy, but exist only to facilitate its celebration.

To say that singing carries with it a note of solemnity is also to ask this question of each community at each celebration: has every song effectively enriched the celebration? It is quite possible to have people singing at times simply out of habit, without any enthusiasm and without any real merit. Today we sing in the vernacular simply because we once were obliged to sing the same songs in Latin. The following rule should be followed: every time the quality of the music is not equal in value to the quality of the silence it is breaking, it is better not to sing at all. To state this in a positive way: it is always necessary to sing with such perfection that the community will be *edified,* in the most beautiful sense of that word. Vatican II will hopefully bring about an end to all poorly performed music.

## 2. SINGING INCREASES THE EFFECTIVENESS OF THE TEXT

In his encyclical, St. Pius X discusses this subject:

> And since its chief duty is to clothe the liturgical text, which is presented to the understanding of the faithful, with suitable melody, its own special object is to make that text more efficacious so that the faithful through this means may be more easily moved to devotion and the better disposed to receive the fruits of grace which have their one source in the celebrabration of the holy mysteries.[34]

According to the *Constitution on the Sacred Liturgy,* "sacred music gives a sweeter expression to prayer *(orationem suavius exprimens)."*[35] The Instruction of March 5, 1967, expresses the same idea in identical terms.[36]

The very "clerical" manner in which the Constitution and the Instruction are expressed is undoubtedly regrettable. For the adjective "sweeter," which is part of this clerical vocabulary, has little impact upon present-day men and women. Of course, the fundamental idea is unquestionably sound: through its "sweetness," singing gives the texts a greater effect; clothing them in splendor makes them more persuasive. Singing is to the spoken word what poetry is to prose, or what an artist's painting is to a photograph. And, in the eyes of the Church, this fact has a certain importance. Thus, the Church recalls that God himself made use of poetry throughout his Word. Two-thirds of the Bible, including the more important revelations, is clothed in poetic splendor and rhythmic beauty.

The concern to make the texts more effective through the magic of music is not at all new, as the quotation of St. Pius X demonstrates. What is new since Vatican II, however, is the approach to the problem. According to pre-conciliar texts, the reasoning probably ran along these lines:

— Singing increases the effectiveness of the texts;
— Gregorian chant and polyphonic music are the songs of the Church (Roman rite);
— therefore, Gregorian chant and polyphonic music of the 16th century increase the effectiveness of the texts.

The Church now asks that the community be taken into account; that is, it is necessary to determine whether a particular song in a particular community will effectively achieve its ministerial function. We can no longer content ourselves with abstract reasons in this matter or with authoritative statements. A melody can, indeed, be more or less "sweet," tasteful to one type of congregation, yet repulsive to another; a syncopated rhythm can be most pleasing to an African ear but a shattering experience to a European one; a dissonant harmony can seem quite pleasant or extremely irritating, depending on the degree of musical sophistication of the listener.

The effectiveness of a song, its ministerial function, is then relative to the community.

This is particularly applicable in view of the many different cultures which do not necessarily like the same melodies. In *Musicae Sacrae Disciplina,* Pius XII stated that:

> . . . from all antiquity, the Catholic Church has always wanted to spread not only its sacred rites but its music as well, whenever messengers of the Gospel were sent out to regions where the light of faith had not yet shone. Gregorian chant will attract these people to the faith by its melodic nature and thus more easily persuade them to embrace the truths of the Christian religion.[37]

The present evolution of liturgical music in the mission countries reveals that Pius XII's judgement about the "sweetness" of Gregorian melodies (in other words, European melodies) was just a bit too optimistic. The extraordinary flourishing of native musical creations shows that the missionary communities, in Africa and elsewhere, were only waiting for a sign from the Church to sing Christ in their particular music, a music which completely fulfills its ministerial function. This in no way means that other communities throughout the world who have grown accustomed to the Gregorian melodies must now abandon them. On the contrary, the same reasoning which suggests that some communities create new melodies may suggest that other retain traditional melodies — and this reasoning is the basis of the ministerial function of music.

## 3. MUSIC ENHANCES THE LITURGY WITH BEAUTY

Here is another "service" rendered to the liturgy by music. Since it is a true art form, it endows the liturgical celebration with the indispensible elements of beauty and splendor.

In *Tra le Sollecitudini,* St. Pius X reacted quite strongly to the mundane trivia which dominated the liturgical music of his time. When he speaks of a *Tantum Ergo* whose first stanza is a cavatina and whose second is an allegro, we can easily see the low level to which the music of his day had fallen. Pius, it seems, wanted Church music to be a true art and to possess excellence of form.[38]

Pius XI wanted an artistic clergy. In *Divini Cultus* he asks that seminarians be trained in:

> . . . that more studied art which could more appropriately be called "esthetic," in Gregorian melody and musical art as well as polyphony and the organ, which should be in the clerical domain.[39]

In a mixture of Roman lyricism and clerical emphasis, Pius XII writes:

> The dignity and sublime goal of sacred music consists of this: through its very beautiful tonal effects and its sheer magnificence, it must embellish and enhance both the voice of the priest offering the sacrifice and at the same time that of the Christian people who are praising the Almighty; it raises the hearts of the faithful to God through its own impetus and through a sort of intrinsic virtue; it makes the liturgical prayers of the Christian community more alive and more fervent in order that God, One in Three, can be praised and invoked by all with greater strength, fervor, and efficacy . . . through its art it gives the entire ritual a more splendid appearance.[40]

A better formulation of this ministerial function of music is contained in the Instruction on *Music in the Liturgy* of March 5, 1967:

> . . . minds are more easily raised to heavenly things by the beauty of the sacred rites, and the whole celebration more clearly prefigures that heavenly liturgy which is enacted in the holy city of Jerusalem.[41]

The Instruction clearly emphasizes the "service" that music contributes to the liturgy: it leads man to God. For man on his way to God needs song and music. He needs beauty in order to contemplate God and sing forth his name. His devotion cannot live on theology and rubrics alone. He certainly knows that God is the creator of every splendor: the tenderness of a melody, the warmth of a chord, the pulsations of a rhythm — as well as the smile of a child and the charm of a woman. When the poet writes a hymn, when the musician dresses it with melody, when the sculptor carves into stone the smile of a"holy woman," they are all proclaiming the name of God. The liturgy owes it to itself to utilize all their talents. It sanctifies them by consecrating them to God. To accept such beauty as merely the *semblance* of God would be sin, but to see beyond it to find the *reality* of God himself is grace:

> Now if out of joy in their beauty they thought them gods,
> let them know how far more excellent is the Lord than these;
> for the original source of beauty fashioned them.
>
> For from the greatness and the beauty of created things
> their original author, by analogy, is seen.[42]

The Christian people have always had an appreciation of the beauty which leads to God. The countless number of cathedrals are witness to this in the architectural field; likewise, the Gregorian chant and polyphonic repertory in the field of music. However, at times this importance of beauty has been relegated to a back seat. The Latin and the Gregorian chant style have, in the past, exercised a certain tyranny over popular songs in the vernacular, which were considered less worthy and were therefore discarded from the solemn liturgy. The official music was so jealous of its prerogatives and so complacent in its own perfection that it would not tolerate being replaced by a song in the vernacular. Note, for example, this rule set forth in the Instruction of March 5, 1967:

> However, if there is a reasonable cause (for example, because of an insufficient number of singers, or because of their inexperience in the art of chanting, or even because of the length of the function or some piece of music) such that one cannot chant one or another liturgical text as given in the notations of the liturgical books for performance by the choir, only the following is allowed: that these texts be chanted in their entirety in a monotone (recto tono) or in the manner of the psalms. If desired, organ accompaniment may be used.[43]

Specifically, this meant that if a schola could not sing an Introit, for example, it did not have the right to replace it with a familiar piece in the vernacular but, on the contrary, had to recite the Latin text *recto tono* even though the members did not understand it. Can we seriously say, in this case, that such music made prayer "sweeter" or that it "enriched the sacred rites with a greater solemnity" or made the text "more effective"? Can we really assert that this chanting on one note lifted anyone's mind to the contemplation of "invisible realities" and foreshadowed the liturgy of the heavenly Jerusalem?

The Instruction on *Sacred Music and the Sacred Liturgy* dates from September 3, 1958; the *Constitution on the Sacred Liturgy* of Vatican II dates from December 4, 1963. How far we have come in five years; imagine how much further we have to go!

## 4. MUSIC IS A UNIFYING ELEMENT FOR THE CONGREGATION

Now the last — but not the least — of the "services" that music gives to the liturgical community: it strengthens the solidarity of the congregation.[44] The Instruction of March 5, 1967, strongly affirms this point: ". . . the mystery of the liturgy, with its hierarchical and community nature, is more openly shown, *the unity of hearts* is more profoundly achieved by *the union of voices.*"[45]

Stated simply, an assembly of the faithful, even though situated in the precise limits of a given place — the interior of a church — remains an undetermined group, like a body without a soul, unless it expresses its unity in common activities which signify its reason for assembling. One of the most significant of these activities is singing. In this lyrical expression of faith, each individual person experiences true brotherhood as his voice blends with the voices of his neighbors. The faithful, who were previously only a crowd, become a liturgical congregation through song.

This unity of hearts in the union of voices was hardly mentioned in earlier official documents before the *Constitution on the Sacred Liturgy.* These documents emphasized what the choir was to sing rather than what the people were to sing. Such an attitude was so widespread that the Instruction of September 3, 1958, stated that "the full participation in song must be sought particularly in religious communities and seminaries."[46] In other words, the people were denied the opportunity to sing the Entrance Song, the Gradual Psalm, the Alleluia, the Offertory Antiphon or even the Communion Processional (which represented the third degree of participation according to the Instruction). The people were asked to answer simply "Amen" or "And also with you" (which corresponded to the first degree of participation), or perhaps to take part in the Kyrie, Sanctus, Agnus Dei, Gloria, and Profession of Faith. (If too difficult, these would be sung by the *Schola Cantorum,* which was the second degree of participation.) Under such conditions it would be ironic to insist that the music was encouraging congregational unity! Favored above all was the schola, with its virtuosity in Gregorian chant — or its monochord recitatives, if virtuosity were lacking. The congregation was merely asked to lend a not-too-critical ear and give easy admiration.

On the other hand, pre-conciliar texts were rightly insistent upon a certain world-wide unity by the use of Latin and the chants of the Church of Rome:

> And if in Catholic churches throughout the entire world Gregorian chant sounds forth without corruption or diminution, the chant itself, like the sacred Roman liturgy, will have a characteristic of universality, so that the faithful, wherever they may be, will hear music that is familiar to them and a part of their own home. In this way they may experience, with much spiritual consolation, the wonderful unity of the Church. This is one of the most important reasons why the Church so greatly desires that the Gregorian chant traditionally associated with the Latin words of the sacred liturgy be used.[47]

The unity of the Church was seen here as the union of each individual church to the Church of Rome through the adoption of the same language and the same musical mode. The Instruction of March 5, 1967, just four years after the *Constitution on the Sacred Liturgy* of December 4, 1963, prefers to speak of the unity of the faithful among themselves in their own individual churches. It knows that this unity among the faithful in their own particular groups does not injure the unity of the Church but is, in fact, one of its essential elements. It applies the principle stated in the Constitution *Gaudium et Spes,* December 7, 1967:

> Moreover, in virtue of her mission and nature, she is bound to no particular form of human culture, nor to any political, economic, or social system. Hence the Church by her very universality can be a very close bond between diverse human communities and nations, provided these trust her and truly acknowledge her right to true freedom in fulfilling her mission.[48]

## D. The Essential Question

Is the ministerial function an important question? It is much more than that: it is *the essential question,* the fundamental principle from which have come the best of our current reforms. It is the starting point from which we will be able to grow in intelligent understanding of the liturgy and its potentiality.

This essential question can be stated quite simply:

—How does singing serve the liturgy? How does a particular song serve the liturgy?

—What can be done to insure this "service"?

At this level, the search for an ancient liturgy no longer exists. Rather, a serious reflection upon new and present situations must be made. It is no longer sufficient to have the keys of the past to open the doors to the future. It is no longer enough to modernize an ancient liturgy, as if it were a restored fossil, because, even though perfectly restored, it would be inadequate for today's problems.

Faced with new questions and confronted with the ministerial function, liturgical music after Vatican II finds itself freed of certain useless restrictions and is rediscovering the exciting taste of Christian liberty. It recalls the prodigious affirmation of the Constitution *Gaudium et Spes:*

> But at the same time, the Church, sent to all peoples of every time and place, is not bound exclusively and indissolubly to any race or nation, nor to any particular way of life or any customary pattern of living, ancient or recent.[49]

Liturgical music, which is not tied to any ancient or modern custom, must not be allowed to flounder with its new-found freedom. For its liberty, like that of the children of God, is liberty in the service of the Lord Jesus. It is strengthened and blooms if it seeks to serve the liturgy; it is weakened and withers if it denies the very liturgy which gives it life. The Christian will use this liberty to place every beauty and splendor in the service of the liturgical community. He will seek to put the smile of heaven into his sometimes so rebellious notes.

# CHAPTER II

# THE PARTICIPANTS IN THE LITURGICAL CELEBRATION

In this second chapter, we will discuss the participants in the liturgical celebration, as defined in the Instruction of March 5, 1967, articles 13-26. We will approach this question from a special point of view, one which holds great personal interest for us; namely, from that of liturgical music in the Eucharistic celebration.

In the past, when liturgical music was mentioned, one would think immediately and almost exclusively of the schola or chorale. Today, however, we encounter other extremes. Certain pastors, although they themselves are well oriented toward a more active participation of the people and wish to bring about true reforms in music as well, think only in terms of songs sung by the congregation — perhaps, because they are hampered by a choir with only a very traditional repertoire. There can be people who willingly like to oppose the "musician-congregation" to the "liturgical-congregation," the first being proud about the singing of the choir, the second, about the singing of the congregation. Sometimes, in order to make things simpler, one affirms that the choir has to sing the propers, while the ordinary is sung mainly by the congregation.

Perhaps these classifications may seem a bit elementary. However, they involve affected preferences and customs which are easily but improperly identified with tradition, and do not express the true elements of the liturgy.

Indeed, liturgical song is an integral part of the liturgical celebration. It does not enjoy an autonomous existence as if in the liturgy there existed rubrics and ritual on the one hand, and music and song on the other. Certainly, music possesses an autonomy, but only in the area of technique. Musical technique is a field that has its own rules and no liturgy can dictate the proper chords or structure of the melody. It can simply say that some music is suitable while some is not. As soon as music enters into the liturgy, it becomes subservient to the liturgy, and, like a good servant, must fulfill its assigned ministerial function. The structure and hierarchy of the liturgical celebration are identical with those of the liturgical music and its performers. Therefore, "liturgical services are celebrations of the Church; that is, of the holy people, united under and directed by the bishop or priest."[1] This simply means that priest and people have related parts to play in such a celebration, yet together form the celebrating community.

Each of these participants, priest and people, is assisted by secondary figures according to the needs of the liturgy.

The priest is assisted:

—on the one hand by his ministers, those having received orders: deacons, subdeacons (reader);

—on the other hand, by those who exercise a "ministry": servers, readers, commentators, and choir.

The people are assisted mainly by the choir.[2]

This priest-people structure is essential. It constitutes the celebrating community. This means that the choir or schola does not form a "part" of the congregation, as if the the congregation were split into sections with the priest in one, the choir in another, and finally the people in a third. The choir is not a part *of* the celebrating community, but a part *within* it, having its own specific grandeur. However, to be very clear, we shall treat each of the following:

    a)  The music sung by the priest;

    b)  The music sung by the people;

    c)  The music sung by the choir or schola.[3]

## A. The Music Sung by the Priest

The priest is the leader of the celebrating community gathered in the name of Christ. His position and ministry can be seen from a double point of view.[4]

### 1. IN THE NAME OF CHRIST

He presides over the congregation as the representative of Christ, "in persona Christi."[5] He is, so to speak, the sacrament, that is, a sacred sign of Christ. It becomes evident, therefore, that the most dignified song of the priest and of the entire Eucharistic celebration will be that in which the priest most truly identifies himself with Christ, i.e., the singing of the words of the Institution of the Last Supper with the words of Consecration.

The Eastern liturgies have long realized the dignity of this music which is the heart of the Eucharistic celebration. The priest sings the words of the Institution on a solemn tone; the prayers of the priest become the prayers of the people when they respond with their acclamations. In the liturgy of St. James (and in the Mozarabic rite) each consecration is acclaimed with a triumphant Amen. In the Ethiopian liturgy, a triple Amen is sung, followed by a profession of faith:

> Amen, amen, amen!
> We believe, we confess,
> We praise you, Lord, our God.
> Yes, we believe![6]

In the Coptic liturgy, the people join in the words themselves, thus creating a joyous and solemn dialogue with the priest:

> Jesus Christ, the night he was to undergo his passion, took bread in his holy, immaculate, pure, blessed and life-giving hands; lifted his eyes toward heaven and you, his Father, God, Lord of the universe; gave thanks;
>
> —Amen!
>
> blessed it,
> —Amen!
>
> sanctified it,
> —Amen!
>
> broke it . . . and said:
> "Take and eat this, all of you.
> For this is my body, offered
> for you and for all for the
> remission of sins. Do this
> in memory of me."
>
> —Amen, amen, amen!
> We believe, we confess
> and we give you glory.[7]

Finally, in almost all rites we find an acclamation of praise:

> We praise you,
> We bless you,
> We give you thanks, O Lord.[8]

In this acclamation, the liturgy most admirably shows the Eucharist to be, above all, the act of thanksgiving of people who are truly celebrating. From its origin, the liturgy has sought to grow and develop in the warm glow of joy and praise. Toward the middle of the second century, St. Justin witnessed this festive atmosphere when he wrote: "When the bread, wine and water are carried up, the presiding minister prays and gives thanks *as best he can*. And all the people respond with the acclamation: Amen!"[9]

Roman rubrics have long preferred a profound silence at the Eucharistic prayer, calling it "sacred."[10] This, however, was rather oppressive. Nevertheless, it expressed the veneration and adoration with which the Christian community surrounded the mystery it was celebrating with its priest. But the priest performed the most essential rites of the celebration alone without ever inviting the people to participate openly in the great Eucharistic Prayers. Condemned to silence, they took refuge in individual prayer and were united privately to the Eucharistic Prayer of the priest. During a high Mass the people participated more. The Sanctus was sung before the consecration and the Benedictus afterwards, and, in former times, the people were permitted to sing a motet to the most blessed Sacrament after the Benedictus.[11] But was this not an open invitation to do something other than the priest and thus to be completely detached from the great Eucharistic Prayer?

The solitude of the priest at the altar during the Consecration and the veil of mystery surrounding the Eucharistic Prayer due to the use of Latin did not, however, lack grandeur. The specific character of the ministerial priesthood was thus forcefully shown: only the priest who has received sacerdotal ordination can, according to the Catholic faith, consecrate the Eucharistic bread and wine. However, there was a rather great disadvantage: the priesthood of the faithful seemed to have been forgotten. They, too, offered the Eucharistic sacrifice because of the grace of their baptism, yet they seemed to be separated from the climax of the celebration. This solitude of the priest must be experienced in order to measure all its incongruities — to see the people defer their rightful place and participation to the priest at this deeply meaningful part and to feel the people (especially the children) awaiting the moment when he will be finally "finished" and everyone can again unite in the *Our Father!*

This priestly isolation was emphasized even more in the architectural arrangements of some churches. There were elevated choir stalls and altars, a real "Thabor" which one ascended by a long series of steps and from which the people were largely dominated, and also "communion" rails that should really have been called "separation" rails. Moreover, some choir entrances were separated from the people by an imposing grillwork which seemed to be an ancient reminder of the riches of former times which kept the clergy apart from the laity. Finally, the priest presided over his community with his back to all.

All this was hardly conducive to a dialogue with the people. It responded perfectly to the theology of the Council of Trent, which had so earnestly insisted upon the sacerdotal nature of the priest as being different from that of the faithful. But it clearly does not reflect the theology of Vatican II, which prefers to apply to the faithful the text of I Peter 2:9. "You, however, are a chosen race, a royal priesthood, a holy nation, a purchased people."[12]

## FURTHER CONSIDERATIONS

**a.** It would be best to solemnize the proclamation of the Eucharistic Prayer, especially the words of Institution.

Such solemnization is usually attained through singing. But, as a matter of fact, it is not a question here (any more than it is in the readings, the Preface, or the collects) of strict melody, but of chanting on only a few notes. The general rules of chanting are just as applicable to the Eucharistic Prayer.

This chanting is particularly necessary when several priests are concelebrating. We all know how difficult it is to find priests who can all give a common recitation that has an external air of dignity, for each has his own individual personality, not to mention his own type of voice and preference for this or that tone and rhythm. Very often the sacerdotal prayer degenerates into a helter-skelter anarchy of murmurs, without rhythm or life. Music alone is capable of achieving this "miracle" of unifying the priests' voices so that all keep the same tone and verbal rhythm. Here we see an example of music accomplishing one of the ministerial functions of which we spoke earlier: unity.

When singing is not desirable, either because the celebrant is untrained or the occasion is a simple one, a presidential tone may be assumed in accord with the solemnity of the rite. The narration of the Eucharist is not a story to be told to the community; nor is it a prayer that one murmurs to oneself. Rather, it is a solemn proclamation of the mystery being accomplished.

**b.** For the people to become more fully involved they can eventually respond with more than the Sanctus, the Anamnesis, and the Amen at the end of the Eucharistic Prayer. There can be an acclamation of praise and thanksgiving after each consecration. We shall discuss this more fully later.

## 2. IN THE NAME OF THE CHURCH

The priest presides over the congregation in the name of the Church, "in persona Ecclesiae." The prayers he addresses to God are offered in the name of all the holy people, and principally in the name of those assisting in the Mass and celebrating it with him. The most important chants would be those in which the priest offers to the Father, through the Son, in the unity of the Holy Spirit, the prayers of the ecclesiastical community: the orations and the Eucharistic prayer.

## FURTHER CONSIDERATIONS AND SUGGESTIONS

**a.** The priest's prayers are indeed presidential. Sung or read, they will be proclaimed with great solemnity in a manner which is truly "presidential" (recited by one who is presiding). This intense solemnization can be obtained in a simple diction; because the intensity comes from the texts themselves and not from any emphasis in the voice of the celebrant.

**b.** It does not seem useful to sing all the presidential prayers. Why not? Because one runs the risk of making them all seem of equal importance when there should be a definite hierarchical order. Such order could be as follows:

—of first importance should be the Eucharistic Prayer, the center of the Eucharistic celebration;

—following this would be the Preface and the Doxology which concludes the Eucharistic Prayer because of their "eucharistic" character, and after them the epiklesis and the anamnesis[13] in consideration of their liturgical importance;

—finally would come the orations and other prayers which the reform has envisioned.

These classifications must remain flexible. On the pastoral level, it may well be desirable in a given set of circumstances to put extra stress on a certain prayer. For instance, on the feast of Pentecost, perhaps the epiklesis could be sung to emphasize the descent of the Holy Spirit on the bread and wine.

**c.** The orations pose a more specific problem. Is it necessary to sing them all? Of course not, even in the most solemn celebrations. In fact, in order to sing an oration, it must first be singable. This is not always the case.

As everyone knows, the old orations were written in a rhythmic prose which gave them a noble literary air.[14] When man stands before God's majesty and, begging, extends his hand to receive his kindness, he clothes his words in a holy dignity. Sometimes, however, the transition from Latin to the vernacular can reflect a change from nobility to banality. The translation divests the text of its literary cloak. Sometimes only a skeleton remains. Is it worth dignifying in song?

No one is responsible for this state of affairs in the first years of post-conciliar liturgy. The translators of the orations had no choice; they were not free to deviate from the original Latin. What was really necessary was to create new orations which would have the same literary quality as the Latin ones. This, fortunately, is being accomplished at the present time; the inconvenience now is part of the transitional stage.[15]

These are the problems of the ancient prayers. Prayers composed more recently, when the liturgical tradition was less well known, present other problems. They are filled with pious sentiment but lack literary style. Whereas ancient prayers bear the stamp of their Roman genius and take pride in being concise and sober, the new ones often suffer from verbosity. How can one sing the oration of St. Jane Frances de Chantal?

> O Almighty and merciful God, who willed to add glory to your Church through the new congregation founded by blessed Jane Frances, you inflamed this saint with such a love of yourself that her wondrous strength of soul led her in the way of perfection in every walk of life. May her merits and prayers bring us grace from heaven to overcome everything that hinders us, for we are conscious of our own frailty and trust solely in your strength.[16]

What can we conclude about the singing of orations? The new liturgy is more demanding than the old. Formerly, any oration could be sung with no preparation at all. Latin constructed a shield behind which the celebrant could hide and which protected him from ridicule when he mispronounced words, stuttered, or even skipped a line. The modern vernacular allows no margin for error. Each prayer must be carefully and thoughtfully prepared.

**d.** A final remark about the priest's singing.

With great pastoral sense, the Instruction on *Music in the Liturgy* states:

> Whenever, for a liturgical service which is to be celebrated in sung form, one can make a choice between various people, it is desirable that those who are known to be more proficient in singing be given preference; this is especially the case in more solemn liturgical celebrations.[17]

What was meant by the above statement is obvious. To have a beautiful voice and to know how to use it is a gift that God gives to a few for the benefit and pleasure of the whole community. We must use this charisma. This is equally important when it comes to choosing priests for Mass. It sometimes happens that certain priests, or even those elevated in dignity as monsignors, and, if I may say so, bishops, just do not know how to sing; there are even a few cardinals — heaven forbid! — who cannot put two notes together. Some, it would seem, scorn the exactness of notes and just slide over the scales. The 1967 Instruction puts a curb on these situations by requiring that, all things being equal, the cardinal, bishop, monsignor, or priest who knows how to sing properly should be chosen.

There is, in this note of the Instruction, a profound sense of service to the liturgical community. To celebrate a Mass for the community is not an "honor" accorded to a priest; it is service which the community asks of him. The liturgy requires that this service be rendered as well as possible.

The priest who will first rehearse what he must sing honors the community for whom he celebrates and shows the seriousness with which he treats his sacerdotal ministry. Yet, it sometimes happens that some men have vocations to be priests but not to be singers. What can be done with them? They certainly cannot be cast forever into the shadows of cacophony. The Church, as we know, is motherly and has foreseen all this when she speaks in the 1967 Instruction:

> If, however, a choice of this kind cannot be made, and the priest or minister does not possess a voice suitable for the proper execution of the singing, he can render without singing one or more of the more difficult parts which concern him, reciting them in a loud and distinct voice. However, this must not be done merely for the convenience of the priest or minister.[18]

The Church no longer prefers a solo by a minister who, as in the *Ite missa est* for example, would begin on an arbitrary note, immediately "derail" to another key, and then slide up and down the twelve-tone scale as if on ice, and eventually come to rest on the final note like a plane crash-landing. Instead, the Instruction would prefer today that the priest simply state: "The Mass is ended; go in peace."

## B. The People's Singing

Everyone knows the Council's ardent desire for the participation of the faithful. This "full, conscious, and active" participation, according to the Constitution, is demanded by the very nature of the liturgy, which is not the celebration of any one clergyman nor the singing of any one choir member but rather a celebration of the entire ecclesiastical community. Moreover, it is both a right and a duty of the Christian people, who are "a chosen race, a royal priesthood, a holy nation, a purchased people."[19] Therefore, "the Faithful fulfill their full, active, and conscious participation which is demanded by the nature of the liturgy itself."[20]

Now, singing is one particular form of expressing this participation. However, it still cannot replace the interior participation of the people where "their thoughts match their words, and they cooperate with divine grace."[21] Nor is singing the only form of external participation; many new and desirable forms can be foreseen. Yet singing is, indeed, a special activity in which the private prayers of the community, united with the priest's thanksgiving, share in the joy and praise of the entire assembly. Therefore, the Instruction of March 5, 1967, stated:

> . . . the active participation of the whole people, which is shown in singing, is to be carefully promoted . . . [22]

How do these words agree with older official statements? We will find that the Motu Proprio *Tra le Sollecitudini* of St. Pius X, 1903, can be considered as an excellent beginning in the reform of church music, for it was already speaking of the "active participation" as the "primary and indispensable source" of the Christian spirit.[23] Yet it almost completely ignores the use of music by the people. It demands that "the use of Gregorian chant be reestablished among the people so that they may once again participate in the celebration of the services."[24] But in regard to singing, it only mentions "the songs reserved for the celebrant at the altar and for the ministers." On the other hand, it states that "every other liturgical song is in the realm of the levitical choir."[25] Under such conditions the people's participation was very often limited to listening with devotion to what was sung and to admiring what was done.

Some may call this "participation through listening" — or through "watching" as a spectator. This is perfectly fine for people attending a concert or an opera, but certainly not for Christians celebrating the Mass as a community with their priest. What would you say if a friend invited you to dinner and then asked you just to sit there and look at the meal being served? Or if you were invited to participate in a dialogue and then told to keep quiet and just listen to the conversation? Was this not the condition of the Christian people up until now? Today, however, all the documents repeat like an antiphon: "The active participation of the people must be promoted." Indeed, the Instruction becomes almost lyrical: "One cannot find anything more religious and more joyful in sacred celebrations than a whole congregation expressing its faith and devotion in song."[26]

Now let us simply make a few general observations; those parts of the Mass which are meant to be sung specifically by the people will be treated later.

## 1. CONSIDER THE CONGREGATION

The 1967 Instruction states:

> . . . in selecting the kind of sacred music to be used, whether it be for the choir or for the People, the capacities of those who are to sing the music must be taken into account.[27]

Here is a wonderful novelty! Before this, the only thing to be considered was the official book in Latin. For example, the same Requiem Mass was sung for a thousand people in a city parish, for a monastic community or a seminary, and for the immediate family of the deceased, even though none of them understood a word of Latin. It was always the same *Dies Irae.* Whether the community knew how to sing or not was never considered. No one seemed to care whether the choir had twenty well-trained singers or a single organist. The rubrics did not make such distinctions. Now, however, the principle has been established: consider the congregation!

Of course, it is easy to criticize what is past. It is better to be careful when applying this principle now. Let's take an example. You have to choose a communion song. You open your card-index file and think: "Let's see, out of all these choices, which communion song is the most beautiful, the most inspiring, the most exciting, the most biblical?" If those are your first thoughts, you have missed the point. When choosing songs, "consider the congregation!" Ask yourself: "What kind of congregation is going to celebrate the Mass today? Teenagers or widows of World War I? Little girls preparing for Communion or a large parish group? The best song is rarely the one which is best in itself or the best in your files — it will always be the one that is best for the particular group celebrating a particular Mass.

We must also add that a great deal of simplicity and humility is demanded of the celebrating priest and the music director in such a situation. They must always be ready to sacrifice their own personal preferences to achieve a better celebration for the entire community. Happy is the community where the best song in itself is, at the same time, the best song for the community! Liturgically speaking, this community is truly adult.

## 2. PROGRESSIVE SOLEMNIZATION

Before Vatican II there was a very definite distinction made between a low and a high Mass. The Instruction of September 3, 1958, defined a high Mass:

> The Mass is called a "sung Mass" if the priest celebrant actually sings those parts which are to be sung according to the rubrics. Otherwise it is a "read Mass."[28]

No thought was given to or mention made of the people.

There was also a distinction between a high Mass and a solemn high Mass. It was a solemn high Mass when it was celebrated with "sacred ministers," i.e., with a deacon and a sub-deacon. Again, there was no mention of the people.

To have the required holy ministers, a ceremonial ruse was employed; a priest was disguised as a deacon.[29] As for the sub-deacon, the parish seminarian could fill in that spot.

The distinction between high and low Masses also led to financial consequences. The stipend for a high Mass was always more. It was, and still is, hoped that this delicate and often touchy question of "honorarium" will be happily resolved in the not-too-distant future. Everyone agrees that the musicians or anyone performing a service should be paid for the work they do. But it is just as clear that liturgical music, which honors Jesus Christ, must not be burdened with financial considerations.

To sum up, there were three categories of Masses:

1. the solemn high Mass with a deacon and a sub-deacon;

2. the ordinary high Mass;

3. the low Mass.

These distinctions were by no means simply rubrical fiction; they were serious pastoral considerations. Over and above the pages of the rubrics, these distinctions directly affected the people's participation in the songs. The Instruction on *Sacred Music and the Sacred Liturgy* had even decreed the following law:

> In sung Masses the Latin language must be used not only by the priest celebrant and the ministers, but also by the choir and the faithful.

> In sung liturgical functions no liturgical text translated verbatim in the vernacular may be sung except by special permission.[30]

In principle, then, no high Mass could be celebrated except in Latin. Those who knew Latin and Gregorian chant gladly kept the law. Those who did not, painfully submitted. To the Christian people it looked like a clerical debate around the lectern.

Practically speaking, pastors managed as best they could. Not having the power to simplify the solemn Masses, they solemnized the simple Masses. They celebrated "low" (read) Masses which allowed the people to sing songs they knew in the vernacular or Latin.

The Instruction of March 5, 1967, does not condemn them. On the contrary, very wisely and in consideration of pastoral needs, it states:

Between the solemn, fuller form of liturgical celebration, in which everything that demands singing is in fact sung, and the simplest form, in which singing is not used, there can be various degrees according to the greater or lesser place allotted to singing.[31]

In other words, between a Mass that is completely sung and a Mass that is completely silent, there can be different degrees. The principle of "all or nothing" is no longer liturgically valid. The true principle must instead be: "The community sings what it *can* sing." Or "Every song must be adapted to the community."

There must be a progressive solemnization of every Mass including those celebrated during the week, even with a reticent congregation. Indeed, every piece must fulfill its "ministerial function"; as the Instruction states, it must be executed according to its proper nature.[32] If it is a song, it must actually be sung.

For example, here is the Communion Antiphon for the Sixth Sunday of Easter:

Sing to the Lord, alleluia!
Sing to the Lord, and bless his name . . .

This text [Ps. 96(95):2] invites musical adaptation. So, too, a communion processional completely fulfills its ministerial function only when it is sung effectively. Therefore, should the psalm "Sing to the Lord" be recited on a single note and not be actually sung? Liturgically, this would be ridiculous. Or, if the antiphon must be recited at all cost, should not the text be changed? For example, "Recite to the Lord a recitation, alleluia."

Needless to say, this rule of progressive solemnization must itself be applied gradually. It is not necessary, for the love of liturgy, to upset the little old ladies in the parish uselessly or to bully the faithful into changing from their accustomed habits. The Instruction proposes the following progression:

In selecting the parts which are to be sung, one should start with those that are by their nature of greater importance, and especially those which are to be sung by the priest or by the ministers, with the people replying, or those which are to be sung by the priest and people together. The other parts may be gradually added according as they are proper to the people alone or to the choir alone.[33]

One must never forget that in every celebration the aim of a liturgical law is never "to sing or not to sing," but is rather to achieve the full, active, and conscious participation of the people, whether that be through song, recited prayer, or even silence.

## 3. THE THREE DEGREES OF PARTICIPATION

Putting into practice the principle of progressive solemnization, the Instruction of March 5, 1967, proposes three degrees of participation "according to the capabilities of each congregation." "In this way the faithful will be continually led toward an ever greater participation in singing."[34]

### a. First Degree

In the first stage, we have:

1. in the entrance rites:
   — the salutation of the priest with the people's re-response,
   — the prayer.

2. in the liturgy of the word:
   — the acclamations at the Gospel.

3. in the Eucharistic liturgy:
   — the Prayer over the Gifts,
   — the Preface, with its dialogue, and the Sanctus,
   — the concluding doxology of the Eucharistic Prayer,
   — the Lord's Prayer, with its introduction and embolism,
   — greeting of peace,
   — the prayer after communion,
   — the dismissal.

As we can see, the first degree is comprised of dialogues, prayers, and acclamations, among which is the Sanctus. Strictly speaking, these pieces are not songs but belong to the genre of chant — that is, all except the Sanctus, which is the people's most important song in the Eucharistic liturgy. It should be sung at every Mass. On the other hand, the prayers and salutations need not be chanted at every Mass. The participation of a small group — say, ten — can justify reciting the salutation "The Lord be with you" and the collects; however, this very same group will be in accord with the spirit of the liturgy singing the Sanctus.

This first degree may be employed alone. Theoretically, it is fulfilled, either totally or in part, each time we make use of the second or third degrees.

However, we must be extremely flexible. The first degree merely provides an outline to orient the faithful toward full choral participation. It would be contrary to the spirit (as well as the letter) of the Instruction to emphasize the distinctions of this triple classification, as if they were insurmountable barriers. To do so would render more difficult and even destroy the people's participation; what is really wanted is to provide the principles for progress.

### b. Second Degree

This includes:

1. the Kyrie, the Gloria, and the Agnus Dei;
2. the Profession of Faith;
3. the General Intercessions.

The second degree is comprised of the songs that formerly made up the ordinary (excluding the Sanctus) as well as the General Intercessions. The songs with fixed texts are more easily integrated. Their liturgical importance varies. Therefore, the Gloria and the Profession of Faith are not found in every Mass. Nevertheless, their absence in no way unbalances the structure of the celebration of the Mass.

### c. Third Degree

Here we include:

1. the processional songs of entrance and communion;
2. the song after the Reading or Epistle;
3. the Alleluia before the Gospel;
4. the Offertory song;
5. the readings from Holy Scripture, unless for some reason it would be better not to sing them.

The third degree includes the pieces from the variable Proper, the most important being the Responsorial Psalm contained in the liturgy of the Word. Just as the Sanctus in the Eucharistic liturgy, it must be sung at every Mass.

## 4. THE PROBLEM OF VOCAL QUALITY

What about the problem of quality? How well will the people sing?

This question is sometimes raised in certain esthetic circles. Music or singing, they say, is an art. Our congregations are largely composed of musical "Philistines," so to speak. Under such circumstances, are they able to sing with enough musical perfection?

The fear expressed over the musical quality of the singing, especially if it would impede prayer, does honor to those who think of it. Even if one cannot agree with them, they must still be respected. Besides, this problem is by no means a recent one as a result of Vatican II, as if there had always been good singing before the Council and only bad afterwards. However, it must be considered in a true perspective.

The aim of the liturgy is not to promote the musical education of the people in order to obtain a better musical rendition. The Church is a mystery of salvation, not a conservatory or a music school. The people's singing will always be valuable insofar as it expresses, according to liturgical rules, the participation of the baptized in the liturgical celebration. It would be unthinkable to deny the people this participation merely for esthetic reasons. The Church surely knows that among the *plebs sancta* — the holy people — there are voices that certainly do not belong to any nightingale. Some will quaver and others will go flat. But she also knows that the most important and essential thing is the participation in the mystery being celebrated.

Having said this quite forcefully, it is necessary to add that the people's participation will be better expressed if the people can sing and sing better. However, the goal toward which the Church moves is not to promote the quality of the singing but to foster the people's participation, and this is accomplished through improved singing. Liturgy and art are not at war; the people's participation and improved singing are not contradictory ideas. On the contrary. Liturgy needs art to express itself more fully. People need to sing well so they can celebrate more perfectly.

We must also add that the sound of people singing has a special beauty all its own — one that no choir or polyphonic music with its antiseptic voices and mathematical chords can attain. Of course, quite frequently people will drag out the last note, possibly break into a shrill vibrato, distort the melody, and scream when trying to reach the high notes (a problem which can and must be gradually corrected). But we cannot judge the people with the same criteria used for a choir. The congregation is not a choir. The congregation is not a schola in the pews, but the people of God. When the choir sings, the entire congregation listens, and if, by chance, the musical performance is not up to par, the whole congregation notices it, becomes embarrassed in its prayer, and has every right to criticize it. But when the whole church is singing, no one is listening — except God — because everyone is taking part in the liturgy. And this is exactly what constitutes that special quality of the congregation in song. The union of all voices — the pure voices of the children, the vibrato of the old ladies, the rough voices of the men, and the high brilliant voices of the women, good voices, bad voices — all these many variations and weaknesses express what nothing else can express: the mystery of the Church which unites all men in the praise of Christ. ". . . That, one in spirit, you may with one mouth glorify the God and Father of our Lord Jesus Christ," Paul wrote to the Christians in Rome.[35]

Something like a miracle happens. These voices, with all their faults, form the richness of a choir. These inexperienced singers, none of whom could sing alone, together proclaim the "oneness" of their faith. These musical "Philistines" together attain a unity in

which each person expresses his own personality, thus enriching
all others and reinforcing the bond among them. That miracle can
only be understood by one who has sung in such a group or by the
musician who has had the honor of accompanying the baptised
community on the organ as they proclaim their faith and joy.

## 5. ACTUAL POTENTIAL OF THE CONGREGATION

A final word about the actual potential of the congregation. Two
aspects will be considered, the first of which is:

**a. Never underestimate the people's musical potential, or their
artistic sense.**

People are not stupid. They are aware of beauty and are quite
capable of appreciating it. They can also make some progress,
though perhaps slowly at times, in choral singing. Just look at the
changes you have in popular music. Varied and rhythmic melodies,
thought to be "unsingable" when they first appeared some ten or
fifteen years ago, are now whistled by bricklayers on the job! It
would be a grave error in pastoral judgement to allow a congregation to sing only some parts of the melody, or to sing shortened
antiphons. For heaven's sake, let's not submit our churches to
kindergarten-level repertoires. Quite the contrary, we must allow
the people to sing their joy or sadness, to express all their prayers in
lively and melodic antiphons, to vibrate with pulsating rhythm —
in short, to be treated as adults. It is a plain fact: antiphons learned
in only one minute are most often forgotten the next; those which
make the least impression upon the memory are also the ones which
are the dullest. On the other hand, songs which have a certain vigor,
which demand a bit more effort, are also those which do not easily
become boring. This does not mean that short antiphons are not so
good as longer ones: such a judgement would raise other criticism.
It simply means that one should not underestimate the musical potential of the people.

Our second aspect is:

**b. Never overestimate the people's musical knowledge or their
actual capabilities.**

In order to foster singing among the people, it is best to begin
with the simplest of songs and progress from there. We must first
use songs which even the less "talented" among the congregation
would not find too difficult to sing. Once this has been accomplished, one would not want to close the door to all future progress.
Everyone must take the same train, even if the slow ones must be
carried along for a while until they catch up. The rungs of the
ladder should not be so high that they can't be reached, only just
low enough for everyone to begin to climb up to new possibilities.

# C. The Singing of the Choir

There are many questions concerning the choir. There are also quite a few solutions proposed in the Instruction of March 5, 1967.

## 1. THE MEMBERS OF THE CHOIR

The following question has often been asked: who can become a member of the choir? One might say: "What a strange question! Any of the faithful who are of good will may sing in the choir!" But that was not the opinion and teaching of Pius X in his *Motu proprio*. He saw the choir as the "choir of levites" and concluded:

> Church singers fill a real liturgical function; therefore, since women cannot participate in this office, they cannot be allowed to join the choir nor become a choirmaster.[36]

Therefore, women cannot sing in the choir. At least, that was the law until a few years ago. Of course, it was not observed everywhere, but it certainly reflected a very definite clerical outlook and mentality. In days gone by, in order to show the "priestly" nature of the choir, even though it may have been made up of the parish grandfathers and children, the men were dressed in cassocks and the children (the sopranos and the altos) like miniature priests with surplices over their shoulders and crosses around their necks. This clericalization of the choir was in perfect accord with the teaching of Pius X who stated: "It is most fitting for members of the choir to dress in the clerical cassock and surplice when singing in Church."[37]

Then came Vatican II, and the Church discovered that she was composed of not only men, but also women — almost 50%. The Instruction looks at the consequences of this discovery and states:

> The choir can consist, according to the customs of each country and other circumstances, of either men and boys, or men and boys only, or men and women, or even, where there is a genuine case for it, of women only.[38]

We are therefore witnessing a type of "declericalization" of the choir. This evolution must likewise involve a certain declericalization of the repertoire. This is a very big problem to face. The repertoire must not be representative of the pious style of the 19th century, but rather of the words, rhythms, and melodies of today. Just as it is no longer necessary to wear a cassock or surplice to accomplish a liturgical function, it should no longer be necessary to borrow the format of liturgical songs from the so-called ecclesiastical style.

Certainly, the Church does have the right to impose liturgical regulations, just as it had the right to bar women from the choir. That is not being questioned. A law is not a "raison d'être" in itself. It is justified only with reference to a higher purpose. In liturgy, a law is necessarily oriented toward the celebration of Jesus Christ. The problem is not only for those who obey the law to respect it, but also for those who formulate the law to consider the welfare of the entire Christian community and its new environs. In the history of the liturgy, Vatican II enjoys a privileged position for its renewed insight.

## 2. DIFFERENT TYPES OF CHOIRS

You don't have to be a cleric to know that there are many different types of choirs. For example, some choirs are both large and full of talent, while others are small and not too well-endowed vocally. We also know that the smaller choirs like to imitate choirs of greater renown. This way of thinking goes on every day all around us: the younger brother always imitates the actions of his older brother. Therefore, the small choirs practice long and hard in order to be ready for special occasions — Christmas or Easter — but the rest of the year, they slough off.

At the present time the Instruction asks that we reconsider the role of the choir: must it sing only on great feast days and be silent the rest of the time? To help us in our consideration the Instruction distinguishes three types of choirs:

### a. Large Choirs *(Capellae musicae or Scholae cantorum)*

They are usually found only in basilicas, cathedrals and other major churches, seminaries, and scholasticates. These are exceptional choirs. Normally they perform an exceptional repertoire, since the magnificence of the music is usually in proportion to the magnificence of the building. One doesn't sing the same way in a cathedral as in a country chapel, even though the same intensity of liturgical beauty can be attained in both.

These choirs, says the Instruction,[39] must cultivate the priceless "musical treasures" left us by tradition, as they are to be the guardians of a treasure. But one doesn't guard a musical treasure in exactly the same way a jailer would guard a prisoner. The best way to preserve this music is to sing it and make it popular with the people. The better it is sung, the better it will be preserved. If it is not sung to perfection, or carelessly performed, it will soon be undermined and destroyed.

### b. Parish Choirs

These parish choirs actually stem from the liturgical congregation. The Instruction states: "It would also be desirable for similar choirs to be set up in smaller churches."[40] This should be the golden rule: every Mass celebrated, during the week or on Sunday, should have the participation of a choir — a few singers — coming from the liturgical congregation and directly proportionate to that congregation. Why? Because every Mass has several parts which can only really fulfill their liturgical function if sung.

Take the Gloria, for example. This is the same kind of hymn as the Christmas canticle "Unto Us a Child Is Born," or even "Angels We Have Heard on High." Therefore, the liturgy, along with good old-fashioned common sense, would affirm that this song is supposed to be sung, not recited. What would it sound like if we just recited the following lines on one note?

> Silent night, holy night,
> all is calm; all is bright.

We would surely say it seemed more like a lament and certainly not a Christmas carol. Therefore, this is exactly the type of lamentation we reproduce when we intone the hymn of the angels of Bethlehem on one note:

> Glory to God in the highest,
> and peace to his people on earth . . .

Of course, this is only one example. Others could easily have been chosen, like the Responsorial Psalm, which by its nature requires a psalmist. Yet these examples point out the number of problems we have to face. Their solutions must be sought with a great deal of patience and Christian perserverance and will be gradually found. Liturgical reform never asks that we become so impatient as to disrupt things and upset the people. Yet, we *are* asked to be ready to relinquish secure positions in order to explore new areas. Priests have a special duty to protect inner freedom so that we may more easily welcome change when it comes. Have we become like "confirmed bachelors" who are set in our ways? Have we dared to name as "tradition" things that are really only accepted routine? Some thought all problems were solved when they left the seminary; for dozens of years they had been sincerely reading or reciting *recto tono* pieces which were meant to be sung. Now all is being questioned; yet the person who accepts the discomfort of change in deference to the liturgical wishes of Vatican II does true honor to his priesthood.

### c. "One or Two Singers . . ."

Finally, the Instruction speaks of what could be called "mini-choirs."

> Provision should be made for at least one or two properly trained singers, especially where there is no possibility of setting up even a small choir. The singer will present some simpler musical settings, with the people taking part, and can lead and support the faithful as far as is needed. The presence of such a singer is desirable even in churches which have a choir, for those celebrations in which the choir cannot take part but

which may fittingly be performed with some solemnity and therefore with singing.[41]

So, from the choirs in the large cathedrals and the small parish choirs we come to the "mini-choir" where the director is the only singer. The Instruction wishes each congregation to express itself according to the resources at hand. Thus, the Church has an almost maternal desire to have every parish, even the most modest, sing its faith in Christ in the truth of the liturgical celebration.

## 3. THE FUNCTION OF THE CHOIR

The Instruction points out, in a general way, the dual function of the choir:

> Its duty is, in effect, to ensure the proper performance of the parts which belong to it, according to the different kinds of music sung, and to encourage the active participation of the faithful in the singing.[42]

**a.** On the one hand, then, the choir must perform those parts which are in its domain. It is necessary that the execution of the choir, singing alone before the congregation, be completely valid on the musical level. The choir should sing with such perfection that the people will yearn to tell them: "We want to sing like you. We want to sing with you. What you do is so beautiful that we are enchanted by it. It warms our hearts and greatly helps us to pray. We are literally enraptured by your melodies, your harmony, your rhythms!" But if the choir's singing — heaven forbid! — is as dreary as a rainy night, if the people keep looking at their watches and begin to mumble, "When will they finish bellowing so?" — then their singing is not at all valid on the musical level and should be condemned liturgically as well, for it will not have accomplished its ministerial function.

The Instruction speaks of "parts which belong to it." But which songs belong to the choir? There are certainly no pieces which have the right to be reserved for the sole use of the choir. Although some are designated specifically for the congregation, it must be remembered that the choir is a part of the whole congregation. Still, there is a wide area in which the choir can exercise some influence.

— It can sing pieces that are not reserved solely for the people, like the Gloria.

— There can be a dialogue with the people, as in a procession, the choir singing the verses (eventually in harmony) and the people taking the antiphon.

— It can add to the acclamation of the people in the Sanctus by a polyphonic effect.

— And, finally, with well-chosen motets it can enrich the celebration during the offertory and communion.

**b.** The choir, however, must encourage "the active participation of the faithful in the singing." This is an immense and never-ending job. Practically speaking, the choir is irreplaceable. They either support, correct, and encourage the congregation's attempts at song, or they introduce a new song with a certain amount of forcefulness. As a matter of fact, it has been shown that, when the choir is good both musically and liturgically, the singing of the people also is good, and the entire parish community is exceptionally active and alive. On the other hand, when the choir is musically and scripturally mediocre, so too is the singing of the people, and the parish community itself is often apathetic and lifeless. Music is such an integral part of the pastoral situation that it can, in itself, reveal the strength or weakness that will be found therein.

For this reason, the Instruction specifically notes that the choir "because of the liturgical ministry it performs, deserves particular mention. Its role has become something of even greater importance and weight by reason of the norms of the Council concerning the liturgical renewal."[43]

Therefore, in the opinion of the Church, the new liturgy does not overshadow the choir, but emphasizes its importance. Admittedly, in some parishes, there was probably a certain amount of tension concerning the choir and its activity. The tension resulted in one of two things:

— A misunderstanding about the role of the choir on the part of those responsible for the liturgy. Some priests thought that Vatican II gave them free reign to take over the microphone or to introduce any new song that came along under the pretext that it was "popular."

— Or a misunderstanding on the part of choir directors and the choir itself concerning their proper function. They thought that Vatican II had not changed anything in the choir-loft or at the organ and that they could keep their former repertoire, which was surely a part of the "treasure" mentioned in the documents!

Such tension has gone as far as having the choir suppressed or the director, along with a few of his singers, dismissed. Instances of this kind are most unfortunate and should be deeply regretted, even though they are few in number. Often the choir has stepped more and more into the background, especially when it was in a rut and incapable of acquiring a new repertoire to save it from a stifling routine! Now, however, a great pleasure is it, indeed, for both the musician and the liturgist to note that the work of the past ten years, inspired by the encouragement of the Council, has engendered innumerable parish choirs and singing congregations, where before there was nothing but silence and boredom.

## 4. THE NECESSITY OF LITURGICAL INSTRUCTION

Many difficulties will finally be resolved when the pastor gives
the choir liturgical and biblical formation that will be as valuable as
the musical programs and instructions they receive from their director. The *Constitution on the Sacred Liturgy* of Vatican II made
such a request:

> Composers and singers, especially boys, must also be given a
> genuine liturgical training.[44]

The 1967 Instruction answers this question and develops it more
forcefully:

> Besides musical formation, suitable liturgical and spiritual for-
> mation must also be given to the members of the choir, in such
> a way that the proper performance of their liturgical role will
> not only enhance the beauty of the celebration and be an ex-
> cellent example for the faithful, but will bring spiritual benefit
> to the choir members themselves.[45]

The Constitution stresses the role of children. But we can also
imagine some musicians who are virtuosos at the keyboard and
definitely adults in music, but are children in the realm of liturgy.
There may even be a few priests — very good priests, in fact —
who are completely ignorant in certain areas. In a word, there are
many good Christians who are most devoted and who may be very
well-trained in music but who are "under-developed" from a liturgical and biblical point of view.

All of us, who are the people of God, must set to work with
resolution. It is useless to hope that things will get done on their
own, as if there will be some kind of spontaneous generation. They
need our cooperation and often our sweat. True, it is always good to
place our trust in the Holy Spirit, who, in difficult times, will help us
improvise a solution; but it is far better to confide in the Holy Spirit
to lead us to work for the liturgical formation which is spoken of in
Vatican II.

Allow me to interject a personal story at this point. I was attending a series of lectures in what used to be the major seminary of
Yaounde, in Ottele, in the Cameroun, near the equator. This seminary is about 30 miles from the capital in the middle of a thick
forest. One night after dinner I was out walking and met a negro
who was scantily dressed but proudly carrying his Gregorian *Liber
Usualis* under his arm. I greeted him, "Hi! Do you know how to
sing Gregorian chant?" "Yes, Father," he answered, obviously proud
of this accomplishment. "Can you sing next Sunday's Introit?" I
then asked. That year, I remember, the Sunday in question fell
on August 6, the feast of the Lord's Transfiguration. Without the

slightest hesitation my friend began to sight-read the day's Introit, *Illuxerunt coruscationes tuae,* in the 3rd mode. I congratulated him and asked: "Do you know the psalm you sang so well?" I was referring to Psalm 77(76). This psalm celebrated the love of God who, from the time of the Exodus, led his people as a shepherd does his flock and showed them a path through the waters. The verse, borrowed from Psalm 84(83), speaks in very endearing tones:

> How lovely is your dwelling place,
>     Oh, Lord of Hosts!
> My soul yearns and pines
>     for the courts of the Lord.

My Gregorian "expert" had absolutely no idea about the meaning of these texts. After we had said goodbye, I wondered, "Here is a man baptized in Christ, very well educated by our missionaries in every possible way according to official procedures, who knew the intricacies of Gregorian chant with its *salicus, torculus resupinus* and the rest, but who was completely lacking in knowledge of the Word of God. He knew how to decipher the Gregorian neumes but did not know how to "decipher" the Word those neumes were meant to convey!" I wondered too, "How many choirs around the world have singers so much like this native singer — singers who know their psalm tones better than their psalms!" However, they are all ready to undergo a needed reform, for they are most devoted to the liturgy and eager to learn. All we need to do is to open the door to the riches of the Bible.

What, then, can the members of the choir themselves do to further the reforms proposed by Vatican II? Among many possibilities, I have listed a few. Choirs from the same town or district could meet together from time to time (once a month, for example) to enrich their own knowledge of the Bible and the liturgy under the guidance of a well-trained director. They could prepare the following month's program together or learn new songs so that they would be able to transmit their mutual experiences to the whole community. Members of clubs or societies are happy to come together to discuss their common objectives; why should choir members, who are all "children of light," have less knowledge about their chosen interest than members of fishing clubs have about fishing?

## 5. THE REPERTOIRE

The choir's repertoire also presents a serious problem and deeply affects each member. This repertoire is the very bread of life for the choir.

Formerly, choirs feasted on their bread each Sunday. They also had at their disposal a cheap audience, who, for good or bad, was obliged to listen. Now this audience is beginning to come alive liturgically by really participating in the singing. Now also we are taking the bread out of the mouth of the choir and replacing it, not with Palestrinian cake, but with the coarse bread of the people. Thus certain choirs are wondering, "What will we eat tomorrow? What will we sing tomorrow?"

The traditional Gregorian or polyphonic repertoire is often very beautiful but is not necessarily adaptable to the new liturgy. Therefore, a Gloria sung in four-part harmony from an arrangement of Palestrina is liturgically valid because the Gloria is essentially a hymn. But the Sanctus from the same Mass by Palestrina, constructed upon the same theme and according to the same rules, can hardly be adapted to liturgical regulations because it is essentially an acclamation of the whole community. Moreover, the new modern language repertoire is still suffering from growing pains. It will take some time and much experimentation to create works of art that can be sung by the people — a situation not without precedent. The Patristic period and the Middle Ages produced well over 30,000 hymns, yet only 75 of the 30,000 eventually found their way into the Roman Breviary period.[46] Of those 75, the people of today would recognize and be familiar with only two or three.[47]

Obviously, only the best hymns have survived the ravages of time and only a few of them have become familiar to the people. Likewise, a new repertoire in the vernacular will also take a long time to grow. To rip out the roots would kill the entire organism rather than produce new variations. This points out the fact that we are in a period of transition and that there will be many pieces which are not quite appropriate for the new liturgy but which will continue to be sung in our celebrations.

Each selection from the former repertoire should be analyzed as to its function and usefulness in the new liturgy. If it is no longer appropriate to the function for which it was first intended, it should be eliminated, but it is not necessary to eliminate it completely. It could still be used somewhere else in the service, perhaps in the celebration of the Word. The 1967 Instruction puts it this way:

— Moreover, in these same popular devotions, and especially in celebrations of the Word of God, it is excellent to include as well some of those musical works which, although they no longer have a place in the liturgy, can nevertheless foster a religious spirit and encourage meditation on the sacred mystery.

— As regards the heritage that has been handed down, those parts which correspond to the needs of the renewed liturgy should first be brought to light. Competent experts in this field must then carefully consider whether other parts can be adapted to the same needs. As for those pieces which do not correspond to the nature of the liturgy or cannot be harmonized with the pastoral celebration of the liturgy — they may be profitably transferred to popular devotions, especially to celebrations of the Word of God.[48]

One last remark. The classical repertoire was supposed to outline the change of centuries and the movement of history, and Gregorian chant seemed destined to endure in the Roman Church until the parousia. Let's be careful not to foster the same pretentions concerning the vernacular repertoire now taking shape! Modesty is in vogue. We must accept in good faith that the new repertoire is definitely provisionary. By that I mean that each generation must create its own musical forms and songs according to its needs. It must bake today, in the oven of modern-day inspiration, the bread that is needed *today* to nourish its faith. The next generation will bake its own bread. If future generations find that our bread is still flavorful, they will gladly eat it, but we will not force them. We must let them be free to enjoy the responsibility of expressing their faith for themselves.

Such an attitude in no way closes the door on history as a foundation for tomorrow's liturgy. It is simply the logical consequence of what has already been said about the ministerial function of singing. The effectiveness of a song is relative to the community it serves, varying with time and place. We would judge badly if we simply condemned the repertoire of the turn of the century. Perhaps in that era it was an edifying element of the Church and thus fulfilled its ministerial function. Today, however, such a repertoire is perhaps inappropriate. But then there may be a few people in our communities who are closer to 1900 than to 1970!

The previously quoted thoughts of the 1967 Instruction, based upon the ministerial function of the repertoire and its relative effectiveness, reflect the maternal and loving respect the Church has for her children. The celebrated "treasure" of the Church is there to enrich the lives of the faithful, but the faithful are not there to "guard" the treasure.

## 6. THE LOCATION OF THE CHOIR

Finally, here is a problem whose solution depends solely upon the architecture of each church. Where should the organ be? Where should we place the choir? The choir-loft is an excellent answer to both questions from the point of view of acoustics, but not of the liturgy. What, then, is the true solution? The Instruction of March 5, 1967 states:

> Taking into account the layout of each church, the choir should be placed in such a way:
>
> a) that its nature should be clearly apparent — namely that it is a part of the whole congregation, and that it fulfills a special role;

b) that it is easier for it to fulfill its liturgical function;

c) that each of its members may be able to participate easily in the Mass, that is to say, by sacramental participation.[49]

There is no universal solution to this problem that could be applicable to each particular case. The Instruction clearly states that the physical facilities of the church must be considered. None of our churches built before 1963 were constructed to conform to the new liturgy. They all need to be rearranged. In most cases all that will be needed is a little imagination to come up with a worthwhile solution.

All such problems, however, should be envisaged with a great deal of patience and serenity. They will not be solved with one brutal all-encompassing blow. Rather, solutions will come about gradually, just as Church tradition has come down to us. This fact is just another reason for starting without delay and wasting no time.

This is an exciting task the Church proposes to us. We cannot let ourselves fail or attack it half-heartedly. Essentially, it involves creating the beauty which accompanies prayer. It involves letting the splendor of God shine forth on the community celebrating this liturgical mystery.

# CHAPTER III

# THE DIRECTOR OF THE CONGREGATION

We will discuss here the duties and function of the person who will lead the congregation in song. We can outline our main points as follows:

We are not discussing the methods employed to conduct Gregorian chant, polyphony, or a classical or modern piece of music. The techniques used for a small choir of twenty people will not necessarily be applicable to a crowd of a thousand people who know little about music. There are good directors who know how to direct a motet by Palestrina but who do not know how to lead a congregation.

We are not treating the problem of the organ and the organist. Obviously, a good organist who has a fine instrument to play is a blessing to the liturgical service. If he is well-trained and knows how to use the organ, he can very easily lead the congregation all by himself. In most parishes the organ will be used to unify the congregation.

Nor will we discuss the role of the commentator. In a community rich in human resources where one could easily find a commentator, care must be taken not to confuse the duties of the commentator with those of the choral director. These are two separate functions. The commentator should announce the song; the director should lead the people while they sing. The function of the commentator is particularly important and was recognized as such in the Instruction of September 3, 1958. Its full liturgical value is attained when the directions are "prepared in writing; they must be brief and serious, delivered at a fitting moment . . . "[1] The role loses its value when the directions become too wordy and the person "tells the story of his life" into the microphone!

Nor will we treat the problem of resonance, which, if effective and in good taste, should be a great help in coordinating the people's singing.

All this deserves to be treated in regard to the new liturgy. The organist, choral director and commentator are privileged participants in the liturgy. They are primary collaborators with the priest in the realm of song and the primary servants of the people singing. They have a decisive influence in the celebration. What organist does not feel that the lyrical mood he creates by playing a beautiful prelude does not influence the rest of the ceremony? But we are concentrating here upon the function of the person who, according to the Instruction of March 5, 1967, "leads and supports the faithful" when they sing. In the order of the urgency of problems to be treated, his function must surely be of primary importance.

We are speaking here of both the act of leading and the leader himself, the conducting and the conductor. In principle, the concepts of leading are broader than those of the conductor or director. The act of leading is more than the act of conducting which it includes. If you take both words in a limited sense, conducting is the external activity which consists in guiding the singing. The conductor keeps time for the congregation, choir, or orchestra. But a conductor worthy of the name will never admit that he is nothing more than a human metronome. He thinks, and rightly so, that he has a mission to fulfill, a vocation to be realized. He wants to express to the orchestra, choir, or assembly that there is much more than the notes on the page; he wishes to introduce to them this spiritual zone where music itself takes a back seat to silence and finds a *soul*. He is then the leader who is conducting. In the following pages we will speak of the leader, conductor, or director without making the above distinctions or elaborating the fact that the leader of liturgical singing does not simply conduct notes but most definitively helps form the prayer of the congregation.

We shall first discuss:

— the leader of the congregation

— the leading of the congregation

## A. The Choral Director for the Congregation

### 1. HIS ROLE

The role of the choral director consists of "leading and supporting"[2] the singing of the congregation so as to facilitate prayer. He is the congregation's "security blanket" when they are singing. In this regard, his role is much like that of the deacon or commentator. They are not there primarily to give an intellectual analysis of the text but to create an atmosphere conducive to prayer through a better understanding of the texts. The choral director's first task is not to seek better musical performances but to create that prayerful mood through a better musical interpretation.

For him, the human factor is of prime importance. Any priest can validly officiate at the Eucharist even if he does not celebrate in a beautiful way and is disliked by the congregation. But to do his job in the best possible way and truly to fulfill his ministerial function, the choral director must have a pleasant disposition and must be accepted by the whole community.

He must be so well accepted by the congregation that, in a certain sense, his presence and directions are almost unnoticeable. Whether we like it or not, the choral director's role is always that of a critic; an active critic during the performance, who must use his judgment at all times. One "performance" is never like another. Some will be good, some bad. He is not directing a machine or a robot, but something sonorous and vibrant, come alive by a spiritual breath blowing gently over the congregation. The conductor must sense its movement. If the singing begins to slow down, he must quicken the beat or the congregation will all fall asleep. He is always making a critical evaluation, constantly assuring the steady rhythm and melody for the people. Criticism is most helpful when given in a friendly and constructive way. The choral director should try at all times to be calm, cool, and collected, even when the song is being butchered. We hope that very nervous or quick-tempered individuals will not assume the task of being choral directors.

The director should also avoid looking sad or mournful, as if this would be more pious; the "children of light" do not need a façade of sorrow or piety. A gloomy appearance definitely hinders the congregation's spontaneity and really "turns them off." Rather, he should look joyful, as if he is enjoying his task, thus communicating his enthusiasm to the people through his actions and attitudes. The people should be so caught up in his enthusiasm that, when they respond to the Word of God, there is such a sound that the very "rocks begin to shout . . . "

The role of the people's choral director corresponds in part to that of the singer, mentioned in the 1967 Instruction:

> Provision should be made for at least one or two properly trained singers, especially where there is no possibility of setting up even a small choir. The singer will present some simpler musical settings, with the people taking part, and can lead and support the faithful as far as is needed. The presence of such a singer is desirable even in churches which have a choir, for those celebrations in which the choir cannot take part but which may fittingly be performed with some solemnity and therefore with singing.[3]

Therefore, the singer should be able to introduce simple songs and be able to conduct them at services when the choir does not participate. His presence would still be beneficial at Masses which include the choir, for he could lead the people. It is not good, however, for the choral director and the singer to be one and the same person, i.e., that he direct and sing at the same time (except in cases of emergency, to save a tune from dying altogether). In fact, to direct a song objectively, it is necessary to remain silent while conducting.

A final thought. May a woman assume the role of choral director for the people? Of course. The Instruction of September 3, 1958, already allowed this.[4] After centuries of restrictions and segregation, women were finally given permission on January 15, 1968,[5] to pronounce the readings (with the exception of the gospel). Actually, the former restriction reflects a certain clerical and masculine mentality which used to enjoy emphasizing what Paul said about women, "Let women keep silence in the churches, for it is not permitted them to speak . . . " (I Cor. 14:34). Paul in no way meant to legislate for our century and our present needs, but the Church has acquired certain mental attitudes down through the centuries which weigh heavily on today's thought.

Personally, I don't think you can approach this question on the parish level by asking whether a woman may or may not conduct the singing. Rather, the question should be seen in the light of the ministerial function of the role. To direct the singing is a "ministry," i.e., a service rendered the community celebrating the liturgy. The question to be asked at the parish level should be this: who among all of us, man or woman, can best fulfill this function? If it is a man, we use him for this service. If it is a woman, we use her for this service. Isn't this the easiest and most sensible solution?

## 2. HIS DEMEANOR

The congregation's choral director should have a festive appearance, for the celebration in which he is deeply involved is always joyous.

He must have an impeccable appearance. The most popular liturgy should never be a "shirtsleeves" liturgy. It must be completely dignified, even if this dignity is not expressed as in former times. If I were part of the congregation, I could attend looking sloppy, unshaven or even dirty. The only person I would hurt would be myself for not knowing how to show respect for the community. But the choral director, as a servant of the congregation, should show his respect with a good and wholesome appearance.

Now that we have established the basic principles, it is still difficult to set down specific regulations in this area. Each community has its own customs of behavior; each person will exude his own personal charisma in the way he presents himself to the congregation.

He can, when the occasion calls for it, dress liturgically, i.e., he may wear a cassock and surplice even though he is not a cleric.

However, this statement concerning the use of "choir robes" by the laity must be considered very freely, and applied with thought and discretion. At the present time, there is a change of mind going on in this regard. In the Motu Proprio *Tra le Sollecitudini* of St. Pius X,[6] the singers among the laity were to be dressed as clerics to show that the choir was performing a liturgical function. All apparel which indicated the holy people of God who were not clerics, and therefore did not wear clerical garb, was kept out of the choir. But the time has come to ask whether all functions that are not specifically clerical shouldn't be shorn of their clerical appearance. One such function would be that of the choral director, who does not perform a clerical function. A layman can legitimately assume this role without having to hide his tie beneath a clerical robe.

His comportment — his gestures and facial expression — should be festive. He is in the midst of a celebration. Let him avoid anything that might distract the faithful from their prayer. If he must move about, he should do so quietly and inconspicuously. Discretion and effectiveness are his two most essential qualities.

When I meet a friend in the street, I greet him by shaking his hand. I might even slap him on the shoulder and ask, "How is your wife these days, pal? And your little girl? Didn't she have the measles?" But if I meet my friend during the liturgical celebration, I greet him with, "The Lord be with you," because we are both on a different plane now. We are both involved in the liturgical celebration of the community. Even if I look down at the congregation and see my cousin Mary whom I haven't seen in ten years or my uncle Fred just returned from China, I cannot change my festive attitude: I am in the service of the community which is at that moment celebrating Jesus Christ.

## 3. HIS PLACE

The choral director's place before the congregation is determined in part by his function and also by the physical arrangement of the building. Each church poses a particular problem. Yet we can still put forth a few general suggestions.

— He should be in front of the congregation, not lost in its midst.

— He should be visible to all. His effectiveness depends on this.

— He should be able to see and be seen by the choir so that he can be the link between it and the people.

— He is not to be the central figure. He should not block the altar nor upstage the presiding minister.

— He should not be placed in the pulpit. This is reserved for the reading of the Word (the Epistle, Responsorial Psalm, Gospel, Homily) and the prayers associated with it (General Intercessions, for example).

We can foresee in our churches a fixed pulpit on one side of the sanctuary having some kind of importance and blending in with the architecture of the altar and the seat of the presiding minister. On the other side would be a simply constructed lectern from which the congregation can be directed. The pulpit and the lectern have two distinct liturgical functions:

— The pulpit is the venerable place where occurs the mystery affirmed by Vatican II: "He is present in His word, since it is He Himself (Christ) who speaks when the holy Scriptures are read in the church."[7] The dignity of the pulpit in the church can be compared only to that of the altar.

— The lectern is the place where the congregation is given all needed directions whether they be for the singing, the ritual of celebration (the procedure for receiving communion, for example), or any other messages relative to the parish community life.

## B. The Direction of the Congregation

### 1. A GENERAL PRINCIPLE

The choral director's primary goal is not to give a better musical performance but, rather, to foster better prayer by means of such a performance. Let's not forget the hierarchy of values here. The Lord asks us to pray well, not necessarily to sing well. But we must ask ourselves whether we couldn't get our community to pray better by having them sing better. We should remember that it is necessary to pray ourselves, if we hope to inspire prayer in the congregation when it sings.

### 2. PREPARING THE SONGS

Obviously, the songs to be used should be chosen with some thought beforehand, but not just ten minutes before the start of Mass. Then, too, they should be properly prepared. Start with the existing repertoire. The old repertoire need not be thrown away under the pretext that it has been criticized. After all, the faithful can express themselves sincerely in songs that are not necessarily perfect. It is useless to prepare a magnificent program that cannot be accomplished. Consider the 1967 Instruction, which states:

> In selecting the kind of sacred music to be used, whether it be for the choir or for the people, the capacities of those who are to sing the music must be taken into account.[8]

We must immediately add that consideration of the present abilities of the people should not become an excuse behind which to hide when songs are multilated. We must progress. Just as a child who refuses to grow will surely die, a community which refuses to progress will perish of boredom.

In order to progress, the choral program should be prepared for the year, the quarter, or the month. Such a program could be established on the parish, district, or diocesan levels. Anyone who is responsible for the liturgy should also be consulted in this planning: the pastor, the assistants, the choir director, the organist, the sacristan, the altar boys and commentators, and, as much as possible, the singers themselves. We must learn to work together in a democratic way. Choosing songs for the entire community cannot be the privilege of one person, for whom the Holy Spirit has reserved his rays of wisdom.

If this kind of planning is not done, then we necessarily condemn ourselves to last-minute preparations, and, by accepting the bonds of using the same songs over and over again, we succumb to mediocrity and tired disenchantment. As a result, the congregation is the loser.

There are, of course, exceptions to the rule when unforeseen circumstances make it necessary to improvise on the spot. But such improvisations are made more easily when there is a fully-prepared repertoire to fall back on in such an emergency.

When making our selections we must also note the verses and antiphons. Otherwise, the first two or three which are known by heart might be repeated indefinitely, even though they may not be the most appropriate. Other songs which stress a particular aspect to be emphasized in the service are preferable.

No new song should be introduced to the people unless they have received sufficient instruction about it. What if you should, for example, want the community to sing Psalm 25(24) during Advent? You believe that this psalm would enhance the liturgical tradition of Advent, the period of waiting for the Messiah to come, and could effectively replace the "O come, O come, Emmanuel" that lulled us to sleep when we were young. Very well. Begin to preach about this wonderful psalm for two Sundays. Have the Bible club devote a session to it. Keep emphasizing it until the faithful come to you and say: "Father, when are we going to sing this beautiful psalm you've been praising so much?"

Keep in mind that the best song is not one that is musically perfect, or the best in your hymnal, but rather, the one that is best for the particular community celebrating the mystery. As previously mentioned, we should realize that the ministerial function of a song is relative to the celebrating community.

### 3. NO DIRECTION

The golden rule for directing the congregation should be:

— A *minimum* of intervention

— A *maximum* of effectiveness

D. Julien put it quite nicely when he wrote this rule-of-thumb which all choral directors should learn by heart:

When a sentence will do, don't make a speech.

When a word will do, don't use a sentence.

When a gesture will do, don't use a word.

When a look will do, don't use a gesture.[9]

Such discretion on the part of the director can be most effective. There are times when it is better not to intervene or direct at all:

— In a very homogeneous community, a religious community or a seminary, for example. All the needed directions should be given in practice, but not during the celebration.

— In a community (homogeneous or not) that knows the song so well that it does not need to be directed; directions would be given only when necessary, as, for example, at the beginning or end.

Let's take another example — a parish community which has sung "Holy God, We Praise Thy Name" for heaven knows how long. Liturgical reform now presents this community with a choral director. If he starts to direct "Holy God," this particular community could rightfully tell him, "Thank you very much for your help, but we prefer to be left alone. We, as well as our fathers, grandfathers, and even our great-grandfathers, have always sung this correctly without any kind of help at all. Direct us when we need it, when we sing some new antiphon we are just learning."

Then, too, whenever directions would interfere with the quality of prayer, they should not be given. It is never necessary to change a prayer in song into a song about prayer, or, in other words, into a musical performance. "He who sings, prays twice," it is said. This is most desirable. But he who sings too well, risks not praying at all.

### 4. INTRODUCING THE SONG

The song can be introduced in two different ways: one emphasizing the text of the prayer and one stressing the music of the prayer.

#### a. Introducing the Text

The choral director (or commentator) can give the congregation a brief monition that the prayer or song is about to take place. He must prepare the spiritual and biblical climate for the song. For example, the introduction of "There Is One Lord"[10] can be drawn from the Epistle to the Ephesians 4:4-6.

> One body and one Spirit, even as you were called
> in one hope of your calling;
> one Lord, one faith, one Baptism;
> one God and Father of all,
> who is above all, and throughout all, and in us all.

One can see how this introduction is appropriate to the song itself.

We will return to this song later. There are a number of biblical texts which treat the unity of the Church and which are extremely suitable for this hymn. John 10:16 is of particular interest.

> Other sheep I have that are not of this fold.
> Them also I must bring, and they shall hear my voice,
> and there shall be one fold and one shepherd.

But this text, as beautiful as it is, does not directly evoke the hymn, "There Is One Lord." You need a short introductory note such as:

> "Let us sing to the Lord who has gathered us together
> in the unity of one faith and one baptism; of one God
> and Father."

From this the entire congregation will be able to recognize the song which is to be sung. The introduction should not only present the song, but should also introduce the words. As a result, the community will be much more at ease and feel more comfortable knowing what is to come.

Or what if you wish to sing *Maranatha*? The director might simply say: "Take your hymnal and let us sing Hymn No. 8" or even "Let us sing *Joy to the World* on page 16." Such a short indication might be used when there is no time to spare. However, I think there are more inviting ways to encourage the congregation to sing. At any rate, such shortened introductions should never be given to a congregation in the middle of the celebration. Instead, one should say:

> "With the Apostle Paul, with Christians of all ages,
> let us continue the prayer of the Church by singing:
> 'Maranatha! Come, Lord Jesus.' "

Of course, any introduction should be prepared. True, we can trust the Holy Spirit to help us improvise in an emergency — but we can also rely upon Him to help us in our preparations. Besides, we know that the best improvisations are those which have been very well prepared and given only after careful consideration.

### b. Introducing the Music

The music can be introduced either by a few bars on the organ or by the tone given by the choral director himself. However, intoning a song is a true art. Three musical elements must be considered:

— melody,

— rhythm,

— harmony.

### 1) MELODY

Here are two remarks concerning melody:

a) We have to remember that the musical work does not begin with the congregation but with the intonation, which is what first creates the lyricism. It, then, must be an integral part of the song itself. It cannot be a hybrid, with no link to the main body, but must be connected to the music in the same way that the introduction is to the text.

For example, suppose you want to sing "Keep In Mind."[11] If the organist intones some freakish concoction like:

Keep  in  mind that  Je - sus Christ has  died  for  us...

he has broken the melodic line and killed its poetic content. Such carelessness can even be seen in excellent musicians from time to time. They are in such a hurry to have the people begin the song that they don't seem to care how carelessly they intone it. It should always be remembered that the melody is to be kept intact:

Keep  in  mind    that  Je - sus...

How many songs have been destroyed in this way, as have been Gregorian chants in the past! A melody has character, a face of its own; it lives and breathes and has a rhythm just as if it were alive. We don't scar such a face. We don't shoot down a bird in flight!

Very often the best solution is simply to play the entire first
line of the musical phrase.

Keep      in      mind      that      Je - sus      Christ

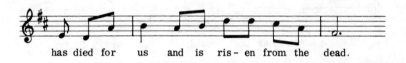

has died for      us      and      is      ris - en from the      dead.

b) The most adaptable tessitura[12] must be chosen for the congregation. The composer most certainly writes his song in the key
that seems best to him, in the range that is best for the melody. But
there may be occasions in which it will have to be transposed to suit
the congregation at hand. In this respect there is a fundamental difference between the execution of a classical composition and that of
a song sung by the people. The performance of the former must conform fully to the intention of the composer. Thus, you should not
perform the *Toccata in F Major* by Johann Sebastian Bach in any
other key. But when you accompany a large group of singers, the
song must be adapted to the range most comfortable for them.
Therefore you might easily:

raise the key

    — when only men are singing;

    — in the afternoon or evening;

    — when the atmospheric pressure is high
      (good weather);

or lower the key

    — when there are only women singing;[13]

    — in the morning;

    — when the atmospheric pressure is low
      (bad weather).

Let's take, for example, the hymn "Glory and Praise to You."[14]
If you have a good choir at your disposal, you can easily sing it in
B-flat, as it is written. Perhaps, if the community sings well, you
might even do it in C-major and it will sound magnificent! But, if
you have only one voice and the song is being sung at a morning

Mass for little school girls, don't hesitate to lower it a third (major or minor), even a fourth if need be:

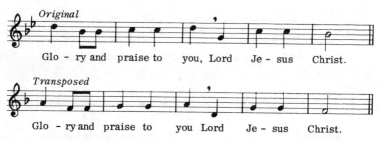

Undoubtedly, every song is not that easily transposed. In the example given above, transposition is easy because the melody is expressed in intervals of a major sixth.

Remember, too, that the range of a congregation which has had some training and is accustomed to singing is much better than the range of one which has just begun to sing. The first group could easily reach high E, but the second had better settle for a C (or a D) as its upper tone, lest it meet with certain disaster.

### 2) RHYTHM

Here are three remarks regarding rhythm:

a) The rhythm given in the intonation is the one which the congregation is to follow. It must therefore be clear and exact. A good example here is "Wonderful and Great."[15] If the intonation is presented like this:

it is evident that the congregation will not catch the correct rhythm, which is really:

b) Whatever was said about melody pertains likewise to rhythm. The rhythm of the intonation must be linked directly to the beginning of the song. Take the same example as given above (Alleluia).

If there is a vague silence between the end of the intonation and the beginning of the song, it will be extremely difficult for the congregation to begin on time or together:

*Intonation (Cantor or choir)*          *Congregation*

The beginning of the song must be rhythmically connected to the end of the intonation. In the following example the connection is perfect and the congregation will sing as a single unit:

*Intonation (Cantor or choir)*          *Congregation*

c) Choose a tempo that is suitable for the congregation. The following rules can thus be observed:

— If the congregation is musically trained, the tempo or pace should be ideally the one intended by the composer.

— It should be slower if there is a great number of people singing or if the tonal structure of the building and the amount of reverberation would both tend to make the song be sung at a slower pace. The reason for this is obvious: a large group necessarily moves more slowly than a small group. The natural echo of the building itself has the tendency to "make the stones sing," as it were. If you do not take into account this natural resonance, the beginning of many phrases will be overlapped by the end of those preceding (reverberation). The result will be a melodic chatter and a smothering effect upon the hymn itself.

### 3) HARMONY

Harmony will be useful and at times necessary to establish the modality of the melody. To have the melody heard with desirable clarity, it will often be useful to begin the intonation with a single note and to add the harmony only when the congregation really knows its part. For instance, the antiphon "Alleluia, Amen"[16] can be introduced to the congregation in the following manner:

This intonation is much better than one cluttered with a harmony that would only confuse the parishioners. The organist who introduces the hymn and accompanies the congregation must shine in the sobriety of his harmony.

## 5. DIRECTING

Choral direction has a two-fold aspect:

— direction of the rhythm;

— direction of the melody itself.

We will not discuss the esthetics of direction here, for that contains too many nuances and applies more to the choir.

### a. Directing the Rhythm

Directing the rhythm is most important. It consists of pointing out the basic rhythmic tempo, whether it be a measure of two, three, or four quarter time. Naturally, the congregation need not know what two, three, or four quarter time is, but it should be guided in the desired rhythm. Here are a few basic elements for the rhythmical choral direction of large groups:

— It is important to indicate the fundamental rhythmic balance of the melody — the alternation between *rise* and *fall:*

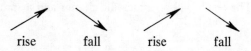

To signify the fall, lower the arms; to signify the rise, raise the arms. The lowering gesture is made from left to right; the raising from right to left. These gestures must always be made "outside" the frame of the body. This is done to make it as easy as possible for those in the last pews to follow your directions. The last row always needs much more direction than the first.

The amplitude of the gesture should correspond to the importance of the congregation. The following rules can easily be followed:

— To direct smaller groups, less exaggerated movements should be employed.

— The larger the congregation, the more obvious the gesture.

— The more obvious the gestures, the more sparingly they should be used.

— In order to have your directions seen by all, your hand should not appear to be a dead weight attached to the forearm, but rather the focal point of your direction.

— The body should remain immobile. You should not sway back and forth or up and down.

### b. Directing the Melody

Such direction consists of pointing out the melodic line to the congregation, i.e., the progression of the melody upon the different degrees of the tonal scale. This method has been quite popular in the past. It is particularly helpful when the congregation does not yet know the melody or when it is used with children.

## C. Conclusion

We should not be surprised if we cannot immediately find accomplished choral directors in all our parishes. Such directors are not born by spontaneous generation, but are formed only after much study and practice. Nor should we deceive ourselves into thinking that the grace of the priesthood or of religious life as enjoyed by brothers, monks, and nuns, automatically gives one the charisma to direct a congregation. No, here, as everywhere, grace does not replace hard work.

One final remark. The principles set forth here should not be taken as gospel truth. Rather, accept them in good humor and freedom, applying them with discretion, knowing full well that, although there are a thousand ways to accomplish something, there are also a thousand ways to go astray.

Finally, each choral director should keep in mind his saint, Jesus himself, whom tradition calls "choregos," i.e., the true choreographer of the soul, for he is the one who directs the prayers of

redeemed mankind, as Clement of Alexandria eloquently said
(† about 215):

> The word of God forsakes the lyre and zither, instruments
> without soul, and through the Holy Spirit is adapted to our
> world and especially to that microcosm man, to his body and
> soul. He uses this instrument of a thousand voices to celebrate
> God. His word is sung through this instrument that is man . . .
> Man is an instrument of God, harmonious, in tune and holy.[17]

# CHAPTER IV

# ACCLAMATIONS AND DIALOGUES

The songs used by the Liturgy in its Eucharistic celebrations are not all of the same structure or form. There is a world of difference between an ornate, jubilant alleluia and the simple chanting of the Gospel or the Lord's Prayer. The structures vary and are influenced by the type of liturgical action: a litany is not a hymn, nor is a hymn a Responsorial Psalm. Each song has its own particular visage, its own lyric movement, its own liturgical personality. All of these qualities generally increase to the same extent that the song realizes its particular ministerial function.

By considering only the songs used in the Mass of the Roman rite we can establish the following categories:

— the acclamations and dialogues;

— the Responsorial Psalm;

— the Kyrie and Agnus Dei litanies;

— the processional hymns: Entrance, Gospel, Offertory, and Communion;

— the Gloria and the Profession of Faith;

— the readings.

As acclamations and dialogues we can classify all the songs which the Instruction on *Music in the Liturgy* considers the first degree of participation in the Mass:[1]

— the priest's greeting, "The Lord be with you," and the people's response, "And also with you";

— the Amen at the end of the prayers;

— the acclamations to the Gospel;

— the introductory dialogue to the Preface and Sanctus;

— the Amen concluding the Canon;

— the wish, "The peace of the Lord be always with you," and the response, "And also with you";

— the dismissal, "Go in the peace of Christ," and the response, "Thanks be to God."

Each of these acclamations and dialogues is subject to the principle of authenticity or truth. We can define that principle thus: whatever the form expressed, whether sung or spoken, a dialogue must be an *actual* dialogue and an acclamation must be a *true* acclamation.

The dialogue must be an actual dialogue. It must address itself to someone and call for an answer. If the priest says, "The Lord be with you," while he timidly lowers his eyes and looks down at the floor, he is not having a dialogue with the congregation. And, if the people respond in a half-hearted manner, one might think that they don't care or that they do not realize the liturgical truth contained in the salutation of their priest.

What we priests have to do is to learn or relearn how to celebrate Mass in a modern language. There is a way to address the congregation which does not evoke a response; there is another way which, within the limits of the liturgy, not only calls for but encourages a unanimous, joyful response. We must consider seriously our physical attributes, especially our voices, which express our souls, so that our dialogues will always remain authentically human and expressive. This problem involves much more than music; it is, above all, a problem of human authenticity. The dialogue must:

—be suited to the size of the congregation — you don't say "The Lord be with you" to ten people in the same way you would say it to a crowd of a thousand;

— express to some degree the personality of the presiding minister and that of the congregation. Each priest and each congregation speaks, prays, and sings with its own particular characteristics in accordance with its own special charisma given by God.

The acclamation, too, should be marked with a sign of authenticity. We don't say, "Thanks be to God," in the same way that we say, "Lord, have mercy." Or take this comparison. Imagine a crowd at a football or baseball game. Notice how spontaneous and whole-hearted are their cheers: "Let's go!" "Go, team!" "Hurrah!" "Charge!" They even groan "Oh!" when the goal is lost. There are similar acclamations in the liturgy: "Amen!" "Alleluia!" "Hosanna!" "Glory to you, Lord!" "Thanks be to God!" Of course, the liturgy is not a football game. Indeed, it is much more; therefore the participation of the congregation in the celebration of the Euchar- istic act should be infinitely more intense and profound than that of the sports fans "attending" a game. In the Mass, it is the "crowd" itself that "plays"; the entire congregation is celebrating. Their ac- clamations should, therefore, be much more convincing and humanly authentic.

Several of the acclamations and dialogues pose no particular problem. We need only take the official formulas and carry them out with dignity. For this discussion, then, we shall restrict ourselves to the following points:

a) the dialogue: "The Lord be with you";

b) the response: "Amen";

c) the acclamation of the Sanctus;

d) the Eucharistic Acclamations or Anamnesis.

# A. "The Lord Be With You"—"And Also With You"

## 1. BIBLICAL SIGNIFICANCE

In the Roman liturgy every time the priest wants to address the people he begins by saying, "The Lord be with you." This wish is not a catch-all formula, meant simply to get the attention of the dozing community. Rather, it is one of the most essential revelations of the Word of God.

### a. The Wish: "The Lord be with you."

The affirmation of God's presence in the midst of his people is a part of the formula of the Alliance contracted with Abraham:

"I am the God of your father Abraham;
fear not, for I am with you.
I will bless you and multiply your descendants . . ."[2] *Gn. 26:24*

In the setting of Deuteronomy, the formula "I am with you" evokes the saving protection surrounding the people of God.[3] In the literature of the exile it is most naturally concerned with the themes of return and restoration:

"Behold, I will deliver you from the far-off land,
your descendants, from their land of exile;
Jacob shall again find rest, shall be tranquil and undisturbed,
for I am with you, says the Lord, to deliver you."[4]     *Jr. 30:10*

This saving presence, through which God accompanies his people on their journey toward the New Testament, was to be fully realized in the Incarnation of Jesus Christ. He is the Emmanuel, *God with us*.[5] The messianic times began when the angel said to Mary, the Daughter of Sion:

"Hail, full of grace, the Lord is with thee."[6]          *Lk. 1:28*

Thus began the definitive residence of God among his people. Moreover, the Gospel affirms:

"And the Word was made flesh, and dwelt among us.
And we saw his glory."          *Jn. 1:14*

And the prophet of the Apocalypse responds:

"Behold the dwelling of God with men,
and he will dwell with them.
And they will be his people, and God
himself will be with them as their God."[7]          *Ap. 21:3*

Such is the mystery of glory evoked by the priest when he says to his people: "The Lord be with you." It signifies the descent of the Eternal into time, the descent of the tenderness of Jesus into human distress, the descent of an inaccessible God, visible otherwise only after our death, but now in our midst through the mystery of the Word and the veil of Bread. Moreover, the Lord's promise itself is expressed in the liturgy thus:

"And behold, I am with you all days,
even unto the consummation of the world."          *Mt. 28:30*

### b. The Response of the Congregation: "And also with you."

The response "And also with you" is a simply translated Hebrew phrase. St. Paul uses it almost liturgically when greeting the Galatians:

"The grace of our Lord, Jesus Christ
be with your spirit, brethren. Amen."          *Gal. 6:18*

Similarly, he says to his disciple Timothy: "The Lord Jesus Christ be with thy spirit," and then adds to his greeting to the community the words: "Grace be with you." (2 Tim. 4:22)[8]

By their response, the members of the celebrating community accept the priest's good wishes for them, and they assure him that Christ is also by his side as he guides them in prayer.

Indeed, ever since Hippolytus of Rome (circa 215), liturgical tradition has insisted upon this Hebraic formula without ever using any other.

## 2. SINGING

When the priest says, "The Lord be with you," to the congregation and the congregation replies, "And also with you," both the salutation and the response should contain the respect due the meaning of the text and the solemnity of the religious occasion. However, the question arises: is it necessary to sing this dialogue? At every Mass? When two friends meet, they don't sing "Good morning," at

least not in our society. When the priest meets his congregation —
in the context of today's society — must he sing his greeting?

Let us suppose that the problem of the melody used for the above
text has already been solved. It is the "official" melody used everywhere. It is neither elaborate nor anything out of the ordinary. It
is not supposed to be. It is simply the most convenient melody almost everyone can sing. When sung well, it can certainly give added
significance to the text.

The Instruction on *Music in the Liturgy* answers our question in
this way. The chanting of the dialogue "The Lord be with you" with
its response belongs to the first degree of participation. This first
degree must be realized every time the elements of the second and
third degrees are used. In other words, when the Sanctus or Gloria
is sung, the dialogue must also be sung.

This point of view expresses the juridical aspect of the question
as it was presented in the legislation of March 3, 1967. It would be
good to add the following considerations.

In order to pass a fair judgment, any song or chant should be
considered in light of its own ministerial function to see what it
should be giving to the assembled congregation. Singing, according
to the Instruction, should give the following services:

— be an element of solemnization;

— give greater effectiveness to the texts;

— enhance the liturgy with beauty;

— be a unifying element.

It seems to us that none of the first three services is directly
achieved by singing the dialogues. In fact, the melody seems too
much of a monotone to make any impression on the congregation.
Can it seriously be said that singing the dialogues lifts the soul "to
heavenly things" and "prefigures that heavenly liturgy which is
enacted in the holy city of Jerusalem"?[10]

Only the last service remains: singing as a unifying element.
When dealing with a large congregation, this is quite obvious. Indeed, a small group — let's say, about twelve — can respond in
a single voice with dignity without having to sing their response.
A large congregation — let's say, about 100 — cannot. If the
responses are spoken, the voices will be uneven, straggling, dis-
united, and will totally disintegrate into low mumbling. Hence, a
large congregation can express its unity only when its words are
unified by a definite rhythmic pattern and a precise vocal pitch;
that is, by singing. It seems best, then, that a large congregation
should sing all the dialogues and acclamations in order to express
most effectively its oneness.

This rule is instinctively followed in every linguistic grouping of the tonal languages in Equatorial Africa. In these languages, which are poor in concepts yet rich in expressive possibilities, every word is a song and each song has rhythm. Each community expresses itself as a community; the faithful "reciting" their prayers can only recite them together, and only in song. One never hears the loud droning so prevalent in our congregations. The voices are instinctively regrouped into a rhythmic pattern, and they modulate in distinctive tones. Marvelous music rises from these people in prayer. The Lord's Prayer is sung just as the Act of Contrition, the catechism lesson, a page from the Gospel, or a sermon from the Fathers. Once heard, it is never forgotten. It possesses a rhythmic majesty like that of palm trees swaying in the evening breeze. It is a surging melody that constantly renews itself like the turbulent rapids of the Congo, a melody that breathes and flows in a rhythm naturally inherent in the words.

Our European languages, so adept at conceptualization, have lost such a sense of rhythm and melody. In order to unify and regroup the voices, we must call upon music and chant.

## 3. FURTHER THOUGHTS AND SUGGESTIONS

We mentioned above that the dialogues should be as real as possible, as authentic on the human level as they are on the liturgical. But if some priests say them mechanically, without conviction, they could soon become unnatural, fixed formulas which are far from authentic. "The Lord be with you" is a wonderful wish, but it was used much too often in the "old" Mass:

— in the Prayers at the Foot of the Altar,

— before the Collect,

— before the Gospel,

— before the General Intercessions,

— before the Preface,

— before the Postcommunion,

— before the final blessing.

Seven times in all! It is difficult to repeat the same phrase seven times with exactly the same intensity each time. If I greeted my friend by saying "Good morning!" to him seven times during our conversation, he would be right to question my reason and could conclude that my greeting was not altogether sincere. This is exactly the situation in which the rubrics had placed the priest.

Of course, a few may disagree. "The Lord be with you" is not always used as a greeting. At times it is employed simply to attract the congregation's attention. That is why it is used before the Gospel.

Very well. But why not simply say, "Brethren, give your attention to the words of the holy Gospel"?

Anyway, the new 1969 *Order of Mass* removed some of "The Lord be with you" dialogues. But the problem remains. For instance, why does the priest have to wish this presence of the Lord in the congregation by saying "The Lord be with you" just after the communion (no. 113) when the people have received the living Christ?

The problem could easily be resolved if the priest could freely use other "wishes," whether composed by himself for the particular needs of his congregation (a Mass for children, for example) or drawn from age-old biblical verses. The Bible is indeed a treasure house of phrases filled with theological grandeur. Here are a few (which could possibly be used in the celebration of the Word):

Grace and peace from God our Father
and from our Lord Jesus Christ. *Ep. 1:2; Gal. 1:3; 2 Cor. 1:2*

Grace, mercy, and peace from God the Father
and from Christ Jesus our Lord.             *1 Tim. 1:2*

The grace of our Lord Jesus Christ,
and the love of God,
and the fellowship of the Holy Spirit
be with you all.             *2 Cor. 13:13*

Peace be to the brethern, and love with faith,
from God the Father and the Lord Jesus Christ.
Grace be with all those who have
a love unfailing for our Lord Jesus Christ. Amen. *Ep. 6:23-24*

May the peace of Christ reign in your hearts!    *Col. 3:15*

May our Lord Jesus Christ himself and God our Father,
who has loved us and has given us through grace
everlasting consolation and good hope,
comfort and strengthen your hearts in every good
   work and word.          *2 Th. 2:16-17*

May the peace of God
which surpasses all human understanding
guard your hearts and your minds in Christ Jesus.   *Ph. 4:7*

Here are two eschatological verses which are most appropriate for Advent:

May the Lord make you to increase and abound in charity
towards one another, and towards all men
just as we do towards you,

that he may strengthen your hearts,
blameless in holiness before God our Father,
at the coming of our Lord Jesus Christ. Amen.   *1 Th. 3:12-13*

May God our Father keep you secure unto the end,
unimpeachable in the day of the coming of our Lord Jesus
   Christ.
God is trustworthy, by him you have been called
into fellowship with his Son, Jesus Christ our Lord. *1 Cor. 1:8-9*

The statements inviting *praise and thanksgiving* are particularly
deserving of enrichment. The ones now used have been worn out
by repetition ("Lift up your hearts" — "We have lifted them up to
the Lord"). The domain of doxology and praise is especially rich in
the Bible.[11] What a pity that the faithful do not know these magnificent biblical doxologies!

To God be glory in the Church
and in Christ Jesus
down through all the ages of time without end.     *Eph. 3:21*

In all things honored through Jesus Christ,
To whom are the glory and the dominion forever. *1 Peter 4:11*

The God of all grace who has called us
into his eternal glory, in Jesus Christ,
will himself, after we have suffered a little while,
perfect, strengthen and establish us.
To him is the dominion forever and ever.     *1 Peter 5:10-11*

Now to Him who is able to preserve you without sin
and to set you before the presence of his glory,
without blemish, in gladness, to the only God our Savior,
through Jesus Christ our Lord,
belong glory and majesty, dominion and authority,
before all time, and now, and forever. Amen.     *Jude 24-25*

Nor can we neglect to mention the "hymn of jubilation" (Luke
10:21-22 and Mt. 11:25-27), reflecting Jesus' attitude toward his
Father and showing his praise:

I praise thee, Father, Lord of heaven and earth,
that thou didst hide these things from the wise and prudent,
and didst reveal them to little ones.
Yes, Father, for such was thy good pleasure.

Each of these doxologies could be used to revitalize the statements
of praise and thanksgiving, especially at the end of the Eucharistic
Prayer.

The formula for the *final blessing* (coming at the end of the Mass)
could perhaps be given new life and meaning by using the blessing
of Numbers 6:24-26.

> The Lord bless you and keep you! Amen!
> The Lord make his face to shine upon you
>     and be gracious to you! Amen!
> The Lord look upon you kindly and give you
>     peace! Amen![12]

Perhaps the priest could humbly put himself on the same level
as those he is blessing by saying: "May the Lord bless *us*."[13] The
people, then, would not have to say in turn, "The Lord bless you,
too." Doesn't it seem to be an anomaly that the priest blesses but is
never officially blessed in return?

Finally, let us say a word about dialogues. The Roman liturgy
has been so insistent upon the ministerial priesthood that the dialogues between priest and congregation have been reduced to mono-
logues, ratified by the people's Amen. Later on, we will speak of
the profoundity of this Amen. However, it is evident that other responses should be considered as well. Here are three statements
borrowed from the Pauline writings which could be used by the
people in the final doxology.

Priest:
> May God supply your every need
> according to his riches,
> in glory in Christ Jesus!

People:
> Now to our God and Father be glory for endless ages.

*Phil. 4:19-20*

\*     \*     \*     \*     \*

Priest:
> Grace and peace be to you from God the Father,
> and from our Lord Jesus Christ,
> who gave himself for our sins,
> that he might deliver us from the wickedness of this present
>     world
> according to the will of our God and Father.

People:
> To him is glory forever and ever!                    *Gal. 1:3-5*

\*     \*     \*     \*     \*

Priest:
> May the God of peace who brought forth from the dead
> the great pastor of the sheep, our Lord Jesus,
> in virtue of the blood of an everlasting covenant,
> fit you with every good thing to do his will;
> through Jesus Christ.

People:
> To him is glory forever and ever!                 *Heb. 13:20-21*

There is, as you can see for yourselves, an immense and un-explored domain which Latin had hidden from us and which the ver-nacular fortunately reveals, even if with a certain brutality! The fact that sometimes our acclamations seem to spring from weariness rather than spontaneity may be due to over-repetition of the same phrases, which, although quite good, eventually stifle any sort of life. The congregation's lack of affection for such formulas lies not in a lack of interest for the liturgy, but rather in an exacting love for authenticity and truth in the celebration.

## B. Amen

### 1. BIBLICAL SIGNIFICANCE

Amen: One of the smallest words in chant yet one of the most powerful in the liturgy — a word full of majesty and glory.

*Amen* comes from a semitic root (amân) which means *firm, solid*. From this primary meaning the Hebrew language quite naturally passed on to the idea of truth and fidelity. These two new meanings may seem to us as already representing a spiritualization of the primitive image, but for a Semite they are only the application of their primary meaning. What we can feel and touch in our hands, what offers a certain consistency and solidarity is "true"; on the other hand, a friend on whom we can rely is considered "solid" and "firm."

Amen is perhaps both an affirmation (in the sense of "It is so") and a prayer (in the sense of "So be it").

The Apocalypse places in true perspective the solemn affirmation of the Amen when it juxtaposes it with the "yes" affirmation in the vision of Jesus Christ, the First-born among the dead:

> To him belong glory and dominion
> forever and ever. Amen.
>
> Behold, he comes with the clouds,
> and every eye shall see him,
> and they also who pierced him.
> And all the tribes of the earth shall
> wail over him.
>
> Even so. Amen.                                    *Ap. 1:6-7*

The Amen which concludes a request for a blessing or the invoca-tion of God's name upon the congregation is a prayer. In this case we can cite the formula for benediction used in the Book of Num-bers, 6:24-26 (given above). Each invocation is followed by the people's Amen. The people thereby intensify the prayer said for them by seeking to make the benediction their own.

### a. Amen, the Name of the Lord Jesus

In the Old Testament, God reveals himself as God-Amen:

> And he who takes an oath in the land shall
> swear by the God of truth (God-Amen). *Is. 65:16*

The God-Amen is the sure and firm God who can be relied upon as a steadfast rock; he is also the faithful God whose Word lives forever. In the new Alliance, the God-Amen is Jesus Christ himself, according to the witness of the Apocalypse (3:14):

> Thus says the Amen, the faithful and true witness,
> who is the beginning of the creation of God.

Amen is the personal name of Jesus. It is a part of his royal and messianic title; it introduces epithets particular to him: *Witness* (literally: the martyr, i.e., the one who gives witness) and the *True and Faithful One*. By giving the Lord such an utterly superb name, John does not mean to show only that God was indefatigably faithful to his Promise through the ages, but also that the truth of the God-Amen is incarnate in humanity in the very Person of Jesus Christ. Amen is no longer simply a "divine attribute"; it concerns Christ, who reveals himself as the ineffable truth and fidelity of the God of our fathers.

When the Christians of today's liturgical celebrations sing their Amen, do they know they are saying the name of Jesus Christ?

### b. The Amen of Jesus

Jesus himself used the Amen in a very unique way not found anywhere else: *Amen, Amen, I say to you*. This expression should have made a great impression upon his contemporaries, for it was brimming with power and solemnity.[14] By prefacing his words with the Amen, Jesus both proclaimed that what he said was sure, solid, and worthy of his listener's trust, and at the same time affirmed himself as the Amen, the True and Faithful One. No phrase could be more powerful. Nothing in the Old Testament could compare to it, except perhaps "This is the word of the Lord." What the prophets proclaimed in the name of Yahweh in the Old Testament, Jesus now proclaims in the name of his Father:

> Amen, Amen I say to you,
> we speak of what we know
> and we bear witness to what we have seen. *Jn. 3:11*

> He who sent me is true,
> and the things that I heard from him,
> these I speak to the world. *Jn. 8:26*

Christ is affirmed, according to St. Augustine, as the Word giving witness to itself.

### c. The Amen of the Church: a Response to the "Yes" of God

Christ is the gift *par excellence* that the Father gives to humanity; he is also the only true way through which humanity reaches the Father. It is, then, through him that we receive God and through him that we also return to God. Paul beautifully depicts this double aspect when he writes:

> For all the promises of God find their "Yes" in him;
> and therefore through him also rises the
> "Amen" to God unto our glory.                    *2 Cor. 1:20*

Therefore, the Amen of the Church is the response to the "Yes" of God. The "Yes" of God, the realization of his promises, is Christ and it is through Christ that the Father proclaims his "Yes" to humanity. The Amen of the Church is also Christ and it is through Christ that this Amen reaches God.

Doubtless, it is best to read the end of the Apocalypse in this light. We, indeed, find a passionate dialogue — a dialogue of love! — between Jesus, announcing that his coming is at hand, and the Church-Spouse, who, in the Spirit, is begging her Lord not to wait too long. To paraphrase this dialogue in its essential structure, it could be presented as follows:

"I am the descendant of David, the bright morning star."

The Spirit and Spouse say:

"Come!"

"Yes, my return is near."

"Oh, yes! Come, Lord Jesus!"

Amen.

The Lord's parousia will in some way reiterate the mystery of the Incarnation, i.e., the mystery of the coming of Christ among his people. It will be God's supreme "Yes" to humanity when they are invited into eternity for a vision that is no longer veiled and for love without limit. Through this Amen the Church affirms its faith in the parousia; desiring this love with all her ardor, the Church begs the Lord to show himself at last. This Amen which closes the last Book of Revelation is the Church's response to all of God's plans. It is her final prayer; in it she gathers God's every word, from the first words "In the beginning" (Gn. 1:1) when he created heaven and earth, to the Word in the person of Christ (cf. Prologue of St. John), to this final word in the Apocalypse "Yes, my return is near," which will introduce us to God's silence.[15]

### d. The Amen in the Doxologies

Amen ends almost every biblical doxology.[16] The doxology takes different forms. At times, it is simply a matter of a brief acclamation — a kind of exclamation — which is inserted into a discussion to lift the mind to God, who is blessed forever.[17]

To our God and Father
be glory for endless ages.

Amen.                                                                   *Ph. 4:20*

Glory and dominion to Jesus Christ forever.

Amen.                                                               *1 Peter 4:11*

In both of these quotations the *Amen* is found in a context of *glory* which is proclaimed to be eternal, *for ever and ever*. This glory (in the biblical sense of the term) is not that which God receives from man's praise. Rather, it is primarily and essentially that which he possesses himself, a glory rich in power and light. To such a reality, man's praise can add nothing; it can simply be acknowledged by his Amen.

Some doxologies, beautifully composed, are developed in a quasi-liturgical fashion. Such is the case in the two solemn acclamations we read in the first Epistle to Timothy:

To the King of the ages
who is immortal, invisible,
the one only God,
be honor and glory forever and ever!

Amen.                                                               *I Tim. 1:17*

Jesus Christ, who is the Blessed and only Sovereign,
the king of kings and Lord of lords;
who alone has immortality and dwells in light inaccessible,
whom no man has seen or can see,
to whom be honor and everlasting dominion.

Amen!                                                           *I Tim. 6:15-16*

The most beautiful of all the doxologies is the one in the Epistle to the Ephesians (3:21) whose Christological and ecclesiological accent is unique in all the literature of the new Testament:

To God the Father be Glory
In the Church and in Christ Jesus
down through all the ages of time without end.

Amen.

When seen in this context of glory, power, honor, and eternity, our Amen takes on an astonishing importance. It is not the "little" word added automatically at the end of a short prayer to show that it is over; quite the contrary, it is a powerful acclamation introducing us to God's world of eternal praise.

### e. The Amen of the Angelic Myriads in the Heavenly Liturgy

Finally, we encounter the Amen in the heavenly liturgy of the Apocalypse, which is seen through the four animals (i.e., Angels) who attest to the praise of the angelic myriads and of every other creature:

> And I beheld, and I heard a voice of many
> angels round about the throne, and the living
> creatures and the elders, and the number of them
> was thousands of thousands, saying with a loud
> voice,
>
>> "Worthy is the Lamb who was slain
>> to receive power and divinity and wisdom
>> and strength and honor and glory and blessing."
>
> And every creature that is in heaven and on the
> earth and under the earth, and such as are on the
> sea, and all that are in them, I heard them all saying,
>
>> "To him who sits upon the throne, and to the Lamb,
>> blessing and honor and glory and dominion,
>> forever and ever."
>
> And the four living creatures said, "Amen."[19]     *Ap. 5:11-14*

Bossuet makes this wonderful observation: "The chosen are represented to us in the Apocalypse as forever saying Amen before God. In its holy meaning, Amen is an urgent and affirmative "Yes" which gives assent or, better yet, the entire heart. This is the way God is loved in heaven; shall we not do the same thing on earth? O Holy Church, you are in this place of exile while your dear sister, the New Jerusalem, triumphant in heaven, sings this Amen to God! Will you not answer this divine song like a second choir, led by the voice of Jesus Christ Himself?"[20]

## 2. SINGING THE AMEN

We can predict the problem which may arise due to these notes on the biblical meaning of the Amen. If the melody is to serve the text faithfully, it will have to re-adorn the Amen in glory, power, and majesty. The word Amen is short, too short; there's hardly enough time to grasp it before it's gone. Think of the final chorus in Handel's *Messiah* where the Amen is treated with such magnificence, or of the Amen at the end of the Credo in the *Coronation Mass* by Mozart — these ideal solutions in the musical sphere are useless in the ordinary celebration of the liturgy.[21]

We must take a good look at what can be done on the pastoral level. In fact, each Amen in the Mass does not carry the same weight, nor should they all be solemnized in the same way. The following rule could easily be followed: the importance of the Amen should be in direct proportion to the importance of the prayer it affirms.

Some Amens are said without being sung, such as the Amen at the communion through which the faithful attest to the statement "the body of Christ" and which is equivalent to a profession of faith. This personal ratification is particularly important: "Through his Amen the communicant affirms and shows his partaking in the Body of Christ which is the Church, and his will to live in charity and unity."[22] St. Augustine explains:

> If you wish to understand what the Body of Christ is, listen to the Apostle who tells the faithful: "Now you are the body of Christ, member for member" (1 Cor. 12:27). If, then, you are the Body of Christ and his members, it is your mystery being celebrated on the Lord's table. It is your mystery that you receive. You answer Amen to what you are. You subscribe to it by responding. You hear: "The body of Christ" and you answer "Amen." Be a member of the Body of Christ so that your Amen be true.[23]

This Amen at communion can be considered a personal echo of the Amen sung collectively at the end of the Eucharistic Prayer. Still others are said by the entire congregation at the end of a song, such as the Amen in the Gloria and the Profession of Faith. But these songs are not of primary importance liturgically. They cannot have a place in every Mass without threatening the balance of the liturgical celebration.

Finally, there are some Amens which ratify the presidential prayer. These are most important, especially:

— The Amen concluding the Collects.

— The Amen concluding the Eucharistic Prayer.

### a. The Amen in the Collects

The celebrating community ratifies the presidential prayer through its Amen. At one time, this ratification by the people was especially enthusiastic and resounding. According to St. Jerome, the Amen used to resound in the Roman basilicas like a thunder-bolt from heaven.[24] How wonderful if today the people's Amen would sound — if not thundering — at least forceful and convincing! We would assume, of course, that such an Amen would be "called forth" by the presiding minister with equal conviction and strength. If the priest sounds bored with the prayer, the people will respond with a lifeless Amen; if, on the other hand, the prayer is said with true conviction, the Amen will "spring forth" from the congregation and ring throughout the church.

Some congregations like to accompany the Amen with organ or choir. In principle, no solution that would emphasize the Amen should be rejected *a priori*. We should be careful, however, that the organ or harmonization with the choir does not hide a silent congregation. Instead, it should sustain and intensify the people's acclamation.

### b. The Amen of the Eucharistic Prayer

The great Eucharistic Prayer, which continues from the Preface to the doxology preceding the Lord's Prayer, is the heart of the Eucharistic celebration. If the Amen is to be in proportion to the importance of the prayer it ratifies, this Amen must be the most important and the most solemn; it requires an atmosphere of glory and majesty.

We possess a wonderful witness to this Amen in the first complete description of the Mass we have, which comes from St. Justin and dates from about 150:

> Bread and wine are brought to the minister presiding over the assembled brethren. He takes them, gives praise and glory to the Father of the universe in the name of the Son and the Holy Spirit. Then he says a long prayer of thanksgiving for having been judged worthy to be celebrating this mystery. When he is finished, everyone present acclaims in a loud voice: "Amen!" Amen is a Hebrew word meaning: "So be it." When the celebrant has ended his thanksgiving and everyone has made the acclamation, those who are called deacons distribute the consecrated bread, wine, and water to each one present and then take some to those who were absent. We call this food "Eucharist."

In describing the liturgy of the Lord's Day, St. Justin writes also:

> As was said above, when the prayer is ended, bread, wine and water are distributed. The presiding minister then says a few prayers and makes his thanksgiving after which all the people respond with the acclamation: "Amen."[25]

The liturgy of Justin, as we can see, revolves around a theme of praise and thanksgiving, set in an atmosphere of enthusiasm that should make us jealous. The presiding minister gives *thanks,* the people sing their Amen or *thanks,* and both are called an action of *thanksgiving.* But this Eucharist, in the strictest sense of the word, does not belong to the priest alone but to all Christian people. Justin, himself a layman, had a keen sense of his role among the faithful, of his royal priesthood, a role which is his in the Eucharistic celebration. He is to make the priest's thanksgiving his own through the acclamation "Amen." All the people acclaim by saying "Amen."

What can we do? Obviously, the two small syllables "A-men" are not "weighty" enough to ratify the long Eucharistic Prayer. The Eastern liturgies have solved the problem by tripling the Amen, an action which gives the acclamation its full value. This solution is both liturgically and musically valid. The following formula can be proposed:

First formula

This formula has the "official" air of the doxology, a tone which takes its inspiration from the Latin melody (the A-natural of the altos in the final chord is optional).

Here are two more tonal formulas. The first is better suited to a celebrant who has the vocal range of a tenor or baritone:

Second formula

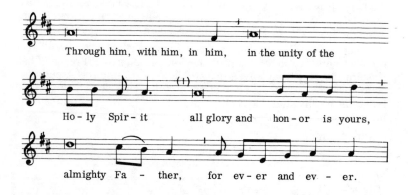

Through him, with him, in him,     in the unity of the
Ho - ly Spir - it      all glory and   hon - or  is yours,
almighty Fa  -  ther,     for ev - er and  ev  -  er.

A - men,      A - men,      A - men!

The next is better suited to a celebrant with the range of a bass or baritone:

Third formula

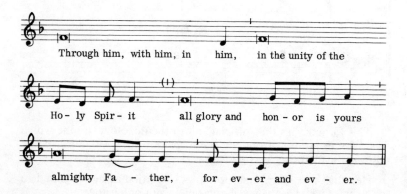

Through him, with him, in   him,    in the unity of the
Ho - ly Spir - it      all glory and   hon - or   is yours
almighty Fa  -  ther,     for ev - er and  ev  -  er.

Instead of singing the doxology, the celebrant can, if he deems it necessary, simply proclaim it (or at least proclaim the final "for ever and ever"), on the tenor F (first formula), A (second formula), and F (third formula), so as to "call forth" the triple Amen from the congregation.[26]

## C. Holy, Holy, Holy Lord

If the value of a song is defined by its relation and proximity to the Eucharist, the Sanctus, which is situated in the heart of the Eucharistic Prayer, is the most important acclamation in the Eucharistic liturgy. If the congregation could only sing one song, it would be the Sanctus. It could even be said that the Sanctus is the on hymn that should be sung at every Mass.

This song is for the people what the Preface is for the priest. The Preface is said by the priest alone, but it envelops us all in its thanksgiving to the Father through the Son in the Holy Spirit. The Sanctus adds to the prayer of the priest the exultation of the people.

### 1. BIBLICAL AND LITURGICAL SIGNIFICANCE

The Sanctus is a centon of biblical acclamations. By placing them in the celebration, the liturgy in no way lessens their original biblical substance but further enriches them in their new setting. These acclamations are four in number (one of which is doubled):

Holy, holy, holy Lord, God of power and might,

heaven and earth are full of your glory.

Hosanna in the highest.

Blessed is he who comes in the name of the Lord.

Hosanna in the highest.

#### a. Holy, Holy, Holy Lord

The first acclamation is borrowed from the biblical account of Isaiah's vision at the beginning of his ministry. The prophet is in the Temple. The heavens are opened before him and God appears to him in glory and majesty. He is seated on a raised throne. The train of his royal robes, spread on the long staircase which reaches down to the Holy of Holies, fills the entire sanctuary. The Seraphim, beings of fire and light, serve as acolytes to the divine throne. Deep in ecstacy, Isaiah hears them sing:

> Holy, Holy, Holy, Lord Sabaoth![27]

God's holiness represents the most profound quality of divine nature in an infinitely luminous purity and an eternal stability. It is the holiness of his love. Placed after the Preface, the acclamation to divine holiness creates a tremendous echo.

In the Preface the priest sings his thanks to God for the goodness with which he surrounds his people. In the Sanctus the people recognize the universality of this goodness that comes to them through his holy love.

Music, too, has sought to express this mystery. In the ferial Mass XVIII, the melody of the Sanctus continues the theme of the Preface. Thus the sequence of the melodies underscores the sequence of the thanksgiving and prayer.

The Sanctus is also placed before the Consecration at the beginning of the Eucharistic Prayer. Likewise, the request for the sanctification of God's name is put at the beginning of the Lord's Prayer:

> Our Father who art in heaven,
> hallowed be thy name!

On the musical plane, we should always take care to keep the Preface, the Sanctus, and the Eucharistic Prayer in the same melodic atmosphere.

### b.  God Sabaoth (God of Hosts)

God Sabaoth means "God of armies, of multitudes." The expression retains an epic flavor and recalls heroic times when Yahweh led the armies of Israel, destroying the enemy and fighting for his beloved people. By the side of these armies — let's say, soldiers — there are, we must also point out, the "heavenly" hosts, i.e., the stars mobilized by God at critical moments when the enemy seemed to be getting the upper hand.

As the old song of Deborah tells us:

> From the heavens the stars, too, fought;
> from their courses they fought against Sisara.[28]

Under the influence of the prophets these celestial troops were spiritualized and became the angelic hosts. Angels are indeed soldiers of God and make up his "camp."[29] The angelic hosts and

the stars have always managed well together. They both enthusiastically greeted the creation of the world when the Lord set the
cornerstone of the cosmos:

> While the morning stars sang in chorus
> and all the songs of God shouted for joy.[30]

God Sabaoth, therefore, should really be interpreted in a very
broad sense. The divine "armies" comprise the entire realm of
created beings who are mentioned in the account of the creation:
"Thus the heavens and the earth were finished and all their array."[31]
Justified too, then, is the latest version of the Order of Mass, which
substitutes "God of power and might" for "God of hosts."

### c. Heaven and Earth Are Full of Your Glory

The biblical concept of "glory" is a technical term to signify the
radiant and luminous manifestation of God's presence among his
people. Glory appears for the first time in the Church of the desert
after the crossing of the Red Sea. Then it is shown at Sinai, where
the Covenant was made; it fills the Meeting Tent and later the
Temple of Solomon.[32] And, as we know, John takes this theme in
the prologue to his Gospel:

> The Word dwelt among us, and we saw his glory.[33]   *Jn. 1:14*

The liturgy makes two minor changes in Isaiah's text. The biblical text says: "The earth is filled with *his* glory." The liturgy dares
to say: "with *your* glory." The somewhat impersonal song, which
the Seraphim repeat while covering their faces in respect for God's
transcendance, becomes a very personal hymn of praise addressed
to the Father. "His glory" is a factual statement. "Your glory" is an
action of praise, of thanksgiving, already a "eucharist." And such
enlargement of the acclamation became better understood by the
second and more important change. The biblical text says: "May the
whole earth be filled with his glory." The liturgy substitutes: *"Heaven
and earth* are full of your glory." The perspective is greatly enhanced. Terrestial praise is combined with heavenly praise; the earth
becomes one with the heavens. It is no longer the Temple alone that
resounds with the Trisagion.[34] It is on earth and in heaven: angels,
men, and all the creatures in the universe unite to give eternal praise
to the Father. Thus the liturgy really seems to be the descent of the
Eternal into time or, if you wish, the ascent and insertion of terrestial acclamation into celestial praise.

### d. Hosanna in the Highest

*Hosanna* literally means: "Save us!" or "Grant us salvation." The
expression comes from Psalm 118(117):25:

> Oh, Lord, grant salvation!
>
> Oh, Lord, grant prosperity!

This psalm is part of the Hallel, Ps. 113(112)-118(117), and, as such, was recited by our Lord at the Last Supper. The acclamation Hosanna, however, became quite popular and thereby lost its original meaning. On the last day of the Feast of the Tabernacles, the people used to wave palm branches and cry "Hosanna!" as they walked seven times around the altar in a procession. As a result, the day became known as the *Great Hosanna*. Obviously, then, this kind of acclamation was instinctive to the people, for when Jesus made his solemn entrance into Jerusalem it was in an atmosphere of praise and frenzied shouts of joy coming from an impromptu procession:

> Hosanna to the Son of David!
>
> Blessed is he who comes in the name of the Lord!
>
> Blessed is the kingdom of our father David that comes!
>
> Hosanna in the highest![35]

"In the highest" is a Hebrew idiom. It means: to God, who lives in the highest heavens above. Out of respect and veneration for divine transcendance, Jewish piety avoided the very mention of God's name, *Eloim*, and preferred to use phrases of circumlocution. Jesus wholeheartedly adhered to this custom when he spoke of the Kingdom of *heaven* (which is the Kingdom of *God*).

### e.  Blessed Is He Who Comes in the Name of the Lord

Just as the preceding phrase, this acclamation also is taken from Psalm 118(117):26. As the pilgrims sang their Hosanna while entering the Temple in procession, they were greeted by the priests' statement of welcome:

> Blessed be he who enters in the name of the Lord.

It was, then, a blessing "in the name of the Lord" given to the pilgrims as they entered the Temple. But the temptation was too strong not to change its original meaning of a blessing in the Lord's name to that of a blessing for him who came in the name of the Lord. Without the slightest hesitation the Greek translation of the Septuagint succumbed to this temptation and threw the doors wide open to this messianic interpretation:

> Blessed be the one who comes in the name of the Lord!

It is under this form that the Gospels quote the psalm both at the solemn entrance of Jesus into Jerusalem[36] and in the eschatological passage referring to the city which is a killer of prophets.[37]

The early communities understood the term "He-who-comes" as an apocalyptic reference to the personal name of the Messiah. When John asks Jesus "Are you the one who is to come?" he really is asking, "Are you the Messiah?" This word is a perfect expression of the mission of Jesus Christ: he is the one who came in the mystery of his Incarnation.[38] Moreover, this idea is often repeated elsewhere. He is the one sought in the Apocalypse, "Come, Lord Jesus!"[39] and it is Jesus whom the Eucharistic liturgy celebrates "until his coming."[40] He is the one who is to come again on the Day of the Lord in glory and majesty. Besides meaning the bodily coming of Christ, "He-who-comes" can also signify his sacramental coming in the Eucharistic celebration, and his eschatological coming in the parousia. By including the acclamation "Blessed is he who comes in the name of the Lord" in its liturgy, the Church once again remembers its pilgrim state and reminds us that we are moving toward an eternal celebration and in some way have already reached the shores of eternity. Moreover, the heavenly liturgy of the Apocalypse, which is the archetype of our own terrestial liturgy, also sings of God's holiness and infinity at the same time:

> Holy, holy, holy, the Lord God Almighty,
> Who was, and who is, and who is coming!                    *Ap. 4:8*

If the biblical meaning of the Benedictus were taken into account, this fourth acclamation would not be sung on a half-tone to mark its separation from the beginning of the Sanctus. This custom derived from polyphonic Masses when the Benedictus was sung after the Consecration and it was musically opportune to have an adagio after the allegro of the beginning, a piano after the forte, a piece for the soloist or for three voices (usually soprano, alto, and tenor in the Masses of Palestrina) after the intial sections sung by the whole choir. But such musical treatment is in no way justified from the biblical point of view. The Benedictus is the "Hurrah!" shouted by the crowd of disciples to Jesus on his messianic entrance into Jerusalem. Thus it should be quite evident that the Benedictus is neither adagio nor piano. Therefore, we can see that the setting of the Benedictus, as well as that of the preceding acclamations, was made "in the crowd" amidst shouts of joy.

To summarize, the biblical setting of the Sanctus is one of enthusiastic celebration amidst overwhelming joy. The singing of the Sanctus should evoke the royal theophany of God Sabaoth, the myriads of angels and heavenly hosts, the cosmic praise toward the Master of the universe, the celestial glory overflowing to earth, the royal and messianic liturgy of the psalms, the coming of the Lord in the New Testament! The Sanctus sung by parsimonious voices, economically conserving their breath and whispering softly, is not really textual. The singing of Isaiah's Seraphim made the very walls of the Temple resound with their voices! There is never enough breath to sing in this way; there are never enough notes to express such joy!

In early Christian liturgy, perhaps the Sanctus was sung in the the Jewish tradition, i.e., during matins. We first see it mentioned as part of the Eucharistic celebration in the two works quoted earlier: the *Euchologion of Serapion* and the *Apostolic Constitutions*.

The Benedictus is first mentioned in the *Apostolic Constitutions* as a communion acclamation in response to the bishop's proclamation: "All holiness be to God's people." The people answered:

> The Holy One, one Lord,
> Jesus Christ is blessed forever
> in the glory of God the Father! Amen.

> Glory to God in the highest,
> On earth, peace to men of good will!

> Hosanna to the Son of David!
> Blessed is he who comes in the name of the Lord!
> The Lord our God has manifested himself among us.
> Hosanna in the highest![41]

The first mention of any connection between the Sanctus and the Benedictus is found in the writings of St. Cesarius[42] (†542). This usage became widespread in the East by the beginning of the 8th century. However, we should not forget that the acclamation belongs to Psalm 118(117), which is a part of the Hallel. In this regard, it was sung by Christ at the Last Supper. It is in union with Christ and the Apostles that the faithful repeat it in the Eucharistic celebration.

## 2. THE SONG OF UNITY

The Sanctus is the song of unity *par excellence* of the Eucharistic community:

> — unity among the angels who "thrill to the same gladness,"

> — unity of men who, along with the angels, sing with one voice,

> — unity of angels and men who join their voices: "With the angels and archangels, with the Seraphim, with the Cherubim, we sing of your glory."

And so it is in keeping with tradition that the Instruction on *Music in the Liturgy* states that the Sanctus be sung by the entire congregation:

> It is preferable that the Sanctus, as the concluding acclamation of the preface, should normally be sung by the whole congregation together with the priest.[43]

The General Instruction to the 1969 *Order of Mass* (No. 55), states also:

This acclamation (the Sanctus) forms part of the eucharistic prayer, and all the people join with the priest in singing or reciting it.

"With the priest" — priests, and eventually bishops, will find it helpful to remember that they, too, are part of the congregation. When one bishop was bemoaning the fact that, while the Sanctus was being sung at a low mass, he didn't have anything to do, someone remarked: "Why not pray with the congregation, your Excellency?" Fortunately, the Instruction has foreseen such instances when priests may think they are "out of work" if they don't do everything by themselves.

> It is desirable that the priest, and the ministers of every degree, should join their voices in the voice of the whole faithful in those parts which concern the people.[44]

Christian antiquity had a very strong sense of this unity in the Eucharistic praise. In his letter to the Corinthians, which dates from the years 95-96, Clement of Rome writes:

> Consider the entire multitude of angels who
> remain before him to do his will. The Scripture
> notes:
>
> "Ten thousand myriads stand before him,
> And thousands upon thousands serve him.
> They cry out: Holy, holy, holy
> Lord Sabaoth!
> All creation is filled with your glory!"
>
> And we, too, reunited through the communion of feelings into
> one body, cry in one voice to him for an immediate
> sharing in his great and glorious promises.[45]

The Seraphim of Isaiah, acolytes to Yahweh's throne, have become ten thousand myriads and countless thousands who stand before the heavenly throne![46] Liturgical tradition enthusiastically accepts these new recruits in the celestial armies for the Trisagion. The Seraphim of Isaiah are never again left alone in their role as singers.

The anaphora of Serapion, Bishop of Thumis in Lower Egypt, introduces us to the Egyptian tradition of the mid-fourth century. The text, which is given as the official prayer of the Church, is without doubt much older:

> Around you is made a cortege of thousands upon thousands,
> and myriads upon myriads of Angels, Archangels, Thrones,
> Dominations, Principalities and Powers. Beside you stand two
> august Seraphim who sing your holiness. Along with theirs,
> receive our acclamations to your holiness:

> Holy, Holy, Holy Lord Sabaoth!
>
> Heaven and earth are filled wth your glory.
>
> Heaven is filled, earth is filled
>     with your wonderful glory![47]

Here is what is noted by the *Apostolic Constitutions* of around the year 380:

> A countless multitude of Angels adore you with the Arch-angels, Thrones, Dominations, Principalities, Powers, Virtues, and eternal armies such as the Cherubim and Seraphim. With thousands upon thousands of Archangels and myriads upon myriads of Angels, they never cease to sing in one unending voice. May the people say with them:
>
> Holy, Holy, Holy Lord Sabaoth!
>
> Heaven and earth are filled with his glory!
>
> Blessed is he for ever. Amen.[48]

In the context of our own culture we admire the eastern literary lyricism but prefer a bit more discretion. Nevertheless, we must — and the richness of the music makes it quite possible — achieve the same atmosphere of glory, joy, and majesty in the unity of our Eucharistic praise.

## 3. THE SANCTUS IN THE GREGORIAN REPERTOIRE

It remains for the individual community to choose the Sanctus which can best express its Eucharistic acclamation:

— if it thinks that it can best express itself in Latin, then, by all means, let it use Latin in the greatest spirit of Christian freedom;

— if it thinks it can sing best by using Gregorian chant, then, by all means, let it keep the Gregorian music;

— if it prefers to use very ornate melodies such as *Sanctus IV* and *VII,* let it go ahead and do so.

Such choices are perfectly possible, and at times preferable: in privileged communities or monastic communities, for example. But such communities are rare and represent only a minute part of ordinary Christian communities. The following proposals are directed to the latter.

— The Sanctus is an acclamation. In principle, an acclamation is an acclamation only if it is acclaimed. For example, there are some Gregorian melodies that are very beautiful but are not suited to the ministerial function of the Sanctus. Such is the case with the Sanctus from Mass VIII *(De Angelis),* which is quite well-known This Sanctus was most fitting for the liturgy before the Council when the priest continued the Eucharistic Prayer in a low voice (while stating in the Preface that he was singing "una voce," in one voice with the community) and when the Consecration came between the Sanctus and the Benedictus. But now, if the priest sings the Sanctus with the congregation — as he should — and if he then recites the presidential Eucharistic Prayer aloud, this Sanctus retards more than enriches the liturgical action. It should be kept only when there is no other Sanctus available. Meanwhile, a better, shorter, and more powerful Sanctus — though just as beautiful — should be taught to the congregation.

There are some Gregorian melodies which are both beautiful and true to their ministerial function. These are the syllabic chants. The following are particularly noteworthy:

— The ferial *Sanctus XVIII.* Sung with power in conjunction with the Preface, it is of incomparable majesty. Besides, it cannot be worn out; a melody whose movement is so closely wed to the rhythm of the Latin phrasing cannot become tiring.

— The easy *Sanctus XIII* with its strongly affirmative triple *Sanctus* plus the beautiful sequence of *Pleni sunt coeli et terra.*

— *Sanctus X,* gracious and as fresh as a spring morning.

— *Sanctus I,* which separates the acclamation from the melody. Its notes ring out, calling forth the light and joy of the Easter Season.

— *Sanctus XVI,* which was at one time fostered by the Instruction on *Sacred Music and the Sacred Liturgy,*[49] September 3, 1958, and was to be taught to "the faithful throughout the world." Despite gallant efforts, it was not too successful. Obviously, this piece did not meet pastoral requirements, the difference between the two parallel melodies of its Hosanna being just too much for the people to master. Consequently, as is often the case, time — the supreme judge — made the decision. This decision was rejection.

— There is a special problem for monastic communities (both male and female), seminaries, or scholasticates. They are free to open their doors to the faithful or keep them shut tight. But if they do welcome the faithful into their midst, they are no longer a singular group of monks, nuns, or seminarians, but rather a moral body of all the baptized persons who may be present. These others, too, must be included in their singing, especially of the Sanctus. Thus there arises a pastoral problem concerning the choice of music which cannot be ignored.

— Finally, a hierarchy of the various hymns in the Mass should be established. The highest, of course, should be the Sanctus. No other song can rightfully even pretend to its magnificence. True, the Gloria celebrates the magnitude of God's glory, but it does not have the same dignity as the Sanctus. It is a more recent ecclesiastical composition, outside the realm of specific Eucharistic thanksgiving.

When we sing the Sanctus, however, we are at the heart of the Eucharist, in union with heaven and earth and "their entire army." If anything should be sung, it is the Sanctus.

In the past it was the custom to enhance the Entrance Song with full organ and the entire choir, whereas the Sanctus was often hurriedly sung in Gregorian chant. This was a mistake. Every musical resource should be made available for the Sanctus (full organ, choir, trumpets, etc.), and only then should other parts of the Mass be enriched as well.

## 4. FURTHER CONSIDERATIONS

### a. Holy, Holy, Holy ...

These three small words have often presented a problem, especially when they are said at a break-neck speed: "Holy-Holy-Holy." Not, however, when they are sung properly: "Holy! Holy! Holy!" with a slight pause between each word. Furthermore, their triple enunciation is a Hebrew idiom which we translate by the superlative or some similar expression: "You are *indeed* holy" — the *vere sanctus* of tradition. Today, however, no one would dream of beginning a sentence by using the same adjective three times. For example, "Strong, strong, strong is the lion," or even "Great, great, great is the Lord." To carry over such Hebrew idioms literally into the vernacular is, indeed, doing the translation an injustice.

Still, there is something that merits a closer look. It concerns the presence of the Sanctus in the Mass. The acclamation is introduced, as we know, by the mention of angels in the Preface, angels who are the brothers of Isaiah's Seraphim who sing the Sanctus. In other words, without the angels in the Preface, there would be no Sanctus, and this acclamation to God's holiness would be merely accidental to the liturgy.[50] The reason is that holiness is a constant theme in the writings of Isaiah; it is a perfectly venerable theme, just as is the theme of justice in Amos, love in Osee, the new alliance in Jeremiah, and inner religion in Ezechiel. Perhaps it might be better, on the pastoral level, to use also other acclamations to some of the other attributes of God — acclamations to the transcendance of his love, for example.

### b. Hosanna in the Highest

Like the Sanctus, this is an exact copy of the Hebrew phrasing. Constant usage has made it a very familar phrase and it has become quite effective. But in practice it is difficult to make any sense of it at all. In fact, no one says "Hosanna" any more, nor do you hear "in the highest" used in everyday conversation. If the acclamation "Hosanna in the highest" were changed to "Praise be to heaven," it would cause quite a stir.

## c. The "Hallel"

This poses the following question: couldn't we improve the text of the Sanctus or, better yet, conceive several different acclamations, just as rich in biblical content, but theologically more significant and pastorally closer to the people than "Hosanna in the highest"? Thus there would become possible a choice between the traditional Sanctus and any of the several new forms.

The answer is simple. The Last Supper, celebrated by Christ with his disciples, was rich in festive atmosphere as seen in the songs of the Hallel, Psalms 113(112)-118(117). It would be very easy to find, in this treasure-chest of psalmodic prayers, acclamations that would be perfectly adaptable to the celebration which we sing in union with Jesus Christ who sang them at the Supper.

Take these few verses from Psalm 118(117) as an example:

> Give thanks to the Lord, for he is good,
> For his mercy endures forever.   (v. 1)

> My strength and my courage is the Lord,
> And he has been my Savior.   (v. 14)

> Blessed is he who comes in the name of
> the Lord!   (v. 26)

Here are a few possibilities from Psalm 116(115):

> Gracious is the Lord and just;
> Yes, our God is merciful.   (v. 5)

> To you will I offer sacrifice of thanksgiving,
> And I will call upon the name of the Lord.   (v. 17 or v. 8)

> I shall walk before the Lord
> in the lands of the living.   (v. 9)

By reviving such splendid texts — and structuring them as acclamations — we will be going back to one of the oldest traditions imaginable, a tradition established by Jesus Christ himself.

## d. The Acclamatory Character of the Sanctus

Resuming the whole tradition, the General Instruction to the Roman Missal, 1969 (no. 55b), presents the Sanctus as an acclamation. But, in fact, the text is not so acclamatory. The statement *Heaven and earth are full of your glory* is not an acclamation at all, but, rather, a simple affirmation. However, an atmosphere of festive celebration can be achieved by using *Hosanna in the highest* as a refrain. It supposes, of course, that the musical setting proposes an acclamatory melody, perhaps by repeating *Hosanna,* as in the following example:

The structure would be the following:

*Hosanna, hosanna, hosanna in the highest!*
Holy, holy, holy Lord,
God of power and might.

*Hosanna, hosanna, hosanna in the highest!*
Heaven and earth are full of your glory.

*Hosanna, hosanna, hosanna in the highest!*
Blessed is he who comes
  in the name of the Lord.

*Hosanna, hosanna, hosanna in the highest!*

## D. The Anamnesis

The anamnesis is the prayer which, after the Consecration, brings to mind (in Greek *anamnesis*) Jesus Christ, especially in the mysteries of his passion, resurrection, and second coming. In the Roman Canon (the first Eucharistic Prayer) this Prayer corresponds to the *Unde et memores.* Through the anamnesis the Church shows that she is performing the Lord's request: "Do this in memory of me."

In all the ancient liturgies this prayer is directly connected to the recitation of the Institution of the Eucharist. Therefore the anamnesis in the *Apostolic Tradition* of Hippolytus of Rome (circa 215) reads as follows:

> " . . . When you do this,
> do this in *memory* of me."

> We *commemorate,* then, your death
> and your resurrection,
> We offer you bread and wine,
> We give you thanks for finding us worthy
> to stand before you and serve you.[51]

In some Eastern liturgies this prayer, which is not necessarily sacerdotal, is sung by the entire congregation. In our present liturgy it has been revived as Eucharistic Prayer II. For St. Paul stated: "For as often as you shall eat this bread and drink the cup, you proclaim the death of our Lord, until he comes." (1 Cor. 11:26).

Several texts for the anamnesis have been suggested. The simplest is:

> Your holy death, O Lord, we remember. Amen.
> Your blessed resurrection we proclaim. Amen.
> Your coming in glory we await. Amen.[52]

The following anamnesis ends with a prayer of supplication:

> We recall your death,
> We proclaim your resurrection,
> We hope in your return.
> Lord, have mercy on us.[53]

The next one is concluded with a statement of praise which seems to conform better to its Eucharistic setting:

> We recall your death,
> We proclaim your resurrection.
> We hope in your glorious return.
> Lord, we bless you.[54]

In the new Eucharistic Prayers a great effort was made to propose new texts of anamnesis, which are:

> (a)   Christ has died,
>        Christ is risen,
>        Christ will come again.

> (b)   Dying you destroyed our death,
>        rising you restored our life,
>        Lord, Jesus, come in glory.

> (c)   When we eat this bread and drink this cup,
>        we proclaim your death, Lord Jesus,
>        until you come in glory.

(d)   Lord, by your cross and resurrection
      you have set us free.
      You are the Savior of the world.

All these anamneses are good in that they are favoring the participation of the people. But perhaps other ways can be found. Indeed, they are more affirmations than acclamations, and, following the rule of the ministerial function, an acclamation is an acclamation only when it acclaims. Let us add also that the text (c) would have a better place before the communion than after the consecration. Finally we know that the priest in the prayer which follows (see 1969 *Order of Mass*, no. 66, 78, 85 and 94) repeats in a certain way what the people have sung, but the liturgy does not favor too much duplication.

## E. Further Considerations

It has been remarked that the Eucharistic prayers are not very much like dialogues. "Why is Father talking all the time?" asked young Vincent, nine years old, during the Mass on Pentecost. Actually, Vincent had many things to say and sing during the celebration of the Word, but as soon as the Eucharistic Prayer had begun, he felt a little "left out" because it seemed I didn't need his participation.

The Eucharistic monologue of the priest does have a theological basis. Since the Reformation had placed in doubt the unique role of the ministerial priesthood (all the faithful are priests), the Catholic counter-reform liked to emphasize this uniqueness by having only the priest say the Eucharistic Prayer, during which the faithful must remain silent. All they have to do is to ratify the priest's prayer with the Amen which concludes the doxology.

Now, tradition, which is the wisdom of the past, has learned to invent and use may diverse and effective forms in order to express the participation of the people. Therefore, in the coptic liturgy, the people intervene with their Amen and their acclamations at the very heart of the account of the Institution. The meaning of these acclamations is as follows: the *entire* community celebrates the Eucharist and, in a certain sense, says the Eucharistic Prayer, each individual on his own level. The priest must keep his irreplaceable role, which is to speak the words of Christ; likewise, the people retain their irreplaceable role, which is to participate in this prayer by their acclamations and Amen.

Of course, we do not have to "orientalize" our liturgy and just mimic what others are doing. But we can gain inspiration from their wisdom.

a. First example:

Let us take the following antiphon:

We give you thanks, we wor-ship you, we
sing your praise and glo-ry, Lord our God.

Borrowed from the ancient liturgies, the text is particularly good. In it the people say, *Eucharistoumen* — in other words, *"We are giving thanks."* This acclamation might be integrated at the heart of the Eucharistic Prayer, when the priest shows the Eucharistic bread and wine (in place of the earlier "My Lord and my God" which was very well situated psychologically). When we take, for instance, the Eucharistic Prayer II, the structure would be the following:

> *Priest:* Before he was given up to death,
> a death he freely accepted,
> he took bread and gave you thanks.
> He broke the bread,
> gave it to his disciples, and said:
> "Take this, all of you, and eat it;
> this is my body which will be given up for you."

> *Congregation:* *We give you thanks,*
> *we worship you,*
> *we give you praise and glory,*
> *Lord, our God!*

> *Priest:* When supper was ended . . .
> this is the cup of my blood,
> the blood of the new and everlasting covenant.
> It will be shed for you and for all men
> so that sins may be forgiven.
> Do this in memory of me.

> *Congregation:* *We give you thanks,*
> *we worship you,*
> *we give you praise and glory,*
> *Lord, our God.*

b. In certain celebrations which are particularly solemn, some communities like to integrate a Eucharistic acclamation into the interior of the whole Eucharistic Prayer; in this way there will be a rhythm established between the prayer of the priest and the participation of the assembly. In Eucharistic Prayer II, the structure would be the following:

*Priest:* Father, you are holy indeed,
and all creation rightly gives you praise.
All life, all holiness comes from you
through your Son, Jesus Christ our Lord,
by the working of the Holy Spirit.

*Congregation: We give you thanks . . .
Lord, our God.\**

*Priest:* From age to age you gather a people to yourself,
so that from east to west
a perfect offering may be made
to the glory of your name.

*Congregation: We give you thanks . . .
Lord, our God.*

*Priest:* And so, Father, we bring you these gifts.
We ask you to make them holy by the power of your
Spirit,
that they may become the body and blood
of your Son, our Lord Jesus Christ,
at whose command we celebrate this eucharist.

*Congregation: We give you thanks . . .
Lord, our God.*

*Priest:* On the night he was betrayed . . .
Take this, all of you, and eat it:
This is my body which will be given up for you.

*Congregation: We give you thanks . . .
Lord, our God.*

*Priest:* When supper was ended . . .
So that sins may be forgiven.
Do this in memory of me.

*Congregation: We give you thanks . . .
Lord, our God.*

Performed in this way, there will always be a living dialogue between the congregation and the priest.

You can use also this other antiphon:

We give you thanks and glory, Alleluia!
For your love is without end, Alleluia!*

The words, "For your love is without end," belong to Psalm 118 (117), which is a part of the "Hallel Psalms," which the Lord sang at the Last Supper.

Whichever other antiphon you choose, you must pay attention not to break the literary structure of the Eucharistic Prayer. The best solution, of course, would be to have other Eucharistic Prayers in which the acclamations of the people are perfectly integrated.

*For musical settings of these antiphons, see L. Deiss, *Biblical Hymns and Psalms,* vol. II, p. 100-101.

# CHAPTER V

# THE RESPONSORIAL PSALM

The restoration of the Responsorial Psalm is one of the most profound reforms undertaken by the new liturgy. It is important not only in the realm of singing, where it totally transforms the present status of the Gregorian gradual and thereby revives its ancient and austere beauty, but also in the domain of God's Word, which it enriches with a new reading. This restoration has learned how to combine the boldness of renewal with the richness of tradition. It is not a mere "re-animation" but, more properly, resembles a resurrection — the resurrection of a piece that was dead, buried under the weight of nearly thirteen centuries of history. Yet it does not revive its original look clothed in the robes of the sixth century or in the dusty shroud of history. No purpose would be served by unearthing such a mummy and parading it into the liturgy of the twentieth century as an archeological curosity. Rather it concerns itself with the resurrection of the *function* of the psalm, a function established in the past with the look of "yesterday," and now restored with the look of "today."

The Instruction on *Music in the Liturgy* of March 5, 1967, underlines the importance of the Responsorial Psalm:

> The song after the lessons, be it in the form of gradual or responsorial psalm, has a special importance among the songs of of the Proper. By its very nature, it forms part of the Liturgy of the Word. It should be performed with all seated and listening to it—and what is more, participating in it as far as possible.[1]

In the same way, the General Instruction to the 1969 *Order of Mass* (no.36) affirms that "the psalm is an integral part of the liturgy of the word . . . . "

The communities who have made serious efforts with the Responsorial Psalm have been able to enjoy the psalms in a new light and have enriched their own faith by much new splendor. On the other hand, the congregation in which the lector links the Responsorial Psalm and the reading by running one into the other like two verses of the same hymn has carried this psalm as a burden. It took this burden by obedience to the rubrics, which is highly commendable. However, the reform is encouraging an obedience that is lucid and enlightened. Then today's burden will be tomorrow's joy.

## A. The Meaning of the Responsorial Psalm

The Responsorial Psalm is the response through which the community greets the Word of God.

### 1. BIBLICAL SIGNIFICANCE

Salvation's intervention into history was far from being a monologue imposed upon earth by heaven. Rather, its goal was to open a dialogue between the majestic freedom of men and God's own divine love. The Word calls upon the community. It steals into its heart and demands a choice. Not to answer would be to refuse. Anyone who has encountered God will no longer be calm, or rather, his tranquility will be found in never interrupting the dialogue once it has begun. Indeed, this dialogue without end or pause will continue in the liturgy of the new heaven and earth for all eternity as a source of peace and jubilation. The Apocalypse presents a wonderful picture of this mystery: God wipes the tears from the eyes of those who are saved and they unceasingly give him thanks in this heavenly psalm:

> Alleluia! For the Lord our God almighty now reigns!
> Let us be glad and rejoice and give glory to him;
> for the marriage of the Lamb has come.
> Blessed are they who are called to the marriage supper
> of the Lamb![2]                              *Ap. 19:6-7, 9*

In its simplest form this response is expressed through the Amen with which the people ratify the Word. Thus it was at the proclamation of the Law to the people of Sichem after they had crossed the Jordan. They ratified each statement of the Law with an Amen so powerful that it echoed through Ebal and Garizim.[3]

In transcribing this Amen, the Bible does not succumb to the use of a literary cliché. On the contrary, it signifies man's "yes" to God, the welcoming of his Word, the thanks for his mercy. When God intervenes in his life, what else can men do but happily kneel before him and give him thanks? We recall the lovely story, in the Yahwistic tradition, of the marriage of Isaac and Rebecca. Upon the order of Abraham, a servant returned to the land of his master's birth with ten camels to find Isaac's future bride. He came to the village of Nahor and stopped at the well just as evening was descending upon the land. Women came to fetch water. Humbly he asked for a sign to distinguish the chosen one: it was to be the one whom Yahweh caused to offer both him and his camels a drink. When he received the sign, when God designated the beautiful Rebecca, as Genesis tells us, he prostrated himself and worshipped Yahweh, saying:

> Blessed be the Lord,
> the God of my master Abraham,
> whose constant favor to my master has not ceased.    *Gn. 24:27*

To the word of God, the servant answers with a "Response" of thanksgiving and praise.

When God's intervention is particularly prodigious and decisive, when deliverance makes the heart exceedingly joyful, when a single cry of praise seems too short to express the radiance of the soul, then the gratitude of the faithful man is increased and he shouts it in a long litany of joy until it becomes a "canticle" or psalm. The Bible is filled with such instances:

### a.  In the Old Testament

— God delivers the people of Exodus, and they cross the Red Sea. Moses and the children of Israel answer God and sing of their Savior and Father, he who conquered their enemy, who opened the sea and made walls of the waves, who led his people to the holy mountain. Miriam lent her tambourine to their song by praising Yahweh "who is gloriously triumphant; horse and chariot he has cast into the sea" (Ex. 15:1-18, 21).

— God delivers his people from the hand of Sisera who for twenty years had besieged the children of Israel with his nine hundred iron-filled wagons. Deborah and Barak answer Yahweh, the hero of all the ancient combats, and praise him; he is the one who, amidst the trembling of the earth and the stars and the seething of the sacred torrent of Qishon, swept up the enemy and crushed their rulers (Judges 5:2-13).

— God delivers Anna from her barrenness by making her the mother of the infant Samuel. Anna makes her response to God through her canticle; she rejoices in God her Savior, who lifts the poor off their dunghills and who gave joy to her barrenness seven times over (1 Sm. 2:1-10).

— God delivers King Ezechiah from the illness which was to carry him off in his prime, like a shepherd's tent in a desert sand storm. Ezechiah answers God, who released him from the grasp of death, in his canticle (Is. 38:10-20).

— The canticle of Jonah is already well-known. Imprisoned in the belly of the whale, he glimpses his deliverance and, amidst the seaweed, he composes a moving song of distress and thanksgiving (Jon. 2:3-10).

— God delivers Tobias the elder from his blindness; he recovers his sight, sees an angel, and sings of his deliverance (Tob. 13:1-17).

— God preserves the three youths, Ananias, Misael, and Azarias, from the stain of idolatry and from the fiery flames. They thank him with their song, "Blessed are you, and praiseworthy, O Lord, the God of Our Fathers" (Dn. 3:26-90).

— God delivers his people from the hands of Holofernes. The community sings its deliverance in the canticle of Judith (Jdt. 16:1-16).

### b. In the New Testament

— God realizes the messianic deliverance through the coming of Jesus among men. Mary, Daughter of Sion, the most pure and most intense realization of the mystery of the Church, sings the *Magnificat,* which is the song *par excellence* of the entire messianic community.

— God intervenes in favor of Zachary the unbelieving, who then believes. Zachary answers by praising God, "who has visited and wrought redemption for his people" (Luke 1:68-79).

— God reveals himself to Simeon, who sings the *Nunc dimittis:* holding the infant Jesus in his arms, he can finally say that his eyes "have seen thy salvation," i.e., *Jesus* (Luke 2:29-32).

It is interesting to note here that, for the most part, these canticles are not a part of the primitive accounts handed down to us today.[4] In other words, they were born in different contexts or even came from different sources, and were then put into the mouths of inspired singers, who are supposed to have retold them. By weaving them into the fabric of today's biblical narratives, tradition underscores how natural it is for man to respond in song to the saving actions of God and to sing to him with praise and thanks.

A response can dress up the various forms of prayer. It is especially pleasing in the form of the biblical "benediction," which includes the thanks given for the wonders of God.

— In the Old Testament, a most significant example is the great Hallel, Psalm 136(135), where each of God's marvelous deeds is proclaimed with praise: "For eternal is his love."

— In the New Testament we have, of course, the *Magnificat* of the Virgin Mary as she exults in God, her Savior, whom she carries within her.

## 2. LITURGICAL SIGNIFICANCE

The reading of the Word of God in the liturgical community is not simply a reading taken from the archives of God's people in the Old and New Testaments. It is, rather, the *actualization* ("*Today* this scripture has been fulfilled," Luke 4:21) of the events and the prophecies which announce and proclaim Jesus Christ for the benefit of the liturgical community. It is a real celebration of Christ present in the Scriptures.

To such a proclamation of Christ in his Word the community responds with the Responsorial Psalm. The following parallel can be drawn: just as in the history of God's people the community answers the "mirabilia Dei" (the marvels of God) through the biblical "canticle," so the present liturgical community answers the Word — which recalls the "mirabilia" — through the Responsorial Psalm. Therefore, this psalm expresses their praise and thanks for God's Word.

As a summary:

— In biblical history the community responded to the wondrous deeds of God through the "biblical canticle." To the *actio Dei,* responds the *reactio* of the community.

— In the liturgical celebration the community responds to the proclamation and the fulfillment of God's wondrous actions through the Responsorial Psalm.

## B. The Form of the Responsorial Psalm

It may be

— a reading

— a psalmody

— in responsorial form.

## 1. A READING OF A PSALM

Early liturgical tradition used the Responsorial Psalm as a reading of the Word of God. This psalm would be given in its entirety to the psalmist who would intone it in degrees *(gradus)* on the scale (thus the name "gradual"). Such was still the practice in the fifth century during the time of St. Augustine (†430 A.D.) and St. Leo the Great (†461 A.D.). In time, however, the psalm became the prey of the vocal virtuosity of the cantor, who was himself enlightened by zeal for the house of God. For God and his greater glory, he always wanted a beautiful, a more beautiful, indeed, the most beautiful rendition possible. The pattern of notes became more complex; they rose and descended, tracing a thousand graceful arabesques. Naturally this musical complexity led to the reduction of the psalm text. Only two verses survived the attack, the *versus* and the *responsus* (indicated in the old books by a V and an R). By the time of St. Gregory (590-604) this evolution was already well-established. The appearance of the schola,[5] whose existence was recognized for the first time in the West under Pope Sergius I in 687, definitively stabilized this situation. The *versus* and the *responsus* furnished a text ample enough for the composition of beautiful melodies, but inadequate for the presentation of the Word. Music took precedence over the psalm and engulfed the Word of God in a myriad of notes. If the psalms are to present Jesus Christ to the Christian Community; if there is a story of Jesus in the psalms, as Jesus himself bore witness (Luke 24:44); if, on the other hand, the melodies are only robes to clothe the Word of God — we can, indeed, say that the presentation of Jesus Christ had been obscured and replaced by the splendor of his clothing. Beautiful musical robes are, of course, praiseworthy; it is precisely in the Gradual that human genius has offered some of the most beautiful Gregorian melodies to God. However, we must always keep in mind the purpose for which these melodies were created. The aesthetic venerates the garment; the faithful adores the Person.

## 2. PSALMODY

The psalm is a lyrical composition. The psalter is not only a book of readings but is really a book of "song and prayer,"[6] just as it was for the postexilic community and is now for the messianic community. It is correct, then, to introduce the psalm with a certain lyricism, so as not to destroy its character or ruin its unique beauty. However, its musical beauty is not a part of the message of the Word but of its presentation. It has its own importance because its ministerial function is precisely to "add a greater effectiveness to the text."[7] To read the psalm without its lyrical cloak would be merely to present the text of the psalm to the community but not the psalm itself.

In order to attain this minimum of lyricism, psalmody or chant seems to present the best pastoral method. Other ways are possible and must, of course, be sought, but always in connection with the literary genre of the psalm. However, music should not claim too great an importance in either the melodic or the harmonic sphere. The tones or the harmonies must not overpower the Word of God nor impede the faithful from perceiving the message, which is the image of Jesus Christ.

## 3. IN RESPONSORIAL FORM

Those assembled actively participate in the singing of the psalm by way of a short refrain, according to St. Augustine: "To the reader (i.e., the psalmist) we answered by singing."[8] Tradition has insisted upon the importance of this participation. St. John Chrysostom explains:

> If you sing:
>
>> "As the hind longs for the running waters,
>> So my soul longs for you, O God."
>
> You conclude a pact with God; you sign a pact with him without ink or paper. Your voice proclaims that you love him above all else, that you prefer nothing to him, that you burn with love for him.
>
> Let us not sing the refrains out of sheer habit, but rather take them anew every time. Each verse can teach us much wisdom.
>
> Even if you are poor, even if you are too poor to buy books, even if you have books but no time to use them, at least take care to keep in mind the refrains of the psalms you have sung not once, twice, or three times, but often, and you will receive great consolation. See what a great treasure the refrains have opened for us!
>
> I urge you not to leave here with empty hands, but to gather the refrains like pearls, to keep them forever with you, to meditate upon them, to sing them to all your friends and relatives.
>
> If your soul is troubled, if greed, anger, or any other passion torments your soul, sing them assiduously. That is how we will enjoy peace in this life and how we will store up eternal rewards in the next, through the grace and love of our Lord, Jesus Christ.[9]

Therefore, it is in perfect accord with tradition that the Instruction on *Music in the Liturgy* of March 5, 1967, states that the Responsorial Psalm, as far as is possible, be executed with the participation of the entire community.[10]

## 4. A SONG OF MEDITATION?

A number of missals presented the Responsorial Psalm as a song of meditation. Therefore, the faithful are invited to meditate upon the Word of God while they listen or sing. In itself, the suggestion is good. It is just as commendable to want a few moments for a personal thanksgiving after having received the Lord's Body and Blood in the Eucharist.[11] For here, too, we have received Christ through his Word, and a brief moment for reflection is not out of order. But this practice should not become exaggerated nor should it be prolonged after the Epistle and the Gospel. The liturgy is a celebration — not a meditation. In principle, when the faithful are united together, they are not assembled to savor the "joy" of community silence. There are other occasions, the rest of the day or the rest of the week, to meditate upon the Word at their leisure and in their own particular way.

Moreover, meditation is also a good suggestion when it means the assimilation of the proclaimed Word in both the Epistle and the Gospel, as well as in the Responsorial Psalm. It is even good in regard to other prayers in the Mass.

> "The essential element of worship," teaches Pius XII, "must be interior, for it is always necessary to live in Christ, to be entirely devoted to him, to give in him, with him, and through him, glory to the Father in heaven. The holy liturgy requires that these two elements (interior and exterior worship) be intimately united, and it never tires of repeating it each time an exterior act of worship is prescribed."[12]

But the question to be asked is this: is it right to consider the Responsorial Psalm a song of meditation and thereby surround the psalm with an atmosphere conducive to meditation upon the Word? Without hesitation, we would have to say no.

The reason is simple to understand. We are speaking of the psalms and the psalter as a well-defined repertoire within the Bible. (And it is just that, materially, at least, even though the Bible presents many other psalms which are not in the psalter.) Yet these words hide several different realities. The composition of the psalter is spread out over a thousand years[13] and the psalms found in the psalter contain pieces of quite varied literary genre. There is a world of difference between the litany of the hymn from Psalm 148 and a psalm from the psalter said by Jeremiah. In fact, exegesis distinguishes the following literary genres in the psalter:[14]

— The "liturgies," such as Psalm 24(23), the song of procession for the entrance of the Ark into Sion, or Psalm 134(133), which is "lucernal" (song of the evening office);

— Hymns celebrating the glory of God, such as Psalms 145 (144), 147(146), 148, 150 and the triumphal litany of the great "Hallel," Psalm 136(135);

— Psalms of enthronement, containing the cry: "God reigns," such as Psalms 96(95) — 99(98);

— Royal psalms, celebrating the Davidic monarchy, such as the supplication for the king in Psalm 20(19) and the long polyphony of Psalm 89(88);

— The canticles of Sion (Zionslieder), such as Psalm 137(136): "By the streams of Babylon";

— Psalms of collective and individual trust;

— Psalms of collective and individual supplication;

— Sapiential psalms celebrating the law of the Lord, such as the interminable Psalm 119(118);

— The so-called historical psalms that recount the wonders of the history of salvation, such as Psalms 78(77) and 106(105);

— The prophetic exhortations containing the divine oracles, such as Psalm 50(49).

Now the form of the Responsorial Psalm will be exactly the same as that of the literary form of the psalm it presents. If the psalm is a supplication, the Responsorial Psalm will also be one of supplication; if it is a hymn, the Responsorial Psalm also will be a hymn; if it is a lamentation, it, too, will be a lamentation; and if it is a psalm of the kingdom, the Responsorial Psalm also will be the cry of the royalty of Yahweh: God reigns! It could even eventually be a meditation, if the psalm itself proposes a meditation, as in Psalm 119(118) where for 176 verses one meditates upon the Word of God.

Yet here one may encounter an objection: when the liturgy uses a psalm according to a certain form (which is meditation), it may take away the color of the primitive literary genre that the psalm previously had.

Of course, precisely that happened in the past, when the psalter, unfortunately, was considered as cloth from which one cut out a habit for each saint and every feast. That is also precisely what we must avoid today. What comes first is not the choice of a certain number of lines but the psalm as God inspired it, according to its literary genre. We must not disfigure the face of the psalm by singing a meditative melody to texts that are themselves filled with joy or trembling with pain: "You changed my mourning into dancing . . . and clothed me with gladness," Psalm 30(29), or "Lord, incline your ear to my call for help," Psalm 88(87), or still, "Let the rivers clap their hands, the mountains shout with them for joy," Psalm 98(97).

We can, therefore, see that the title "song of meditation" is in no way characteristic of the genre of the Responsorial Psalm. Although it will always be most beneficial to dwell upon the Word, still we must first respect the truth of the psalm by respecting its literary genre.

## C. The Text of the Responsorial Psalm

The restoration of the Responsorial Psalm in the new lectionary is not a step backward to the first centuries of the liturgy. Since the readings had been reorganized, it was also necessary to take another look at the graduals which, as was said earlier, are a response to those readings. The responses had to be in direct relation to the readings so that the celebration of the Word would have a certain unity. To insure this harmony between the reading and the psalm reponse (now called "Responsorial Psalm" instead of "gradual"), the lectionary has employed the following principles:

1. When the first reading quotes a psalm, the lectionary retains this psalm as the Responsorial Psalm. Here is an example taken from Easter Week.

— The Epistle for Monday of the Octave of Easter proposes the text of Acts 2:14, 22-23. It contains the first discourse of Peter and leads to the quoting of Psalm 16(15):8-11. This psalm was particularly important in primitive catechesis on the Resurrection of Christ because it states that God (the Father) could not abandon the One he loved (Christ) to corruption.

— In response to this reading, the Responsorial Psalm uses this same Psalm 16(15):1-2a, 7-8, 9-10, 11, and presents it thus:

> Keep me, O God, for in you I take refuge;
>     I say to the Lord, "My Lord are you."
> I bless the Lord who counsels me;
>     even in the night my heart exhorts me.
>
> 'I have set the Lord ever before me,
>     with him at my right hand I shall not be disturbed.
> My heart has been glad and my tongue has rejoiced,
>     my body will live on in hope,
>
> for you will not abandon my soul to the nether world,
>     nor will you suffer your faithful one to undergo corruption.
> You have shown me the paths of life;
>     you will fill me with joy in your presence.'

2. When the Gospel quotes a psalm, the lectionary may use it as the Responsorial Psalm in anticipation of the reading to follow. Thus the Gospel for the first Sunday in Lent (Cycle C) presents the story of Christ's temptation, according to Luke 4:1-13. Psalm 91 (90):11-12 is also quoted therein. Consequently the lectionary, conforming to liturgical tradition, retains this psalm as the Responsorial Psalm 91(90):1-2, 11-12, 13-14, 15-16b, and adds the meaningful antiphon: "Be with me, Lord, when I am in trouble."

3. The lectionary often uses as a Responsorial Psalm the psalm to which a literary reference is made in the first reading. It is clear that a simple literary reference is not sufficient to motivate the choice of the psalm if the spiritual context of the psalm itself differs from the context presented in the reading. In other words, don't keep a psalm which has merely a few similar words. But, if the spiritual context of both psalms is identical, the literary reference is precious.

For example, a reading of the prophet Jeremiah quite naturally led to a choice of psalms from the Psalter of Jeremiah.

The reading from Jer. 1:4-10, because it contains the consecration of Jeremiah as a prophet "from his mother's womb," led to the Responsorial Psalm 71(70):1-2, 3-4, 5-6:

*I will sing of your salvation.*

In you, O Lord, I take refuge;
　let me never be put to shame.
In your justice rescue me, and deliver me;
　incline your ear to me, and save me.

*I will sing of your salvation.*

Be my rock of refuge,
　a stronghold to give me safety,
for you are my rock and my fortress.
　O my God, rescue me from the hand of the wicked.

*I will sing of your salvation.*

For you are my hope, O Lord;
　my trust, O God, from my youth.
On you I depend from birth;
　from my mother's womb you are my strength.

*I will sing of your salvation.*

My mouth shall declare your justice,
　day by day your salvation.
O God, you have taught me from my youth,
　and till the present I proclaim your wondrous deeds.

*I will sing of your salvation.*

— The reading from Jer. 2:1-13, because it contains the affirmation of God, according to the word of the prophet, "They have abandoned me, *the source of life-giving water,*" suggested the choice of Psalm 36(35), which belongs to the psalter of Jeremiah, with verses 6-7, 8-9, and 10-11, and the antiphon: "You are the source of life, O Lord."

*You are the source of life, O Lord.*

O Lord, your kindness reaches to heaven;
　your faithfulness, to the clouds.
Your justice is like the mountains of God;
　your judgments, like the mighty deep.

*You are the source of life, O Lord.*

How precious is your kindness, O God!
　The children of men take refuge in the shadow of your wings.
They have their fill of the prime gifts of your house;
　from your delightful stream you give them to drink.

*You are the source of life, O Lord.*

For with you is the fountain of life,
    and in your light we see light.
Keep up your kindness toward your friends,
    your just defense of the upright of heart.

*You are the source of life, O Lord.*

4. The lectionary chooses as a Responsorial Psalm whatever may illustrate more clearly what was proclaimed in the Word, even if there is no definite literary reference.

— Therefore, on Good Shepherd Sunday (the fourth Sunday of Easter) the Good Shepherd psalm is used, Psalm 23(22):

The Lord is my shepherd,
I shall not want.

— The reading from Acts 3:11-16, which tells of the healing of the lame man at the Beautiful Gate, suggests Psalm 8 as the Responsorial Psalm because the healing was performed *"in the name of Jesus Christ."*

O Lord, Our Lord,
How glorious is *your name* in all the earth.

5. For specific liturgical times, psalms for the Responsorial Psalm should be chosen that have a special meaning for these cycles. History is the mother of wisdom. While moving forward, today's liturgy uses the wisdom of the past ages as its guide. The Reponsorial Psalm keeps the community in an excellent spiritual atmosphere, an atmosphere the liturgy has wished to preserve for the Church for centuries.

For example:

— For the season of Advent, Psalms 25(24), 80(79), and 85(84) are especially advised.

— For Christmas week, the so-called Kingdom Psalms 96(95), 97(96), 98(97).

— For the Week after the Epiphany, Psalm 72(71).

— For the season of Lent, Psalms 26(25), 51(50), 91(90), 130(129).

— For Holy Week, Psalm 23(22).

— For Easter, Psalms 118(117), and 66(65).

— For Ascension, Psalm 47(46).

— For Pentecost, Psalm 104(103).

6. When no rule is directly applicable, the lectionary employs psalms which have not yet been chosen, so that the Christian com-

munity may become more familiar with the entire psalter. By choosing the best psalms and the best verses from those psalms, the lectionary has been able to form a psalter perfectly adaptable to the Christian community, not only for liturgical use but also for private devotion.

It is up to the homilist to point out the connection between the readings and the Responsorial Psalm. The new liturgy supposes that every Mass, even weekday Masses and those celebrated with only a few people, have a homily. It need not be long, but it should highlight the significance of the mystery of Christ as seen through the reading and the psalm. Neither the person responsible for the musical setting of the Responsorial Psalm, nor the people who participate with their response should be unaware of the importance of this mystery.

# D. Execution

The restoration of the Responsorial Psalm is still too recent for the new liturgy to have had time to find new forms or to perfect traditional ones. Just think of the centuries it took to gather the psalms for the old *Graduale*! Nevertheless, there are now various possibilities which will permit a Responsorial Psalm to be formed that will completely realize its ministerial function.

## 1. RESPONSORIAL PSALMODY

In the responsorial psalmody, the psalmist sings the verses of the psalm, and the congregation responds with an antiphon after each "stanza" or group of verses. This procedure presupposes that the community has a "psalmist" whose voice:

— is sufficiently beautiful to be accepted by the whole community;

— is sufficiently humble and discreet so that he, personally, will not be remembered by the community. Indeed, the psalmist should not be there to perform a "solo," or to enable the community to listen to a beautiful voice. Rather, it is the Word that must be proclaimed and received as the Word of God.

## 2. ALTERNATING AND RESPONSORIAL PSALMODY

Here is another way of presenting the Responsorial Psalm: the community, divided into two sections, alternates the verses of the psalm and sings the antiphon after every second verse (i.e., after every four lines).

For example, let us consider the Responsorial Psalm for Easter Sunday, Psalm 118(117), whose antiphon is: "This is the day the Lord has made; let us rejoice and be glad."

All:          *This is the day the Lord has made;*
              *let us rejoice and be glad.*

1st  Section: Give thanks to the Lord, for he is good,
              for his mercy endures forever.

2nd  Section: Let the house of Israel say,
              "His mercy endures forever."

All:          *This is the day the Lord has made;*
              *let us rejoice and be glad.*

1st  Section: "The right hand of the Lord has struck with
              power;
              the right hand of the Lord is exalted.

2nd  Section: I shall not die, but live,
              and declare the works of the Lord.

All:          *This is the day the Lord has made;*
              *let us rejoice and be glad.*

1st  Section: The stone which the builders rejected
              has become the cornerstone.

2nd  Section: By the Lord has this been done;
              it is wonderful in our eyes.

All:          *This is the day the Lord has made;*
              *let us rejoice and be glad.*

This kind of presentation is particularly adaptable to well-trained communities. It presumes that the people can use either a psalter or a text of the Responsorial Psalm which can be easily distributed. Such a situation makes possible an especially active participation on the part of today's congregations. Indeed, we are no longer living in an age when each church possesses only one copy of the psalter and the people are still learning the alphabet. Today, everyone knows how to read and prefers that he himself respond to the Word with some simple refrain. He does not want some intermediary to answer for him. Thus there has come about a happy blending of listening to the Word in the reading with the subsequent response to that Word in the singing of the community.

Care, however, should always be taken not to divide the congregation into two equal sections, lest a balance of equal intensity and uniformity be created. To obtain a pleasant variation, the community may alternate with a small group such as the choir, for example. The small group may, then, very easily and most precisely set the tone and tempo; it may, if need be, quicken or retard the movement; in other words, it may easily set the pace and help the congregation. This will be impossible if the congregation is divided into two equal components. Once begun, such singing can no longer be guided.

The same procedure applies to the use of two choirs in the singing of the office as well. As for the antiphon, it is always good to
have it begun by a soloist who will be immediately joined by the
community.

## 3.  THE READING

There is also a third possibility: a reader — even the priest, if
no one else is available — reads the verses of the psalm and the
people answer by singing the antiphon. Such a method is always
possible, especially when there is no psalmist available and very
few people are present at Mass. This method is liturgically valid,
although it may be rather weak. For in order to achieve the ministerial function of the Responsorial Psalm, at least the minimum
should be attempted.

## 4.  FURTHER REFLECTIONS AND NEW PERSPECTIVES

The three methods mentioned above have an enormous and obvious advantage: they can be implemented immediately, even in
parishes having few musical resources, because very little music
is required.

However, they do present a major disadvantage. By proposing
universal psalmodies applicable to all Responsorial Psalms, we are
seemingly ignoring literary genres. Whether the psalm is a lamentation or a proclamation of the royalty of Yahweh, whether a hymn
or a supplication, whether an act of thanksgiving or a sapiential
psalm, it will have the same melody, or at least the same melodic
progression of four or five notes. It will be sung:

> All you peoples clap your hands,
> Shout to God with cries of gladness.                    *Ps. 47(46):2*

without the singer's ever dreaming of clapping his hands in exalta-
tion — and it will be sung to the same melody as that of a song
of distress:

> My God, my God,
> why have you abandoned me?                              *Ps. 22(21):2*

Then the same tune will be used for:

> So will I give you thanks with music on the lyre,
> I will sing your praises with the harp.                *Ps. 71(70):22*

without the singer's ever thinking seriously of playing the lyre or
harp in a liturgical office! It will be used for even the lamentation
of Psalm 31(30):9-10, on the one hand:

> Have pity on me, O Lord, for I am in distress;
> with sorrow my eye is consumed;
> my soul also, and my body.

> For my life is spent with grief
>> and my years with sighing;

and on the other, for the cries of joy of Psalm 150:

> Praise God with lyre and harp!
> Praise him with timbrel and dance!

without the singer's ever thinking of dancing in church to the rhythm of a drum! Indeed, the same psalmody will accompany Psalm 88 (87), the saddest psalm in the psalter!

> O Lord, my God, by day I cry out;
>> at night I clamor in your presence.
> Let my prayer come before you;
>> incline your ear to my call for help.

In their extraordinary diversity, ranging from murmurs of imploration to shouts of joy, the psalms possess an unparalleled power of evocation. Doesn't psalmody risk losing all this by placing them all on the same level of a pious drone?

It has been asserted in vain that the use of various "modes" will give each psalmody a personality all its own. The mode of *D* is presumably triumphant, whereas that of *E* is suppliant; or better, the mode of *D* is suitable for hymns and that of *E* for lamentations. Consequently every psalm is found, whether comfortable or not, encouched on the same bed of Procustes and arbitrarily submitted to the same melodic treatment. True, a few psalms, whose splendor of text outshines the melody, resist and thereby save their inspired visage. Others are utterly disfigured.

Gregorian chant shows great wisdom here. For a number of the graduals, it certainly was able to weave a melodic garment which was most personal and which lent to each one a unique splendor. The music lives in symbiosis with the text; it is so much a part of the psalm that to remove it would mean destroying the text as well. Just think of the power of the *Haec dies quam fecit Dominus* and of the exultation of *Confitemini Domino quoniam bonus* from the Gradual on Easter, Ps. 118(117), or of the jubilant trumpets of *Ascendit Deus in Jubilatione* from the Gradual on Ascension Thursday, Ps. 47(46), or of the supplication in *Emitte Spiritum Tuum* from the Gradual of Pentecost, Ps. 104(103), etc. However, this does not mean composing Gregorian for English texts. One would no sooner remake Gregorian chant than rebuild the cathedral of Chartres. Nevertheless, the psalm text must always be presented, even now, with the same respect, the same veneration, the same artistic perfection, as formerly Gregorian chant presented it. Indeed, it will take time to weave a glorious garment for the Responsorial Psalm. No one is responsible for the banality of the present-day psalmodies. Up to now, these crutches were needed to help

ease the psalms into the vernacular, but now we can certainly envision new solutions.

All our remarks have referred to the different ways of proclaiming the Responsorial Psalm and to the participants themselves.
The following basic principle has been followed: the literary genre
of the psalm must be respected. Better still, the proclamation of the
Responsorial Psalm should emphasize the literary genre.

## a. Different Ways of Proclaiming the Responsorial Psalm

From the many possible methods for proclaiming the Responsorial Psalm, we have chosen these three in particular:

— The first presents the minimum of musical solemnization
possible: the simple reading.

— The second employs the maximum musical solemnization
possible: the sung Responsorial Psalm.

— The third is a compromise between the first and second:
psalmody.

In every case the congregation should sing the antiphon.

### 1)  READING

We are not speaking here of reading the psalm because no one
is available to sing it — a rather poor substitute. Rather, we are
speaking of reading as being the best formula, in some cases, for
highlighting the literary genre of a psalm.

In fact, it may be the best method for historical psalms, like Psalm
78(77):3-4 ("What our fathers have declared to us, we will not
hide from their sons") or like certain sections of Psalm 105(104).
These psalms tell stories. Therefore, the text is much more "at
home" when read than when clothed with a melody.

Likewise, certain individual prayers, such as prayers of thanksgiving, confidence, or lamentation, may appear in their truest light
when read. It may not be best to chant a prayer as desolate at Psalm
88(87). When one is "down in the pit" like "a man without strength"
(verse 5), the mood is not quite suitable for singing. The bitterness
outweighs any possible melody.

Thus, reading will sometimes protect a psalm's lyric intensity,
which is to be found in the truthfulness of the text rather than in
a musical artifice. Yet the singing of the antiphon at regular intervals
will generally emphasize this lyricism.

### 2)  SINGING (Durchkomponiert)

Singing is the direct opposite of reading. It is distinguished from
psalmody in that it presents a musical argument of some importance.
Psalmody is a garment which may be well-suited to different psalms;

or the same psalm may even be clothed in several psalmodies. But singing, by contrast, is made to measure. It must be written note for note, the music carrying a specific text and amplifying its lyricism.

Some psalms, belonging to the literary genre of hymns or psalms of the kingdom, can be effectively presented as songs. For these the following principle would apply: a song is not a song unless it is sung. Simple psalmody would not always do justice to the text and might even betray its literary genre. This would be as grave an error as *intoning* the carol "Angels We Have Heard on High."

In conservative communities the traditional musical genre of the Church could quite naturally be used, whether it be classical polyphony or a soloist a cappella, in imitation of Gregorian chant. Many recent antiphons are written in such a style. Some communities like the Gregorian modes. Why deprive them of these? Yet nothing should prevent communities which are more receptive to modern music from preferring more contemporary sounds which are more adapted to their sensibility. Nor should anything prevent them from accompanying their songs with instruments which are usually used for contemporary music and which are really the equivalent of the lyres, harps, lutes, tambourines, and cymbals of Psalm 150. In principle, the organ is not more pious than the drum, nor is the devotion of the drummer any less than that of the organist.

### 3)   *PSALMODY*

Between these two possibilities — reading and singing — is another, that of psalmody. It is suitable for the majority of the psalms. Because it has little musical personality itself, it can more aptly express psalms which do not have strong literary characteristics. This statement in no way indicates any prejudice against the intensity of the psalm's own prayer or its musical beauty. This beauty is really found in the supporting prayer of the community, which is also an inspired prayer.

Two closing remarks: the boundaries separating these three proposals are flexible, not necessarily rigid. In fact, a very plain psalmody will sound like a reading, whereas a more ornate psalmody, when sung with feeling, may very well be a song. This does not cause any great inconvenience, because the literary genres of the psalms themselves are not irreducible either. Rarely does a literary genre exist in a pure state. Nothing is more supple, more alive, more rich than a prayer which goes from praise to supplication, from tears to cries of joy.

Note, too, that several literary genres can be found in the same psalm. Therefore, the first part of Psalm 19(18) has the character of a hymn; the second, that of a sapiential nature. Psalm 22(21) first presents a supplication (verses 2-21) and then a thanksgiving

(verses 22-31). It is clear that psalmody will have to take into account these differences and then emphasize them. Obviously, one
could not psalmodize:

> My God, my God,
> why have you abandoned me?                    *Ps. 22(21):1*

in the same way as:

> I will utter praise in the vast assembly.     *Ps. 22(21):25*

### b. The Participants in the Responsorial Psalm

Who should sing the verses of the Responsorial Psalm? Before
the reform, in communities trained in Gregorian chant, the full
schola would sing the two verses. It should be stated that Gregorian
chant did not have to be sung by a soloist, and that choral singing
responded better to liturgical piety. At the present time, the opposite
position is often stressed. The Responsorial Psalm is given exclusively to the soloist, and no one questions the value of this decision. What can be said about this?

Here again an analysis of the literary genre of the psalm is illuminating and invites us not to fix the positions rigidly.

— Psalms that are individual prayers will preferably be sung
by a soloist.

— Psalms that are collective prayers will preferably be sung by
the community, alternating in two choirs, singing the antiphon after
each group of verses.

— Several psalms are presented as dialogues between two
choirs.[15] We don't mean here, however, a dialogue between the soloist and the congregation, such as that in the great Hallel, Ps. 136
(135), where the people acclaim the verses of the soloist with the
antiphon: "For his mercy endures for ever." Nor is meant a dialogue
between the people and the priest who pronounces a benediction, as
in the "lucernal" Psalm 134(133):3—"May the Lord bless you from
Sion, the maker of heaven and earth." The dialogues discussed here
are those between the two choirs or sections of the congregation,
as is the case in Psalm 121(120):

| | |
|---|---|
| 1st Choir | I lift up my eyes toward the mountains; whence shall help come to me? |
| 2nd Choir | My help is from the Lord, who made heaven and earth. |
| 1st Choir | May he not suffer your foot to slip; may he slumber not who guards you: |
| 2nd Choir | Indeed he neither slumbers nor sleeps, the guardian of Israel. |

It is evident that the psalmody with two choirs (with the antiphon sung after each group of verses) will be the best way to stress the literary structure of such a psalm. It would not be good for the soloist to ask the questions and then give the answers all by himself.

In all other cases, the solution that is most adaptable to the community should be chosen. Thus, Psalm 22(21): "My God, my God, why have you abandoned me?" is really an individual prayer. But if the entire community wishes to say this prayer as did Christ, why prevent them?

In the context of our culture it seems preferable to give the community the opportunity to sing the Responsorial Psalm themselves whenever possible, rather than to condemn them to the monotony of the antiphon. As a general principle: never have others do what the congregation can do for itself.

In the account of the last appearance after the Resurrection, according to Luke 24:44, Jesus speaks to his disciples about what was written about him in the psalms. There is, then, a history of Jesus given in the psalms. No matter how the Responsorial Psalm is sung, the problem will always be for the community to discover the image of Jesus Christ in each of the psalms.

# CHAPTER VI

# PROCESSIONAL SONGS

The Mass according to the Roman rite contains four processions:

— the entrance,
— the gospel,
— the oblations,
— the communion.

Each of these processions is accompanied by a song called a processional:

— the Introit or Entrance Song accompanies the entrance procession;
— the Alleluia accompanies the Gospel;
— the Offertory accompanies the oblations;
— the Communion accompanies the communion.

The processions emphasize the mystery of Christ whose presence they denote. We should remember that the *Constitution on the Sacred Liturgy*[1] gives three modes of expressing the presence of Christ in the liturgical celebration:

— Christ is present in the praying and celebrating community, according to his word: "For where two or three are gathered together for my sake, there am I in the midst of them." (Mt. 18:20)

— He is present in his Word, for it is he who speaks when the Holy Scriptures are read in Church.

— Finally, he is present in the Eucharist.

Every one of these modes of expressing Christ's presence implies a real and effective presence. So, too, the presence of Christ in the Eucharist is said to be real "not exclusively, as if other presences were not, but due to its excellence."[2] Each of these expressions of his presence is signified in a special way in the song that accompanies the rite.

1. *The presence of Christ in the community:*

— This presence is realized specifically when the crowd of Christians in the beginning of the celebration becomes a hierarchically organized assembly.

— The rite signifying this mystery of his presence is the entrance of the celebrant, who represents Jesus present in the midst of the community.

— The song accompanying this rite is the Entrance Song or Introit.

2. *The presence of Christ in the Word:*

— It is realized as much in the Epistle as in the Responsorial Psalm, but it culminates in the proclamation of the Gospel, whereby the people see that "God speaks to His people, and Christ is proclaiming His Gospel."[3]

— The rite denoting this presence of Christ is the Gospel procession.

— The song accompanying this rite is the Alleluia (or some other acclamation to the Word of God).

3. *The presence of Christ in the Eucharist:*

— It is realized in the prayer of consecration which, in the Eastern liturgies, necessarily accompanies the epiklesis.

— There are various rites denoting this holy presence. The most important is the elevation at the final doxology concluding the Eucharistic Prayer. Two processions surround the Eucharist; the first is the offertory procession, when the consecrated bread and wine to become the body and blood of Christ are carried to the altar. The second is the communion procession, when the faithful approach the altar to receive the bread and wine in the Eucharist.

— The songs accompanying these two processions are those of the Offertory and the Communion.

## A. The Entrance Processional

### 1. ITS SIGNIFICANCE

What is the significance of the entrance processional? What is the mystery emphasized by this hymn?

### a. The Coming of Christ

The priest "presides over the assembly in the person of Christ."[4] When he joins the community in the entrance procession, it then becomes the liturgical community. It is at this point that the community is organized on a hierarchical basis and becomes the Epiphany of the Church. In the heart of the priest beats the heart of the Church. The congregation is not a small fragment which, joined to thousands of other fragments, constitutes the people of God. The Church is not a mosaic of particular groups; the full mystery of the Church is found incarnate in each individual group. Christ is present in his community.[5] This is the mystery signified by the priest's coming into the midst of the faithful.

### b. The Entrance of the People

The coming of the priest brings about another mystery: the entrance of the celebrating community.

The community, as well, has an entrance to make. Nor do we mean an entrance processional in which the whole community participates. Liturgical groups wishing to indulge in the luxury of beginning each celebration with such a procession of the faithful would, it seems to me, turn it into a liturgical pageant. If the community likes such a display, it should not be denied.[6] But we are speaking here of an entrance that is important for other reasons: the entrance of the people into a state of celebration, into the celebration itself.

Whenever Tom and Dick or Sally and Jane are outside church, they are Christians isolated in their individuality and situated in the secular domain. When they meet in front of the church, they exchange polite conversation with such amenities as "Hello! How are you?" As soon as they cross the threshold of the church, however, they enter a sacred place. Their conversation ceases and is replaced by the Entrance Song. When separated, they are united together in the invisible mystery of the community of saints. When assembled in church, this invisible tie is visibly signified by the constitution of the assembly. Now the community is ready to celebrate Jesus Christ. Yet their song has no comparison with the overtures announcing artists when they appear on stage, or with the ovations with which players are greeted by their fans in the sports arena. Rather, it is the very mystery of the Church now made visible by the assembled community.

Their song also has the more immediate function of unifying the people present, thus fulfilling its ministerial function, as we have said above. The people coming to church are a crowd, sometimes even a mob. Entering the church, they are still separate individuals, but, when they sing together, they express their unity for the first time. John Chrysostom explains:

> As soon as the singing of the psalm begins, all the voices are united and are gathered into a harmonious canticle. Young and old, rich and poor, men and women, slaves and free men,

we all sing the same melody. The musician plays the various chords of his zither but it is one melody that is heard: is it so astonishing that the power of the psalm and the inspired canticle produce the same result! . . . The prophet speaks, we all respond, together we form one choir. There are no longer slaves, free men, rich, poor, master, nor servant. The inequality which exists in the world has been pushed aside, forming a single choir with equal voices, earth imitating heaven. Such is the nobility of the Church![7]

Because it is necessary to express the unity of the congregation, such a song with its rite will naturally be at the beginning of the celebration. It would be contrary to the laws of the celebration as well as the laws of group psychology to begin an office *ex abrupto,* with perhaps a prayer by the celebrant, offering the community no chance to express its common spirit. However, song is not the only way to exteriorize the unity of the congregation. Therefore, on Good Friday when the community celebrates Our Lord's Passion, it begins by kneeling before the altar to show that it bows in silence and adoration. Other rites are possible, such as the common recitation of a prayer. But among these traditional methods, singing is the simplest and the most immediately effective.

These considerations on the coming of Christ in the person of the presiding priest and on the gathering of the community and its entrance into the celebration lead to a simple solution of the problem posed by each celebration: how long should the Entrance Song last?

Formerly this problem did not exist. Or rather, it was suppressed by the rubrics. The Entrance Song was as long as was needed to sing or intone the official text. But this rubrical point of view has now changed. Today some say that the Entrance Song should last as long as it takes the priest and the procession to reach the altar. "In any case, it stops when the celebrant reaches his seat."[8] But such a suggestion reveals a rather narrow, clerical view of the liturgy. It is not the community who should accommodate its actions to those of the presiding minister, but rather *he* — who is in the service of the community — who should direct his actions in accord with those of the congregation. The celebration is an act of the whole community (of which the priest is a part).

To be liturgically true, we must remember that the Entrance Song has a ministerial function to be realized. It should be long enough to realize this function, i.e., as long as it takes for the community to assemble itself and spiritually acclaim Christ. If only one stanza is needed, then only one stanza should be sung. If five or six stanzas are needed, then five or six should be sung — even if the priest has no more than two steps to take from the sacristy to the altar. Whatever time is needed to unify a celebrating community should be taken.

## 2. THE TEXT

The text, along with the music, leads the faithful to the heart of the celebration. If the feast has a strong liturgical personality all its own, the liturgy chooses the text that best emphasizes the mystery to be celebrated. In the wonderful Christmas Introit, the path to the Lord's crib will be easy to find, if the congregation sings:

> A child is born to us,
> A son is given to us.

At times the liturgy has succumbed to the temptation of accommodating texts in order to adapt them to the feast. The Introit:

> *Resurrexi et adhuc tecum sum.*
> I have risen and dwell among you.       *Ps. 139(138):18*

is in excellent text to portray the mystery of Easter but not to denote Psalm 139(138):18, which says something entirely different.[9]

In some instances tradition has given the text a meaning completely different from that of the original. The Introit for the Sunday within the Octave of Christmas is a well-known example:

> When a profound stillness compassed everything
> and the night in its swift course was half spent,
> your all-powerful word, O Lord,
> bounded from heaven's royal throne.

This text would be excellent, if the following were not attached: "A fierce warrior, into the doomed land, bearing the sharp sword of your inexorable decree." (Wis. 18:14-16) In fact, the passage in question is the chastisement of the Egyptians during the Exodus!

Such misinterpretations — which no one approves — can teach us quite a bit. It tells us that the Church has always wanted to choose texts that were best suited to the needs of her children, even if at times they had to be adapted. She did not think that the celebrating community was assembled to evaluate the texts, but that the texts were collected to serve the community.

Outside specific liturgical times, i.e., during the Sundays after Pentecost, tradition has not been hard to please and has taken refuge in the Psalter. Isn't it in the Psalter that we can always find expressions of adoration, praise, thanksgiving, and supplication? The choir master used to follow the numerical order of the psalms, beginning with the first and ending with the last. He did so not only for the Introit but also for the Alleluia, the Offertory, and the Communion.[10]

What is the desired procedure now?

### a. Translation of the Introit Texts

We cannot be satisfied with a simple translation of the Introit texts. If the Latin in the Missal is valid, we should praise heaven for the riches of past tradition and use them for the benefit of the whole community. However, each particular case should be carefully studied to see whether perhaps a better text can be found. Even the best of Introits can present many problems. What about the Introit on Easter Sunday?

> I arose, and am still with you, alleluia;
> you rest your hand upon me, alleluia;
> your knowledge is too wonderful, alleluia, alleluia.

Aren't there more profound texts in the New Testament to express the central message of the Resurrection? What about the glorious texts from the *Pauline Corpus* which were once a part of the early liturgy?

What about the Introit for Pentecost? The first sentence is filled with grandeur: "The spirit of the Lord fills the world." But what follows is anti-climactic: "and knows man's utterance." As for the psalm, "God arises; his enemies are scattered," it rather weakly denotes the mystery of God's love diffused in our hearts by the Spirit.

### b. Biblical Text or Ecclesiastical Composition?

Is it preferable to choose Entrance Songs with texts from the psalms and other biblical sources, or should ecclesiastical compositions be our choice?

— The Roman liturgy reveals a great variety. Texts from the psalms are often used — a practice which is very old. "Before the middle of the sixth century," writes J. A. Jungmann, "an Introit song, taken from passages in the psalms, was already a well-established custom."[11] The text from the psalms was used as a protection against the Gnostic productions of the Manicheans and other heretic groups which flooded the religious song market at that time. As a counter-move to these heretical hymns, the following principle was observed: nothing less than chants dictated by the Spirit of God himself was to be used. We can therefore state that the use of psalms as entrance songs is a tradition of the Roman Church; any other text could have been used as long as it was not of Manichean, Gnostic or other heretical origin. However, we cannot say that the use of the psalter according to numerical order constitutes a tradition: it is simply a custom. It should not stand in the way of choosing new psalms that are better suited for the needs of our day.

It is a shame that so many psalms were chosen without much forethought and were always responsorial in form. There was, then, a responsorial psalm for an Entrance Song, an Offertory, and even for a Communion Song,[12] not counting the Responsorial Psalm itself. Such a manifold use is a sure way to devaluate the psalms in general and the Responsorial Psalm in particular, since the latter is the most important psalm in the Mass.

— Tradition also uses other biblical texts. The Christmas Introit *Puer natus est* (Isaiah 9:6) and the Introit of Holy Thursday *Nos autem gloriari oportet* (Gal. 6:14) are excellent examples and reveal a perfect choice. Yet other new choices can be foreseen; we have scarcely begun to utilize the biblical treasures. The psalter is not the only wonderful section in the Bible.

— Finally, tradition uses ecclesiastical compositions such as the *Salve Sancta Parens*. It will be in line with tradition to compose new texts. The patristic and medieval periods have left us some 30,000 hymns.[13] This fact simply shows that every age has sung of Christ according to its own particular image of Him. Each period of history has offered to the Lord its own "tribute of praise."[14] Nor must our age fail in the same duty.

Such diversity within tradition is most illuminating. In my opinion, we should not concentrate all our efforts on choosing texts from the psalms, or from biblical texts, or even from old or new ecclesiastical compositions. Keeping in mind its ministerial function, we must find — or create — the best text for the celebrating community, one which will offer the best way for that community to enter joyfully into the celebration.

I personally think there should be popular texts that are simple and meaningful but without theological and metaphysical complexities. They should, above all, reflect the splendor of the Word. The faithful, meeting in Christ at the beginning of the celebration, must experience the same radiant and liberating joy shared by so many of Jesus' contemporaries when they met the Lord on the roads of Galilee. We can hardly picture Jesus countering his accusers with a sermon about the "eternal truths," or with verses from the psalms. However, these eternal truths are important, and the liturgy wisely makes use of the celebration of the Word (readings, Responsorial Psalm, and homily) to expose them to the faithful. But the first contact with the Lord, the first gathering of God's children in Church, should be radiating peace and happiness. In short, the Entrance Song should make the splendid image of the Risen Lord shine upon the community.

It also seems that a variety of texts is not only desirable but almost necessary. A child does not sing like an adult. Nor does a well-trained Christian express himself in the same way as does someone who is still being instructed in the faith. There is a world of difference between a catechism class of children and a congregation of mature Christians. To suggest that the same text be used for all these groups would be just as gross an error as to have Gregorian chant sung by all congregations throughout the world. Paul, who was a good teacher, used to say that he gave those who were still "little children in Christ" spiritual milk, not solid food.[15]

Such diversity of Entrance Songs should, likewise, be found in the celebrations of the same community. You wouldn't celebrate the Eucharist during the week in the same way you would on Easter Sunday. Several possibilities should be sought.

The official agencies in regard to both the national and also the universal aspects of the Church have a large role to play in this area. They must not only accord communities the freedom to experiment, but must also furnish them with new texts, such as those we now have for the Responsorial Psalm. However, they should in no way appear as authorities imposing new texts, but rather as offering the communities a choice so as to develop their freedom. Christianity is the one religion most concerned with individual freedom. The Christian infinitely respects his freedom, venerating it as a grace the Lord has merited for him on the cross. Therefore, it is most natural for the Christian liturgy to be the most free, the most disengaged from rubrical restraints. Just as it is inconceivable that I might force my neighbor to sing a particular text in his celebration of Jesus Christ, so too is it inconceivable that some system or organization should impose a text upon the Christian congregation. However, history is living proof that what is "totally inconceivable" is often the practice of the day. The official bureaucrats have always had a weakness for thinking that the texts they proposed were the best for everyone, and the authorities have at times been guilty of smothering individuality for the sake of conformity. This is a big mistake. It also goes against the teachings of history. No liturgy has ever been created by an official edict; it has always been born within the celebrating community itself. All the Church can ask of every Christian community is to conform itself to the Word of God. An ecclesiastical agency can present to the people a text which has been carefully rhymed and set to music by "official" poets and musicians — but it can't make them think it is beautiful.

Yet it is quite simple for authority to obtain unity — even exterior unity — in the celebrations, while, at the same time, respecting individual freedom. It is simply a matter of suggesting texts that are so wonderful in themselves that they will be freely chosen by every congregation. Thus authority will finally have realized the essential nature of its vocation: to be in the service of the celebrating community.

## 3. MUSIC

### a. Festive Music

The Entrance Song should be festive. It should take the people out of the secular world and place them in a world of festivity and celebration. Such a break from the ordinary is by no means a denial of the everyday world in which we live and to which we are tied by bonds of love, joy, or pain. Rather, it is the coming of this world into the presence of the Father, the entrance of our tears and smiles "into the kingdom of his beloved Son" (Col. 1:13). More than that of any of the other processionals — that of the Gospel, Offertory, or Communion — the music here should in some way bring us away from the secular and ordinary life we lead and guide us toward the divine and the life we wish to lead. It is the road to God. Its function is even more important at this point, when our hearts are still heavy and have not yet been lifted by the Word of God which is to follow. When I meet someone in the street and he suddenly begins to sing, I naturally think that something has just happened to him. For the Christian suddenly to burst into song, something has happened: he has just met Jesus Christ. That is why he sings.

### b. Suitable Music

The Entrance Song should be appropriate. It must be functional; it must fulfill its ministerial function. It must, first of all, be suitable *to the particular community* which is celebrating in a particular set of circumstances. It may be very possible that the same music will be good for different communities (this is especially true, thanks to radio and television, which have made the whole world tend toward a common musical culture).[16] But such a conclusion cannot be accepted *a priori*. Only experience can strengthen or weaken it. Here is a basic rule that can be observed: music must fulfill its ministerial function, and this function must be seen in the light of the celebrating community it serves. Now, communities are many and diverse. Their own liturgical personalities, their particular ways of loving Christ and singing about this love must be respected. In order to show the incomparable richness of Christ, a thousand different musical possibilities are open to communities in Europe, Africa, South America, etc. As the *Constitution on the Sacred Liturgy* says, "the ecclesiastical authority . . . must . . . carefully and prudently consider which elements from the traditions and genius of individual peoples might appropriately be admitted into divine worship."[17] The "prudence" of which the Council speaks will be that of opening the doors of the liturgy as wide as possible to every valid musical form in use throughout the world. The music of every nation is invited to kneel before Jesus Christ and sing his glory.

Even among the same linguistic or ethnic groups, there are infinite varieties of people. One congregation may be middle-aged with a fair musical background and used to singing to the accompaniment of an organ. Another may be composed mostly of young people who are more apt to be using guitars. No one would even dream of saying that in theory one type of music is better than another, but in practice it is quite possible that an organist's accompaniment might be quite poor while that of a guitarist might be excellent. We are simply saying that each community has the right and obligation to express itself in the most authentic way possible.

The music should also be suitable *to the liturgy being celebrated*. The community not only enters a state of celebration, but the celebration of a particular feast — the one presented to us in the day's liturgy. You wouldn't sing the same way on Christmas as you would on the first Sunday of Lent, or on Easter as on a Sunday of the Year. We cannot offer here any great musical solution at this point; the culture and the musical customs of the people will come up with the best possibilities. Here as elsewhere, what Paul said to the early Christians concerning charismatic manifestations is most appropriate: "Do not extinguish the Spirit. Do not despise prophecies. But test all things; hold fast to that which is good."[18]

These reflections on music apply equally to all the processionals. We will not reiterate them, then, in discussing the Alleluia, Offertory, or Communion.

## 4.  THE PARTICIPANTS

Who should sing the Entrance Song?

It seems that this song should be sung by the entire celebrating community. There could be a dialogue between the choir and the people, but it would seem out of place for the Entrance Song to be sung solely by the choir or a soloist. One of the best guidelines is found in the Instruction: "It is desirable that the assembly of the faithful should participate in the songs of the Proper as much as possible . . . ."[19]

Why? Because of the significance of singing. As said earlier, the community acclaims here the coming of Christ and manifests it in the celebrating Church. Because this mystery of his coming is lived by the faithful, they express it in song, a definitive way of uniting a congregation.

## 5.  THE FORM

Different forms are possible and desirable, if we consider the many different communities involved. Let's look at the choices we have:

### a. Gregorian Chant, Traditional Form

Communities who like this form and this tradition could always use it for their own edification and consolation.

### b. Strophic Songs

The German Kirchenlied, the English chorale, and the Latin hymns in the Roman Breviary are particularly good examples of strophic songs.[20] Sometimes it has been said that the strophic songs have a "closed" form, every strophe being complete in itself and the musical ensemble being produced by a juxtaposition of autonomous elements. This might not always be a good type of music to use as a processional.

However, before one makes a judgment upon a strophic song, both the text and the melody must be studied. If the *text* progresses, if it is filled with meaning, then the song itself will be vitalized from verse to verse. No one verse will be like another because each one will be made "special" by the words. The spell resulting from the magic of repetition will become charged with meaning in the last verse.

As for the *melody*, there can be, of course, such strophic tunes which try to rise, but fall down again without breaking down the iron barriers between each strophe. Why does this happen? It is because of the melodic structure itself. If the melody ignores the resources of modulation, if it rests on the tonic at the end of each verse like a person completely worn out, it will never spring to life. Other melodies, however, really know how to take flight because they have been constructed with more skill, with more lyricism, and with that trifle called inspiration, which can transform anything. Who may say that the strophic hymn *Vexilla Regis* is a closed melody and could not be used as a processional, when each strophe leads directly to the next? Let us simply say that there are good melodies and bad, whether open or closed.

### c. The Psalm with Antiphon

In line with practices in the Roman liturgy, we can also consider the psalm with its antiphon. The psalm could be sung either responsorially or with an antiphon. In the responsorial form, the soloist or choir sings one verse, the congregation a second, and then everyone sings the antiphon. Our earlier remarks concerning the Responsorial Psalm can also be applied here.

We must also take care not to give the entrance psalm the form of a Responsorial Psalm, lest we endanger the liturgical integrity of each piece. A longer text and a more important musical structure will be used for the antiphon than for the Responsorial Psalm.

We must also avoid making the mistake of choosing a "closed" musical form; for example, when the antiphon and the psalmody both begin and end on the tonic note (or on the same note) of the scale. Unfortunately, such is the situation with most compositions for psalm and antiphon; the antiphon and the psalmody each constitute an autonomous unit, locked tight as a prison tower. Instead of opening, the melodic line closes up. The antiphon-psalmody succession gives a juxtaposition of musically autonomous elements — prison towers! — instead of a musical dialogue between the antiphon and the psalmody.

The advantages of using a psalm as an Entrance Song are obvious: it is easy to implement. It is adaptable to any kind of a congregation, especially one which is not too musically oriented. But there are also serious inconveniences:

— The verses of the psalm will be given prime importance. What should be an Entrance Song then becomes a psalm sung while entering.

— The true mystery of the feast will not be directly expressed in the psalm; the richness of an Introit composed for a particular feast will be lost. Like steam rollers, the antiphons and psalms will crush the particular character of each liturgical season, thus disfiguring the face of the liturgy of the particular feast.

— This effect will be austere and, in the long run, boring. It will completely lack the festive character necessary for an Entrance Song.

### d. The Psalm with Troparion

In the Eastern liturgies the troparion is a composition of a single strophe, of biblical origin, and in celebration of the mystery of the feast. D. Rimaud describes it in this way: "It seems to be a prose text designed to summon the congregation to enter into the mystery of the day's liturgy. It ends with a short refrain (an acclamation of faith, praise, or supplication) which is a detachable part of the entity and which thereby permits the congregation to participate actively in the celebration of the mystery."[21] Here, for example, is a troparion for the feast of the Epiphany.[22]

> On this day, the Trinity of old
> has shown us the goodness that belongs to it alone:
> The Father who speaks from on high is heard,
> The Son was revealed when he was baptized in the flesh,
> And the presence of the Spirit was seen:
> What we have learned in faith, we now cry in one voice;
> "Glory to you, our God, who has made himself known!"

It is executed as follows: the troparion with its short refrain begins and ends the psalm sung in a responsorial form.

Troparion and refrain: Choir and congregation
    Psalm verse: Soloist (or choir)
    Refrain: Congregation
    Psalm verse: Soloist (or choir)
    Refrain: Congregation, etc.
Troparion and antiphon: Choir and congregation

Such a format has undeniable advantages over the simple psalm with antiphon:

— The freedom of the rhythmic prose text allows a rich formulation of the mystery.

— The choir can take a more important part and thereby enhance the solemnization of the Entrance Rite.

## e. Full Form

In most communities, three variations of the Entrance Song prevail:

— congregational singing;

— choral singing;

— a soloist.

Each of these fulfills a determined function:

— Congregational singing assures the participation of the whole community in the Entrance Rite.

— Choral singing, thanks to polyphony, assures solemnity.

— Finally, the soloist allows the text to be clearly proclaimed and understood by the whole congregation.

Here, for example, is the song "Without Seeing You,"[23] composed with the above plan in mind:

Congregation and Choir (antiphon):

> Without seeing you, we love you,
> Without seeing you, we believe,
> And we sing, Lord, in joy, your glory.
> You are our Savior.
> We believe in you!

Soloist (verse):

> Blessed is he who will listen to your Word;
> He shall truly never see death,
> For by you, he is heir to a new life.

Choir:

> O Lord, to whom shall we go?
> You alone have the words of eternal life!

The last verses, which are an acclamation of the choir, are repeated after each verse by the soloist and musically recall the reprise
of the antiphon by the entire congregation.

Finally, let's not forget the richness lent to the celebration by
the organ. The organ plays the overture to the feast. A beautiful
prelude is, for the community, a blessing from God. Hence the
organist bears a great responsibility for the singing of the people,
not only in accompanying them, but also in preparing them at the
beginning of the service.

## 6.  THE INTROIT, KYRIE, AND GLORIA

In a discussion of Entrance Songs, the Kyrie and the Gloria
must be included. Thus there are three songs at the beginning of
the celebration. However, there is a risk of turning the liturgical
celebration into a musical one; therefore we will rightly speak of
the "importance of the opening songs."[24] This importance is seen
as particularly vital in the light of the vernacular, as we seek to
have "the meaning and proper nature of each part and of each
song . . . carefully observed," as is requested by the Instruction on
*Music in the Liturgy*.[25]

The Entrance Song, indeed, has a specific function to fulfill —
namely, to unite the congregation and introduce the feast. Obviously, if the Entrance Song has already achieved that unity, the
Kyrie and Gloria cannot do the same thing. It is far more likely
that they will only disrupt the prayerful mood and distract the
people's attention. For hardly will the faithful have entered into
the spiritual celebration than they will be jerked back by the pre-
liminary supplication of the Kyrie, which makes the rest seem out
of context. Scarcely will they have entered into the spirit of the
Kyrie than they will be projected into the Gloria, a setting for
praise and thanksgiving. Hardly will they have begun this than
they will be back into the Kyrie again. (The *Domine . . .miserere
nobis* of the Gloria is translated as "Kyrie eleison" in Greek!)
Barely will they have returned to the Kyrie than they will be singing
the final praises of the Gloria! What mind is capable of such gym-
nastics? And if capable, how long can it keep its intellectual sanity
or mental balance? Christian prayer should not be a multiplication
of formulas or mental distraction. Let us always remember the
advice of our Lord: "But in praying, do not multiply words, as the
Gentiles do; for they think that by saying a great deal, they will be
heard. So be not like them."[26]

The Christian community, throughout history, has built up a
self-defense mechanism against the aggression of these three "overtures": the Kyrie and Gloria prayers have been changed into songs.
It is much easier to sing three hymns in a row than to pray them.

But the liturgy today should really question the validity of such a practice.

### a. What should be the desired change?

1) The ideal solution would be to have just one Entrance Song. The community should be able to choose, from among several possibilities, the one most suitable for the celebration.

What is the *finis legis,* the final goal of the liturgy? It is not to have Christians sing at all costs, no matter what text or music! The aim of the entrance liturgy is to greet Christ, to enter into the liturgy that is to be celebrated that day, to show the unity of the community. *Any song fulfilling this ministerial function for a particular community is valid for that community.* In practice, most parishes have for a long time been adopting the practice of solemnizing low masses with song. Legislation now agrees with what is in practice.

2) However, if the Kyrie and Gloria are to be kept in the Mass, they should eventually become entrance hymns.

— The Kyrie would be an excellent Entrance Song for liturgical celebrations with a penitential nature (Advent and Lent, for example). We should remember that the trisagion was once used as an Entrance Song by the Byzantine and the old Gallic liturgies:

Holy is God,
Holy is the Almighty,
Holy is the Immortal:
Kyrie eleison.

Such a format using the Kyrie could be enlarged and serve *ad omnia,* as a sort of common Entrance Song.

— The Gloria would be especially suited as an Entrance Song for the Christmas liturgy.

3) A connection between the Entrance Song and the Kyrie can be made. For example, the old German chorales which ended with the "Kyrie eleison":

Jesus, our Savior, has conquered death, has risen,
and triumphed over sin. Kyrie eleison.[27]

Obviously, the added Kyrie should be treated with due respect and not degraded by some liturgical "tra-la-la" attached to its end. That such an eventuality is not impossible is shown by the German chorales. Nor should this melange give rise to a kind of pious potpourri.

Obviously, as soon as such problems are considered in view of liturgical authenticity, the questions far outnumber the answers. To ask questions is a sign of spiritual health. Yet recourse to authority and the observance of rubrics should not be used as an "easy out" to avoid present liturgical problems.

## B. The Alleluia or the Gospel Processional

### 1. SIGNIFICANCE

The liturgy surrounds the proclamation of the Word, especially the Gospel, with an ensemble of extremely meaningful rites. These rites powerfully demonstrate that the Liturgy of the Word is not merely a pious reading of the Bible, attended by the community, but rather a living celebration of Jesus Christ present in the Scriptures. As the Council states, "Christ is present in His word, since it is He Himself who speaks when the holy Scriptures are read . . . "[28]

The liturgical framework in which the announcement of the Word is sung at Mass forcefully proclaims this presence: "The book containing the Gospels is first placed on the altar."[29] This action confers a very special honor upon the Gospels. The altar is "the sign of Christ himself, the place where the mysteries of salvation are fulfilled, and the focal point for the congregation, who should give it the utmost respect."[30] Therefore, until the ninth and tenth centuries, only the Eucharist and the book of Gospels enjoyed the privilege of being placed on the altar. According to former rites for the consecration of altars, the bishop placed the beginnings of the four Gospels, with the relics of the martyrs, in the altar. Then, too, during the Councils, the book of Gospels was solemnly displayed on the altar to signify Christ presiding in person over the congregation united in his name. Vatican II magnificently recaptured this ritual of enthroning the Gospel.

The meaning of these rites is clear: when the deacon takes the book of Gospels from the altar to proclaim it from the pulpit, the ritual will already have shown, in advance, that "God speaks to His people and Christ is still proclaiming His Gospel."[31]

There are also special prayers to prepare the deacon for his duties:

*A special blessing:* "The Lord be in your heart and on your lips . . . "

*At the outset of his ministry:* " . . . that you may worthily proclaim his Gospel." An early formula is even more meaningful: "May the Spirit of God stay with you as you announce the Good News to the poor."[32]

Such rites and prayers make the ministry of the deacon a "prophetic" one: whoever proclaims the Good News speaks as one sent from God.

Then there is a solemn procession which goes from the altar to the pulpit.[33] In the early Church, before the institution of processions with the Blessed Sacrament, the most solemn of these was the procession of the Gospels. One can envision the splendor of the

Small Entrance in the Byzantine rites. The deacon makes a Sign of the Cross with the book of Gospels raised on high and he proclaims: "Wisdom, arise!" And the choir responds: "Come, let us adore the Lord and kneel before him."[34]

Such are the honors given the Gospels with candles and incense, which recall the royal dignity of the Lord, and by the whole community, which stands to greet the Word. The richness, also, of the books containing the Gospels, which were often covered with gold, ivory and precious stones, like tabernacle doors, was witness to such veneration. Books such as these are among the richest treasures possessed by the Byzantine churches.

Finally, there are the acclamations, "Glory to you, Lord," and "Praise to you, Lord Jesus Christ," which are addressed directly to Jesus Christ.

All of these rites converge toward one meaning and underline the same reality: in the Christian liturgy, the announcing of the Word is not only a reading from the archives of the People of God from the Old or the New Testament, nor merely an edifying recollection of past events, but a true celebration, a true worship, a true adoration of the Lord.

Such is the context of the rites surrounding the Alleluia, which accompanies the Gospel processional[35] from the altar to the pulpit. The Alleluia *is* the Gospel processional.

## 2. THE TEXT

### a. Alleluia

*Alleluia* is the transcription of two Hebrew words: *hallelu,* which means *praise,* and *Yah,* an abbreviation for *Yahweh. Alleluia* therefore means *Praise Yahweh.*

The Alleluia is found as a liturgical acclamation in psalms that are called "alleluiatic": Psalms 106-108, 111-114, 116-118, 135, 136, and 146-150. Essentially, psalms of praise and thanksgiving are involved. Psalms 113-118, part of the Hallel, were recited by Christ at the Last Supper. In this respect, the Alleluia, just as the acclamation, "Blessed is he who comes in the name of the Lord" (Ps. 118:26), is among the oldest songs in Eucharistic celebrations. By its joyful and triumphant nature, the Alleluia evokes song from the redeemed Church. Even in his Ninive of sorrow, to which he had been deported, Tobias the Elder never stopped dreaming of a new Jerusalem where the very houses would shout Alleluia.[36]

In the New Testament, the acclamation is found only in Apocalypse 19:1-9. There we learn of the triumphant songs which denote the fall of Babylon and the victory of those who were saved:

After these things I heard as it were a loud voice of
a great crowd in heaven, saying,

> Alleluia! salvation and glory and
>     power belong to our God.
> For true and just are his judgments.
> Alleluia!

And the twenty-four elders and the four living creatures
fell down and worshipped God who sits on the throne, and
they say,

> Amen! Alleluia!

And a voice came forth from the throne, saying,

> Praise our God, all you his servants,
> And you who fear him, the small and the great!

And I heard as it were a voice of a great crowd, and
as the voice of many waters, and as the voice of
mighty thunders, saying,

> Alleluia! for the Lord, our God almighty, now reigns!
> Let us be glad and rejoice, and give glory to him;
>     for the marriage of the Lamb has come.        *Ap. 19:1-7*

The song in the heavenly liturgy of the Apocalypse is divided
into three choirs. The first choir to sing the Alleluia is one consisting of every creature in heaven; then a defense is made for
every martyr slaughtered for the Word. The second choir consists
of the elect of the Old Testament (the twenty-four elders) and the
angels presiding over the governing of the world (the four Animals).

The third choir is the huge crowd of the saved, who, by their
Alleluia, celebrate the inauguration of the kingdom of God. And
then there is a fourth choir — all the faithful who, with their
Alleluia, acclaim Christ, present in his Word. It is in the context of
this heavenly liturgy that our liturgy on earth is to be found.

At present, during Lent, the Alleluia is replaced by another acclamation of praise, such as "Praise to you, Lord Jesus Christ, King
of endless glory!" Such substitutions are unfortunate, not because
they are not beautiful, but because the season of Lent does not
necessarily require such substitutions. If we make an effort to
emphasize the meaning of Alleluia, we must go back to its original
meaning and retain it. To be more specific, in the setting of the
liturgy of the Word, Alleluia means: "Praise the Lord *(hallelu-Yah)*,
present in his Word." In this sense, the acclamation is valid for
every occasion, including those of penance and sorrow. In fact,
St. Jerome tells us that the Alleluia at the funeral of Fabiola was
so loud that it made the roof of the church tremble![37] Moreover,
when the Christian community comes to understand the deep mean-

ing of the acclamation, it will not be able to see why it is omitted
from certain Masses. When *hallelu-Yah* becomes almost synono-
mous with *Praise to you, Lord,* the congregation will not understand
why, during Lent, it must sing in the vernacular what at other times
is sung in Hebrew. Indeed, there remain some very bizarre customs
in the Lenten liturgy from times gone by, whose primary objective
was certainly not authenticity.[38] If the Alleluia is considered as
merely a simple acclamation of joy to be deleted from certain
Masses, it is then reduced to nothing more than some happy "tra-
la-la" with no real meaning at all.

### b. Verses

The verses in the new lectionary are presented as an introduction
to the Gospel. The revision of the old lectionary in this area has
been particularly well-done, and the proposed texts, in both the
biblical and pastoral formats, are really very good. There are two
types of verse involved:

— Some verses are to be used for every occasion. They are
centered upon the mystery of the Word. Here are a few examples:

Speak, Lord, your servant is listening.           *I Sam. 3:9*

You have the words of everlasting life.           *Jn. 6:69*

Your word, O Lord, is truth; make us holy in the truth.

*Jn. 17:17*

— Other verses, which concern particular Sundays, are taken
from the Gospel of the day. The series for the Sundays of Lent
are especially successful.

On the first Sunday, before the Gospel about the Lord's temptation, we read:

Man does not live on bread alone,
but on every word that comes from the mouth of God.  *Mt. 4:4*

On the second Sunday, whose Gospel concerns the Lord's
Transfiguration:

This is my beloved Son,
Hear him.                                         *Mt. 17:6*

On the third Sunday, whose Gospel tells of Jesus' encounter
with the Samaritan woman:

Give me living water,
that I may never thirst again.                    *Jn. 4:15*

On the fourth Sunday, proposing the Gospel about the man
who was blind from birth:

I am the light of the world.                      *Jn. 9:37*

On the fifth Sunday, whose Gospel describes the resurrection of Lazarus:

> I am the resurrection and the life;
> He who believes in me will not die for ever.                    *Jn. 11:25*

## 3.  THE MUSIC

It now remains for music to clothe the biblical words in a garment of splendor. The Gospel processional deserves music that is both festive and lively. When singing the verses, we should, at all costs, avoid reverting to psalmody. A happy and lively song seems quite appropriate. Using several voices in harmony is quite possible, as long as the text can be clearly understood.

As for the Alleluia verses, plain chant once again teaches us about beauty. During its golden age, it provided the best resources for the Alleluia *jubilus* (the *jubilus* is the melody which adorns the -*ia* syllable of the word *allelu-ia*). The Alleluias for the Masses during Paschaltide are simply marvelous. Their stream of vocalization, endlessly springing forth in praise of the name of Yahweh, is undoubtedly among the most beautiful and purest forms of vocal art ever created by man. In order to create the equivalent in a modern language, much time and much thought will be needed. But perhaps genius itself is really another name for patience?

For the musician who is concerned with only the sheet of music, the *jubilus* will have no precise spiritual significance. He may simply admire the melodic line or rhythmic structure in the same way that he would marvel at the splendor of a rose or the song of a nightingale. Yet the early Church tried to give the *jubilus* a more precise spiritual meaning. St. Augustine explains:

> At harvest time, either in the fields or the vineyards, the people first begin by expressing their joy in the words of a song. But when their joy becomes so great that it can no longer be expressed in words, they forget the text and start to "jubilate." When a "jubilus" is sung it seems as if the heart is working hard to express what cannot be expressed. Who deserves this jubilation more than God who is indescribable? If, then, you cannot explain what you mean and at the same time you must speak, what else can you do except to rejoice (jubilate)? The heart rejoices without words and its joy is not limited by words.[39]

The sole purpose of singing is not necessarily to proclaim an intellectual message; it also involves human sensibility and creates an atmosphere of beauty. That is why song can rise above discursive reasoning and more easily penetrate the inner confines of the heart. It appeals to the whole human person, both his intellect and his heart. Therefore, just as words exist so that a message may be communicated, so art exists for the expression of one's emotions. The *jubilus* is to music what laughter is to happiness and tears are to sorrow. As St. Augustine says, it is "a joy without words"[40] due to an excess of joy.

Thus Gregorian chant shows us that in the Alleluia *jubilus* the liturgy not only requires beautifully worded texts, heavy with meaning, but a beautiful melody as well. Even though some of the notes may do nothing for the text, they are needed just the same for the lyricism.

## 4.  THE PARTICIPANTS

As an acclamation to Christ present in his Word, the Alleluia is sung by the entire congregation. The verses should be sung preferably by the choir rather than by a solist, especially if the Responsorial Psalm has already been sung by a soloist. Nothing should prevent the whole congregation from singing along, if they know the words and melody.

## 5.  THE FORM

It is preferable to double (or even triple) the Alleluia acclamation; such a procedure will provide a more ample setting for a musical rhythm and will make it much easier to learn. The text of the verses can be divided into two parts, so that the antiphon can be sung several times, thus creating a more festive setting. The following would be the ideal format:

| | |
|---|---|
| Choir (or Soloist): | Alleluia, Alleluia! |
| Congregation: | *Alleluia, Alleluia!* |
| Choir: | 1st Verse |
| Congregation: | *Alleluia, Alleluia!* |
| Choir: | 2nd Verse |
| Congregation: | *Alleluia, Alleluia!* |

The choir could also join in on the Alleluia and perhaps enhance it with polyphony.

# C. The Offertory Processional

In the present stage of the liturgical reform, the Offertory Song Proper may be replaced by a hymn; if not sung, it is to be omitted.

We will treat the question of the offertory processional rather briefly by limiting our thoughts to what seems best at this point, no matter what may eventually evolve in the distant future.

## 1.  SIGNIFICANCE

In the offertory procession, the Eucharistic bread and wine are carried to the altar. This procession is noted in the General Instruction to the 1969 *Order of Mass,* no. 49: "At the beginning of the liturgy of the eucharist, the gifts which will become the Lord's body and blood are brought to the altar." P. Jounel writes:

> It is best to restore the offertory procession to its greatest amplitude. This procession involves the chalice and paten, covered with the veil, as well as the hosts for the faithful, placed in the ciborium or some other suitable container. It is also the custom to carry up the wine and water.[41]

This bringing of gifts to the altar is not a privilege of only the ministers or clergy, but also one in which all the faithful may participate. We are speaking here of only the oblations and not of any other gifts the faithful may wish to give. Other offerings should not be placed on the altar.

— It would always be beneficial to highlight this offertory procession with a song. The song, however, should be rather short. The offertory procession itself is, of course, not too long, and it would be senseless to prolong it artificially. As we already know, the importance of a rite does not lie in its length but in its meaning. (How many sermons are long but devoid of any real depth!)

## 2. ELEMENTS FOR A SOLUTION

### a. Offertory Processional

The most appropriate solution is an offertory processional. We do not mean just any song that is performed during the Offertory, but a song that emphasizes the reason for carrying the gifts to the altar. Here, for example, is the song "With A Joyful Heart."[42] The antiphon and verse 3, taken from the Book of Chronicles (29:14, 17), beautifully highlight the Christian offering: we give to God what he has first given us; it is given with an open and happy heart.

Antiphon:
> *With a joyful heart, O Lord, my God,*
> *I give all to you.*

Verses:
> Behold, O Lord, this bread
> Which we now carry to your altar.
> This bread will become your Body.

> Behold, O Lord, this wine;
> Accept and bless it for our gladness.
> This wine will become your Blood.

> We come to you, O Lord;
> We bring the gifts that you have made,
> The gifts we return to you.

Yet another song, "If You Bring Your Gift,"[43] illustrates this to even a greater extent:

Antiphon:

> If you bring your gift to the altar,
> and there you remember that your brother has something
>     against you,
> Leave your gift at the altar.
> *First make peace with your brother;*
> *Then come, offer your gift at the altar.*          Matt. 5:23-24

Verses:

> It is love that I wish, and not an empty sacrifice;
> I desire the knowledge of God, and not a worthless offering.

> Let the man who has bread now share with those
>     who hunger;
> let him clothe the poor man in need, in love and tender
>     mercy.

The biblical passages — into which we have scarcely delved — are so rich in content that they must surely suggest several other possibilities.[44]

It is not necessary that there be a long list of Offertory hymns in the parish repertoire. Two or three will be enough. For if, in their brevity, they are fully adapted to the rite and their function, they will last practically forever. The entire congregation can sing them by heart in the same way as they do a Sanctus or an Agnus Dei.

### b. A Time of Silence and Meditation

The celebration of the Word, if developed in depth, is quite attractive to the faithful. After the Entrance Song, the Kyrie or the Gloria, the two or three readings, the Responsorial Psalm and Gospel processional, the Homily, and the General Intercessions, it is natural to want a moment of silence during which the community can "catch its breath," a moment to dwell upon the Word and to pray in silence. The Offertory, after the liturgy of the Word and before the liturgy of the Eucharist, is a perfect place for a small break. A liturgy is not well constructed if it demands constant concentration and thus creates constant tension. The Christian celebration should be "airy," appealing, and restful. Prayer is to be a relaxing experience for the soul, not an exasperating one.

Hence a period of silence should come immediately after the (short) Offertory processional.

### c. The Singing of the Choir

While the community takes time out to meditate and rest, the choir can be singing:

— perhaps a Gregorian piece that foreshadows the Offertory;

— or a polyphonic selection, chosen from the treasures of classical or modern sacred music.

The Gregorian selections would not be linked to the ritual of the Offertory nor to that of the Eucharist. They would simply be a few examples of Gregorian form with psalm verses. For the Sundays after Pentecost, the psalms would be taken in numerical order. For we are speaking not of Offertory pieces, but of selections sung during the Offertory. We must admit, however, that such pieces seem to be "fillers" — a fact which seems especially true when one looks at their texts. Nevertheless, they will fulfill their ministerial function if they create a mood for reflection and peace of mind for those present.

### d. Playing the Organ

Playing the organ for the Offertory seems to provide the best solution. Obviously, this is valid only for parishes rich in musical talent, with both a beautiful instrument and a good organist. Of course, the organist will not merely play notes but will sustain the silence and prayerful atmosphere of the congregation. Some organists are masters of spirituality. They feel that any distraction created by the organ is a musical imperfection. For their congregations, their playing is a blessing; for themselves, a prayer. How fortunate is any parish to have such musicians!

However, this method has limitations which coincide with the borders of Western culture. The organ is unknown in the Orient, impossible in the tropics (because of the climate), and quite unsuitable for the missions (which involve completely different cultures). Thus the domain of the "king of instruments" is rather small. And whereever it does reign, it still needs an organist to give it a voice, and an artist to give it a soul.

### e. A Song "After the Gospel"

In the Syrian rituals the choir performs a song "after the Gospel," between the liturgy of the Word and the litury of the Eucharist. Here is the text for the song used on Christmas Day:

> I am the bread of life, says the Lord.
> I came down from heaven to earth
> as food for the world.
>
> The Father, the Spiritual Word, has sent me;
> like a farmer, Gabriel has sown me;
> Mary's womb, the fertile earth, has received me;

Now the priests carry me in procession to the altar.
Alleluia! — for the forgiveness of sins.

You who are preparing to receive
the body and blood of the one who became incarnate
for you, the Word of God,
Cleanse your mind of any foreign thoughts;
Open the door of your soul to spiritual things;
Sing with the angels:

> Gates, lift up your lintels,
> Lift them up, eternal gates!
> Let the King of glory enter!

For it is he who has raised us up,
who has placed us in heaven with him.
Here he is before us, for us to receive.
Let us glorify him with fear, saying three times:
Glory to you, O Holy One![45]

It seems to us that it would be difficult for the Roman liturgy, at this moment in the celebration, to make use of such profound texts. The homily and General Intercessions highlight the texts of the readings. A new song is not needed to do likewise. It would serve no other purpose than to weary the congregation, which is preparing to enter the celebration of the Eucharist.

## D. The Communion Processional

### 1. SIGNIFICANCE

By receiving communion the faithful fully participate in the celebration of the Eucharist, according to the Lord's command:

> Take and eat. This is my body . . .
> All of you, drink of this; for this is my blood
> of the New Covenant, which is being shed for
> many unto the forgiveness of sins.           *Mt. 26:26-27*

Anyone who does not receive communion only "attends." He doesn't really participate. Formerly, such attendance was all too common. The faithful often received communion before Mass. During Mass, then, they received symbolically, i.e., the priest received in their stead. Such substitutions were quite frequent in "low" Masses: the priest took the place of the schola by reading the songs which should have been sung, the priest substituted for the reader by proclaiming the readings in his place, and the priest took the place of the faithful by receiving communion for them! Notice how dangerous this kind of substitution is to the spiritual health of the faithful. After all, he who would have someone regularly take his place at dinner and eat only by "delegation," or by "substitution," will not live very long!

Such a state of affairs seriously affected the *Communion Song,* which — in the absence of the communion of the faithful — became a *song after the communion of the priest.* While everyone was seated, the clergy, wearing their birettas, sang the Gregorian antiphon. Because of such procedures the communion hymn lost all significance; it became a song which was used to "get on with" the Mass.

In the early liturgies the ritual of communion was unfolded in a festive setting which was like a dinner at which the Christian family gathered to celebrate Jesus Christ. The *Apostolic Constitutions,* which transmit to us the Syrian liturgy (circa 380), give this account of communion:

> The bishop addresses the people in these words:
> "All holiness to God's people!" to which the
> people respond:
>
> > O Holy One, our Lord Jesus Christ,
> > blessed throughout the ages,
> > to the glory of God the Father! Amen.
> >
> > Glory to God in the highest,
> > On earth, peace
> > to men of good will.
> >
> > Hosanna to the Son of David!
> > Blessed is he who comes in the name of the Lord.
> > The Lord God has shown himself to be among us,
> > Hosanna in the highest![46]

Whatever the ritual for the distribution of communion, whether the people come to the altar or the priest goes out into the midst of the people, as was once the case,[47] or whatever liturgical changes may occur in the future, the Communion Song must always express the joy of an encounter with the Lord.

## 2. THE TEXT

After the many changes that the liturgy has undergone in the course of its history, we still retain the canticles or hymns, the psalms, and the antiphons taken from the New Testament.

### a. Canticles or Hymns

The *Apostolic Constitutions,* quoted above, give us beautiful examples of these compositions. Their inspiration is biblical. They are not, however, direct quotations, word-for-word from the Scriptures. They adapt God's Word to the community by paraphrasing it so that the people may more easily express their faith and joy. In the Scripture readings and psalms, the faithful must adapt themselves to the Word; in these canticles and hymns, the Word is adapted to the needs and the sensibilities of the faithful. That is why every age needs its own compositions, its own canticles and hymns, expressing a personal and contemporary encounter with the Lord.

Such biblically inspired hymns have had a powerful influence upon the people. Certain more successful ones, such as *"J'ai reçu le Dieu vivant"* in French, *"Am lezten Abendmahle"*[48] in German, and *"A Mighty Fortress Is Our God"*[49] in English, are among the more striking examples. They have practically molded the souls of the faithful and have done more for them than the best Eucharistic sermons.

Naturally, you may find both good and bad among such compositions. But this danger is not proper to hymns alone; it is found everywhere. In the end, though, the consequent inconvenience is minor. For good common sense and usage play a hard-hearted game: only that which is valid will survive — and only as long as it is valid.

### b. The Psalms

#### 1) EUCHARISTIC PSALMS

We will first consider those psalms which, according to Christian tradition, refer to the Eucharist.

*Psalm 34(33)*

The use of Psalm 34(33) was almost universal in the fourth century Church. In the Eastern Church, as was witnessed by Cyril of Jerusalem[50] (circa 313-387) and the Armenian liturgy,[51] there is as much evidence of it as in the Western Churches, as was indicated by Ambrose[52] (339-397), Augustine[53] (354-430), and Jerome[54] (circa 347-420). The text was quoted, as we know, both in the Greek version of the Septuagint and in the Latin of the Vulgate. In these versions, verses 6 and 9 are wonderfully adapted to the ritual of communion.

> Look to him (the Lord)
> that you may be radiant with joy. (v. 5)

> Taste and see how good the Lord is. (v. 8)

Verse 8 even offers a play on the word *Christos,* Christ. In Greek, the word for "good" is *chrestos,* which is pronounced like *christos.*

*Psalm 145(144)*

As John Chrysostom said[55] (354-407), the neophytes would constantly use verse 15 of Psalm 145(144) during communion:

> The eyes of all look hopefully to you,
> and you give them their food in due season.

However the liturgy may evolve, these two psalms can always be used as communion songs for any season. In addition, tradition and the liturgy have also emphasized the Eucharistic significance of verses from the following psalms:

*Psalm 23(22) — the psalm of the "Good Shepherd" — verse 5:*

> You spread the table before me
> in the sight of my foes.

*Psalm 42(41) — the "psalm of the deer" — verse 2:*

> As the hind longs for the running waters,
> so my soul longs for you, O God.

*Psalm 43(42), verse 4:*

> Then will I go unto the altar of God,
> the God of my gladness and joy.

*Psalm 84(83), verses 2-3:*

> How lovely is your dwelling place,
> O Lord of hosts!

> My soul yearns and pines
> for the courts of the Lord.
> My heart and my flesh
> cry out for the living God.

*Psalm 104(103), verses 14-15, 27-28:*

> Producing bread from the earth;
> and wine to gladden men's hearts.
> They all look to you
> to give them food in due time.
> When you give it to them, they gather it;
> when you open your hand,
> they are filled with good things.

*Psalm 116(115) — recited by Christ at the Last Supper — verses 12-13:*

> How shall I make a return to the Lord
> for all the good he has done for me?
> Salvation I will take up,
> and I will call upon the name of the Lord.

*Psalm 128(127), verse 3:*

> Your children shall be like olive plants
> Around your table.

*Psalm 136(135) — the great Hallel — verse 25:*

> He gives food to all flesh
> For his mercy endures forever.

*Psalm 147(147B), verses 12 and 14:*

> Glorify the Lord, O Jerusalem!
> Praise your God, O Sion!
> with the best of wheat he fills you.

By an exegesis of these texts *per se,* we will find that their application to the Eucharist is a pious accommodation. Yet such an application does not go beyond the possibilites of intelligence and the Christian prayer of the psalms. The Eucharist will always be the goal of Christian prayer and the highest focal point of its praise as expressed through the psalms. It must be extremely clear, however, that not only the psalm as a whole but also the individual verses themselves must be carefuly chosen according to the function of the community and its biblical heritage.

## 2) PSALMS OF PRAISE AND THANKSGIVING

By remembering that the Eucharist is also an act of thanksgiving which the Church offers to the Father, psalms of collective or individual acts of thanksgiving could be used as well as hymns. Psalms 145(144) and 150 seem particularly suited for this purpose. Here, as always, the choice should take into account pastoral needs.[56] The purpose of the Communion Song is not just to use any psalm, as if the psalms were a universal remedy. They should, instead, furnish a text which can bear the community's personal prayers of thanksgiving to God, while keeping within the traditional framework of the Bible and the liturgy.

## 3) PSALMS ACCORDING TO THEIR NUMERICAL ORDER

Tradition has also used psalms for the Communion Song by simply following their numerical order in the psalter. Such a procedure can be seen either in the Sundays after Pentecost or during the Lenten season. There we find twenty-six ferias, for which twenty-six antiphons are taken from the first twenty-six psalms. Despite its longevity (dating back to the sixth century[57]), however, this procedure cannot be considered a liturgical tradition but only a pious custom. We may even say, perhaps, that it simply shows a lack of imagination or a kind of ecclesiastical torpor. Confronted with the threat of heretical hymns, the lazy ritualist retreated to the psalms, sung one after the other. Indeed, we cannot maintain that it was an authentic effort to find communion songs. Nowadays, when the threat of Gnostic or Manichean hymns is no longer an immediate danger, we would definitely feel pangs of guilt if we were to adopt this ancient method instead of choosing texts more relevant to the ministerial function of the Communion Song.

### c. Antiphons from the New Testament

The Roman liturgy proposes yet another solution that is most valuable to the liturgy: for communion it uses antiphons with New Testament texts, chosen from the readings of the Mass of the day.[58] By doing so, tradition underlines the following reality:

The Mass is composed of two parts: the liturgy of the Word and the liturgy of the Eucharist. These two parts "are so closely connected with each other that they form but one single act of worship."[59] This unique act of worship derives its *schema* from Old Testament assemblies in which:

— God gathered his people together and gave them his word, and

— God sealed his covenant with them in the communion rite.

It was normal that the liturgy would try to express the union of both these realities. At every Mass God again gathers his people around his Word and also signs the Covenant with them in the body and blood of his Son. The liturgy, then, signifies the unity of these two actions in the Mass by recalling the Word in the singing of the Communion Antiphon, when the faithful receive the body "given" for them in the New Covenant.[60]

Here are a few examples:

*The Feast of the Epiphany*

— The story of the Magi coming from the East to worship the Lord is told according to Mt. 2:1-12.

— The community benefits from hearing this story. They understand that they too, like the Magi, must find the star and worship the Lord.

— They seal the covenant and sing the Communion Antiphon:

We have seen his star in the east
and have come with gifts to worship the Lord.

*Easter Sunday*

— The community listens to the mystery of Easter, proclaimed by the Apostle, 1 Cor. 5: 7-8.

— The community applies the Word to its own benefit.

— It seals the covenant in the Paschal communion and sings:

Christ, our passover, has been sacrificed, alleluia:
Therefore let us keep festival with the unleavened bread of
sincerity and truth, alleluia, alleluia, alleluia.

*Pentecost*

— The congregation listens to the account of the first Pentecost, according to Acts 2:1-11.

— It then applies the Word to its own benefit: *"Today* is Pentecost."

— The covenant is sealed by singing:
They were all filled with the Holy Spirit,
speaking the wonderful works of God,
alleluia, alleluia!

*The Common of Virgins*

— The faithful hear the story about the ten virgins, according to Mt. 25:1-13.

— The word is then made relevant by realizing that the Lord's return must be awaited in a vigil of love.

— The Covenant is sealed by singing:

Behold, the bridegroom is coming,
go forth to meet Christ the Lord.

Of course, not every example from tradition has the same liturgical richness. The new reforms should not obviate the possibility of new antiphons, but, on the contrary, should create them from the best of the New Testament texts. Without denying the validity of the psalm texts, one could sing them:

— either as antiphons of the psalms, as long as they are not too long and their meaning complements that of the psalms. To do so should be easy in regard to the Eucharistic psalms and the psalms of praise.

— or in the form of a troparion, in a responsorial setting, if the text is more important. Doing so would create a sort of prelude and conclusion for the Communion Song and would thereby place it in a more explicitly evangelical context.

## 3. MUSIC AND PARTICIPANTS

The remarks already given apply equally well to the communion processional. Let us simply note that the ministerial function of the music is not the same as that of the Entrance Song:

— The entrance processional will always remain marked by the mood of the liturgical season in which it is found; the communion processional, on the other hand, merely requires an atmosphere of praise and thanksgiving. It is more independent of the liturgical cycle. For example, one could not use the same Entrance Song for a Sunday during Paschaltide as for the Sundays Through the Year; one could, however, use the same Communion Song.

— Notice that the Introit has the role of an "ice-breaker." It must conquer the secular atmosphere in which the faithful live and bring them to a state of celebration. Now we can suppose that this task has already been accomplished by communion time. Hence, while remaining festive and joyous, the music may then be simpler.

## 4. THE FORM

There are many possibilities for the Communion Song. Besides the Gregorian antiphons, which can always be recommended, there are always strophic songs, responsorial songs, as well as many other valuable works for the communion processional.

### a. Strophic Song

This form, which includes canticles or hymns without refrain, is possible only when the people know the words and music by heart (as is the case with several German "Kirchenlieder"). Otherwise, it is not suitable for a processional, since everyone who partakes of communion — in principle, the entire congregation — would be proceeding toward the altar with his nose in his hymn book. The congregation's singing would not be natural and spontaneous and therefore the procession would not "flow."

### b. Responsorial Song

For a rite where the processional is composed of the faithful who are singing, this form is ideal. After each stanza the community, without text or notes, repeats the antiphon or refrain like a joyful prayer.

We can suggest the following rule: while singing a hymn whose text changes entirely with each stanza, the congregation should not be in the process of changing from place to place, or, in other words, if the text changes with each reprise, the congregation should remain stationary.

Before and after the responsorial song, the choir can sing a troparion whose text will be based on the Gospel of the day.

### c. Other Alternatives

The duration of the Entrance Song is left to the discretion of the community; the length of the communion processional song is restricted, since it lasts only as long as the rite of communion lasts. When there are many people receiving communion, the Communion Song may be the longest one in the Mass. However, if the verses and their refrain are repeated again and again, the congregation will probably become bored, and thus the ministerial function of the song will not be realized. Consequently, it would be advantageous, in such circumstances, to give the congregation a "break" and "air out" the song. The ensuing respite would not interrupt the devotion.

Of course, the communion rite can be enriched even further by musical paraphrases of the Communion Song on the organ, or by the choral arrangements of a Gregorian or a polyphonic piece. The organist can accomplish this by playing not only *after* the song, but also by playing an interlude every two or three verses *during* the song. His playing would, of course, be a "commentary" on the antiphon or the verses in order to sustain the same lyrical mood. Experience shows that the best length for such an interlude is the duration of one verse and that the best interval is every other verse. A long, complex interlude destroys the rhythm of the song.

In the same spirit, the Communion Song can be enhanced from time to time — after two or three stanzas, for example — by proclaiming a short and profound text drawn from the day's Gospel, followed by a moment of silence. The congregation could therefore meditate upon the Word of God as it receives the Word which is the body and blood of Jesus Christ! Yet all should be done with ease, freedom, and joy! Nothing is more contrary to devotion than an unnecessary excess of ritual, words, and songs. If the congregation becomes tired of singing, it is to the detriment of devotion.

All such variations cannot be improvised. They must be prepared in accordance with the liturgical committee, the organist, the choir director, and the commentator.

# CHAPTER VII
# THE LITANIES

## A. The Kyrie Eleison

### 1. TRADITIONAL TREATMENT

There are three litany prayers in the Mass of the present Roman liturgy:

— the Kyrie;
— the General Intercessions;
— the Agnus Dei.

The history of the Kyrie is closely connected with that of the General Intercessions, fortunately restored in the present liturgy according to the directives of the *Constitution on the Sacred Liturgy* (art. 53).

Concerning the General Intercessions, the Constitution quotes the words of the Apostle:

> I urge therefore, first of all, that supplications, prayers, inter-cessions and thanksgivings be made for all men; for kings, and for all in high positions, that we may lead a quiet and peaceful life in all piety and worthy behavior.      *I Tim. 2:1-2*

The Apostle's recommendation is addressed to every Christian who, in his personal dialogue with God, includes the intentions of the universal Church in his prayers and thereby continues the prayer of Jesus Christ. The liturgical celebration is the special place where such supplications can be most naturally expressed by the whole community.[1]

Some of the first prayers left us by tradition reflect the Pauline tradition. The *Didache* has included the following supplications for the Church in its magnificent "Eucharistic Prayer":

> Just as this bread which we break,
> once scattered over the hills,

has been gathered and made one,
so may thy Church too be assembled
from the ends of the earth into thy kingdom!

.   .   .

Remember, Lord, thy Church,
to deliver her from all evil,
to make her perfect in thy love.
Gather her from the four winds,
this Church thou hast sanctified.[2]

The "Great Prayer" of Clement of Rome, included in his *Letter
to the Corinthians* (circa 95-96), also contains the following supplications:

We beg thee, O Master,
to be our Helper and Protector:

deliver those of us who are in distress,
raise up the fallen,
show Thy face to those in need,

heal the infirm,
bring back the erring of Thy people,

feed the hungry,
ransom our prisoners,

set the infirm upon their feet,
comfort the fainthearted:

let all the nations know that Thou art the only God,
that Jesus Christ is Thy Son,
that we are Thy people and the sheep of Thy pasture.[3]

By the time of Justin we see the first entrance of the General
Intercessions into the Mass. The Sunday celebration, as he describes
it, presents the essential elements of the Christian liturgy: the reading
of the Word of God, a homily by the presiding minister, the common
prayer, and the Eucharistic service.

### Reading from the Word of God

The day called sun-day (i.e. Sunday) was a day when everyone
from the cities and the countryside gathered together in one
place. There the Writings of the Apostles and the Prophets were
read as long as daylight and weather permitted.

### The Priest's Homily

When the reader had finished, the presiding minister took
charge and urged the faithful to put into practice the beautiful
teachings they had heard.

## Common Prayer

Afterwards the entire congregation stood and prayed together.[4]

This text of Justin dates from around 150, A.D. Eighteen centuries later, Vatican II, restoring the General Intercessions, gives them the same honor accorded by Justin. The prayer of the Church is therefore thought of less as an *appeal* from man than as a *response* to God. It is not a cry for help coming out of the dark human night, or a distress signal finding its way into God's heart, but it is, first of all, a response in the hearts of men to the Word of God as proclaimed by the Apostles and Prophets.

Very shortly thereafter, the General Intercessions adopted the form of a litany which responds perfectly to the rhythm of the prayer of a large group. Rather than have the intentions read one right after the other, they were announced separately. The community then affirmed these individual petitions by repeating a general response after each one. This litany format, used by the Eastern Churches since the third century, first appeared in the Roman liturgy toward the end of the fifth century.

The people's responses became fixed in stereotyped formulas. The *Kyrie eleison* was the most popular. In her *Journal* (circa 390), the pilgrim Etheria tells how wonderful it was to observe this prayer in the Church of the Anastasis in Jerusalem at the Lucernian office: In the "infinite light" of the candles the deacon lists the intentions and the many children there respond: "Kyrie eleison," which is translated as "Lord, have mercy," and she adds, "Their voices produced an infinite murmur."[5]

The use of the *Kyrie eleison* in the General Intercessions is confirmed by the *Apostolic Constitution* (which dates from the same era, about 380):

> Then all the faithful pray for the catechumens
> with all their hearts by saying: *Kyrie eleison!*
>
> At every intention stated by the deacon, the
> people, especially the children, respond with:
> *Kyrie eleison.*[6]

According to the *Apostolic Constitution* we see that actually not just one, but four of these litanies were used. This quantity indicates the popularity of these prayers, but it may indicate also their subsequent devaluation. As a matter of fact, the early prayers in the Roman Mass quickly lost their form and original meaning. Pope Gelasius (492-496) introduced them into the beginning of the Mass, where they are today. In so doing, he caused — or contributed to — the disappearance of the old Solemn Prayers which had been in every Roman Mass until the end of the fifth century.[7]

St. Benedict (†543 A.D.) then reduced these prayers of supplication to the simple response of *Kyrie eleison* in the Office of the Little Hours, and also suppressed the proclamation of the intentions. From this Office, the shortened form soon found its way into the Mass, as we can see from the acts of St. Gregory the Great (604 A.D.) some fifty years later; the *Sacramentary* which he published and which testifies to the practices of the Roman Church, speaks of the Kyrie with or without the intentions, as well as of the formula, *Christe eleison*.

About the eighth century, the supplications were reduced further to three Kyries, three Christes, and three Kyries. Thus, as a reaction to the Arian heresy which denied the equality of the divine Persons, the Church wished to indicate their equal status by addressing each Person with the same ardent supplication. By the time it came to the end of its historical evolution, however, the Kyrie had ceased being the prayer which concluded the Liturgy of the Word, i.e., the prayerful response to the dialogue which God had begun. It became merely an entrance ritual. Yet, no matter what the future holds, the Kyrie still remains biblically and liturgically significant.

## 2. BIBLICAL AND LITURGICAL SIGNIFICANCE

In the Greek supplication *Kyrie eleison,* the Church implores the mercy *(eleos)* of the Lord *(Kyrios)*. The term "mercy" *(eleos)*, which the Septuagint usually translated with the Hebrew word *hesed,* is at the very heart of God's revelation. It expresses the compassionate goodness and faithful concern with which God surrounded his people in virtue of their Covenant with him. In the revelation on Sinai, Yahweh showed himself to be a "merciful and gracious God, slow to anger and rich in kindness and fidelity, continuing his kindness for a thousand generations."[8] The Covenant, then, meant precisely the mysterious union of divine mercy and God's people, as joyous and tender as that of a betrothed couple:

I will espouse you to me forever:
I will espouse you in right and justice,
In love and mercy.[9]

Indeed, by imploring the Lord's mercy, the Church proclaims her essential message: "God is love."[10]

However, the sovereign manifestation of God's mercy was reserved for messianic times. It revealed itself to the world by the coming of the Lord Jesus.[11] He is the one the poor of the Gospels follow with their *Kyrie eleison,* like a litany of misery and a refrain of hope, throughout the New Testament. It is the cry of the two blind men begging for light,[12] the tumultuous supplication of Bartimaeus,[13] the bold prayer of the woman from Canaan.[14] The *Kyrie eleison* of the Gospels is filled with every kind of misery in search of Christ's mercy. When, like the poor in the Gospel, the Church uses this litany, she extends the hand of the Lord; she knows that she can really listen to his Word and celebrate his Eucharist only if God "magnifies his mercy towards her," as he did for Elizabeth.[15]

Like the Eucharist itself, the Kyrie possesses an eschatological dimension. Mercy is awaited "until he comes"; "the Lord grant him to find mercy from the Lord on that day."[16] Therefore the Father, "who is rich in mercy," will establish for all eternity the people who "have obtained mercy."[17] Then the Kyrie will change from a supplication to a joyful expression of praise for his glory.[18]

## 3. THE TEXT

### a. The Greek Text

The upsurge of modern languages after Vatican II has deluged the liturgy with such enthusiasm and spontaneity that practically all the "dead language" translations have been swept away. Only a few Hebrew words like *Amen, Alleluia,* or *Hosanna* remain. This fact can be explained as a reaction to the tyranny with which Latin once ruled over the language of the people. However, the *Kyrie eleison* should not be confused with Latin texts and, in our opinion, ought not to be totally discarded from the liturgy. In fact, as a text in the sacred language of the Gospels, it symbolizes the presence of the prayer of the Eastern Churches in our Roman liturgy. It is, indeed, the only Greek prayer the people know. Thus, by giving it an ecumenical aspect, we can preserve the Kyrie and use it occasionally in certain Masses.

Yet we willingly admit that our argument is an emotional rather than a liturgical one. We can pray in union with our Eastern brethren just as well in our native languages. But, in such an ecumenical context, the "emotional" aspect should be considered.

### b. The English Text

We are not discussing here the quality of the English translations of the *Kyrie eleison* (Lord, have mercy) and of the *Christe eleison* (Christ, have mercy). However, new translations should be found which are sound both theologically and linguistically. Still, we would like to add that these supplications of "Have mercy" addressed to the kindness of God are perfectly valid in themselves and have a certain grandeur. When someone is seriously hurt in a car accident and lies moaning on the side of the road awaiting help, his repeated groans say more than a policeman's report stating the necessity for an ambulance and a doctor. Aren't we in the same position as this injured man? We do not have to explain or list in detail our injuries in order that God hear us; all we need to do is simply continue to repeat, "Have mercy."

### c. An Expanded Text

The text of the Kyrie has been enhanced by expanding it to include either invocations or prayerful intentions. The General Instruction to the 1969 *Order of Mass,* no. 30, provides expressly that "a short verse (trope) may be inserted" (in the Kyrie). However, such additions should not change the Kyrie into the General Intercessions. The latter has its place at the end of the readings, and to change the Kyrie into a second General Intercessions would be a sure way to devaluate both prayers.

*Invocations* can be addressed to:

— the Father, the Son, and the Holy Spirit, or, if one prefers to stay within the confines of biblical tradition, to the Father, through the Son and in the Holy Spirit;

— or to Christ alone. In this case, we have some perfect examples from the office of Prime:

> You are about to come into the world,
> Lord, have mercy.                              *(Advent)*

> You who were born of the Virgin Mary,
> Lord, have mercy.                              *(Christmas)*

> You who rose from the dead,
> Lord, have mercy.                              *(Easter)*

### d. Penitential Rite and the Kyrie

The advantage of such formulas is that they adapt the Kyrie to the themes of the liturgical cycle. They are also a good way to point out the different titles of Christ, which may be taken from the different readings of the Word of God, as well as from the Responsorial Psalm. This is an excellent way, perhaps the best one, to keep the Kyrie in life and truth.

The General Instruction to the *Order of Mass,* no. 30, provides that the Kyrie can be included in the Penitential Rite. As a matter of fact, the inclusion of the Kyrie in this rite is the most effective use of this litany. If it comes after the Penitential Rite, it seems a duplication and slows the liturgical action.

## 4. MUSIC, PARTICIPANTS, AND FORM

The Kyrie is a litany of supplication. The music, then, should accent its character.

## a. Litany Form

Gregorian chant provides many examples of the very cries of supplication which emphasize the Kyrie litany:

— the Kyrie from the litany of the saints;

— the *Kyrie XVI, In feriis per annum* (the melodic change on the ninth Kyrie is not prescribed);

— the *Kyrie XVIII, In feriis Adventus et Quadragesimae;*

— the Kyrie from the litany of the Blessed Virgin;

— the so-called *Gallican Kyrie,* which uses one of the simplest and most beautiful structures.

Such simple yet effective melodies are perfectly valid in today's liturgy. When the Kyrie is sung in the vernacular, the melodic structure remains that of a suppliant prayer.

If the "two-part" structure is adopted, the soloist (or choir) can alternate with the congregation: two Kyries, two Christes, two Kyries. This method is certainly the easiest and the most popular.

However, the new Order of Mass permits the use of older musical settings with the "three-part" format. If such a structure is preferred, the following methods, which avoid alternation, are better suited by way of continuity:

First possibility —

1st Kyrie: Soloist (or a small group)

2nd Kyrie: Choir

3rd Kyrie: Congregation (plus choir)
etc.

Second possibility —

1st Kyrie: Soloist (or a small group)

2nd Kyrie: Congregation

3rd Kyrie: Choir (plus congregation)

In actual performance the second possibility has proved to be a better choice than the first. In the first, the congregation is often "lost" while waiting to sing the third Kyrie. In both possibilities the soloist opens the spontaneous dialogue, yet it is better that, as in the second possibility, the choir sing the third Kyrie (with the congregation) in order to enrich the melody line with polyphony.

### b. Strophic Form

The text of the Kyrie can be considered as if it were the text of a canticle or a hymn in three stanzas and treated musically as such. The *Mass for Christian Unity* provides an excellent example:[19]

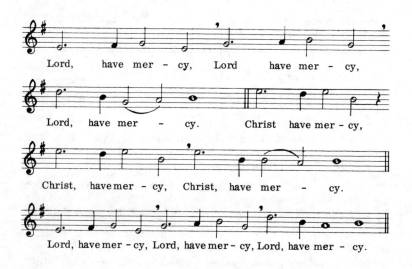

In such a case the congregation sings the whole Kyrie without alternation.

### c. Ornate Form

In almost every one of its Masses, Gregorian chant employs ornate forms of the Kyrie. The supplication of the prayers is treated like the jubilus of a song. In fact, during the eighth century the expression "kyrieleisare" practically became synonymous with "jubilare." The last syllable of *Kyrie* or *Christe* was elided with the first of *eleison* and result was *Kyrieleis, Kyryoleis, Chrisleis,* etc.[20] These Gregorian creations, from the tenth century on, were often melodic masterpieces. Think, for example, of the entreaty of *Kyrie V;* of the tenderness in *Kyrie X,* sung on the feasts of Our Lady; or of the profound solemnity of *Kyrie I* in Paschaltide! No one would dare question the splendor of these musical creations. For anyone who has used them, they remain unforgettable. But we must note that they do not fulfill the function of the Kyrie. The text itself is drowned in a flood of vocalization, which one could literally call a "kyrielle" of notes. To return to the comparison given earlier, one could hardly imagine an injured man lying on the side of the road gaily singing:

Help _____ etc.

On the contrary, he would cry out in anguish in the hope of being heard:

Ky-ri -e  e - le - i -son!

What we have said about the ornate structures of the Gregorian Kyrie applies equally well to the Kyrie in the polyphonic Masses of the classical or romantic masters. In Palestrina or Orlando de Lassus, for example, the text of the Kyrie provides the principal support for the harmony. If need be, the word *Kyrie* or the phrase *Kyrie eleison* was repeated indefinitely, according to the needs of the melody or harmony. (In the first chorus of the *Mass in B minor* by J. S. Bach, the sopranos sing the *Kyrie* fifteen times and the *eleison* forty-nine times on a single melody; however, it sounds marvelous!) No one would say that the music is not superb; it simply has no place in the Kyrie of the Mass.

## B. The General Intercessions

After a silence of a thousand years, the Council requested that the ancient common prayers (General Intercessions) be restored to the liturgy:

> Especially on Sundays and feasts of obligation, there is to be restored, after the Gospel and the homily, "the common prayer" or "the prayer of the faithful." By this prayer, in which the people are to take part, intercession will be made for holy Church, for the civil authorities, for those oppressed by various needs, for all mankind, and for the salvation of the entire world.[21]

The Instruction *Inter Oecumenici*[22] of September 26, 1964, the new *Ritus servandus* of January 27, 1965 (art. 51), as well as the directory published by the *Consilium*[23] and the General Instruction to the 1969 *Order of Mass,* no. 45-47, specified the ways in which this prayer could be reinstated in the Mass.

The swiftness with which the General Intercessions were restored in every parish shows that this rite, one of the most popular in the whole reform, answers a substantial need. In former times, the prayers of the people, in which the community presents their intentions, their hearts, all their desires and frustrations to God, were scattered throughout the Mass. Once stifled in the melodies of the Kyrie, these prayers had practically invaded the Mementos of the Canon. Then, squelched by the Latin of the Canon, they were incorporated, in French-speaking countries, in the prayers said after the Gospel (in Germany known as "Allegemeines Gebet"). When there, too, they were blown away by a recitation of mumbo-jumbo ramblings, they sought refuge in the prayers after Mass — in the three *Aves,* the *Salve Regina,* and the two prayers said for the conversion of Russia. Those who knew the Mass in Latin — face to the wall, back to the people — remember that these prayers were once the only real dialogue between the priest and the people. One almost had the impression that the priest was saying something like this: "We can finally start to pray seriously together for the conversion of mankind" — as if the entire Mass were not supposed to be an intense intercession!

All that is no more than memories now. Today the General Intercessions unite all the intentions of the Christian community into a common supplication.

## 1. GENERAL INTERCESSIONS AND THE KYRIE

What is the reciprocal importance of the Kyrie and the General Intercessions of liturgical reform?

**a.** The presence of the Kyrie at the beginning of Mass should not be overemphasized, even in penitential rites.

On the one hand, if the *text* of the Kyrie is broadened, it becomes a duplicate of the General Intercessions, which are much more suitable after the Liturgy of the Word than at the beginning of Mass. On the other hand, however, if the *musical score* for the Kyrie is expanded, it duplicates the Entrance Song. Therefore the proximity of the Kyrie to the Entrance Song which precedes it and to the presidential prayer which follows it considerably reduces its importance in the celebration.

**b.** Obviously, then, the greater importance should be attributed to the General Intercessions since they conclude the Liturgy of the Word. The following rules logically apply.

— No celebration of the Eucharist without the real proclamation of the Word.

Or better still: no celebration of Christ present in the Eucharist without a celebration of Christ present in his Word. The time is gone forever when the priest reads the Scripture to himself, but even only one person at Mass would be enough to fulfill the mystery expressed by the Lord: "Where two or three are gathered together for my sake, there am I in the midst of them." (Mt. 18:20)

— No proclamation of the Word without a homily.

We speak here of a real homily, not of the uttering of a few mystical remarks. For the homily is essentially and quite simply the presentation of the Word of God so that it will be of practical benefit to the celebrating community. It doesn't have to be long — a few sentences will do — but it must be authentic. The best example of a homily in the Old Testament is that given by Ezra during the feast of Tabernacles, after the Israelites' return from captivity. Ezra read in the book of the law of God (in Hebrew) and translated (into Aramaic) and explained it so that the people understood the reading.[24] The best example in the New Testament is the homily Jesus gave in the Synagogue of Nazareth (Luke 4:16). After reading the text of Isaiah 61, as Luke tells us, he rolled up the scroll, gave it to the sacristan, and sat down: "And the eyes of all in the synagogue were gazing on him. But he began to say to them, 'Today this Scripture has been fulfilled in your hearing.' "[25] There is no essential difference between the homily of Ezra and that of Jesus. The homily should always be a "translation" of the Word — not a translation from Hebrew and Greek into English (which can easily be found in all Bibles), but a translation of the Word so that it may truly become a presence and an active force in our lives. To understand Scripture is not simply to hear the meaning of the words, but to grasp its relevance in the "today" of God.

— No homily without General Intercessions.

The General Instruction to the 1969 *Order of Mass* states that "it is appropriate that this prayer be included in all Masses celebrated with a congregation . . ." (no. 45) As we know, two people (for instance, the priest who celebrates and another person) are a good congregation: Christ is present in their prayer! Practically speaking, it is appropriate to include the General Intercessions at every Mass. Just as a priest, celebrating alone, face to the wall, should stop for a few moments to give himself the homily and to ask himself in the silence of his heart, "What is God saying to me in his Word today?" — so should he also stop for a few moments to pray for the needs of the universal Church.

Of course, this is not obligatory. It is simply a question of excellence. No one is obligated to use something excellent. (We are not even obligated to celebrate Mass every day!) Moreover, it is not so much God, but we ourselves who benefit from the General Intercessions at every Mass. As St. Augustine once asked — is it the sun that benefits when we warm ourselves in its rays? Is it the fountain that benefits when a man's thirst has been quenched? Likewise, it is primarily the celebrating community who benefits from the General Intercessions of each Mass.

For continuity,[26] the homily could close with a phrase such as "Here is what we shall now pray for together" or "Let us pray together for the intentions presented to us today in the Word." The General Intercessions are therefore the response of the community to the Word.

Thus the rites for the celebration of the Word go together very logically in the following manner:

— In the readings the community listens to the Word.

— In the Responsorial Psalm the community responds to the Word through the Word; its response of praise and thanksgiving is from the psalm.

— In the homily, the community grasps the relevance of the Word which is presented.

— Finally, in the General Intercessions, the community responds with an entreaty; they present to God all the intentions he himself has aroused in their hearts.

## 2. NATURE

The directives for the implementation of the *Constitution on the Sacred Liturgy* describe the General Intercessions in the following way:[27]

### a. It is a supplication addressed to God.

The nature of this prayer is to be an act of petition. It deals here, obviously, with the General Intercessions in the Mass. In other celebrations, such as Vespers for example, it would be preferable to have the General Intercessions characterized as a doxology or be of a Eucharistic nature; there the people could respond with "Glory to you forever" or some other expression of praise and thanksgiving.

### b. It asks God especially for universal blessings.

It prays for the whole Church, for the world, for those in need, and for the faithful present in the congregation. In other words, the General Intercessions are not a prayer for the *universal intentions of the celebrating community,* but for the *intentions of the universal Church.* The particular needs of the community are not forgotten, however; they are included in the prayer of the universal Church. Linked to the prayer of the Church, they more profoundly reach God's heart.

### c. The faithful are directly involved.

Those participating in the celebration are directly involved in the sense that the congregation responds to the invitations of the minister and is not limited to a single acclamation at the end of the entreaties expressed by the minister alone. In a certain sense, every prayer in the Mass is the prayer of the celebrating congregation, even those said by the priest, because he, too, is part of that congregation and prays in its name. But the General Intercessions are to be distinguished from the presidential prayer:

— on the one hand, because they are not reserved for the priest alone;

— on the other hand, because the people respond after each intention, as in a litany,[28] and not only at the end, as is done in the Collect or the Eucharistic Prayer.

## 3. STRUCTURE AND TEXT

The General Intercessions are composed of:

— an invitation to prayer given by the priest,

— the announcement of the different intentions,

— the people's response after each intention,

— a concluding prayer said by the priest.

Each of these elements can be given in a general format valid for every Mass and each community. But each can also be based on the Liturgy of the Word according to the needs of the celebrating community.

### BASED ON THE LITURGY OF THE WORD

If we have emphasized the importance of the readings and the homily, it is because they carefully prepare the prayer of the community. As we have seen, the Liturgy of the Word does not end with the reading of the Gospel. It continues into the homily and is concluded in the General Intercessions, which are the response of the Church to the Word. "The General Intercessions are in some way made more profound, more solemn, 'augmented' by the weight of the Word proclaimed and received."[29] It will always be advantageous, then, to personalize the prayers in some way, so as to fix more effectively the attention of the people and open their hearts to God. It is permissable to use "stock" phrases in dire necessity; for instance, in cases when there is not enough time to prepare a suitable text. But it is preferable that the necessary time be found to prepare a personalized prayer, inspired directly by the Word.

### AS A FUNCTION OF THE CELEBRATING COMMUNITY

Let us remember this elementary pastoral principle: if you want someone to understand you, you have to speak his language. In some instances where a certain text is prescribed, as in the Gloria or Credo, such an adaptation cannot be made. But here the principle can and should be fully applied. If the congregation is composed of children, you must speak to them in terms that children can understand (but don't be childish). Each community should be addressed in terms of its own special personality, in terms that will make the message of Jesus Christ meaningful to it.

### a. Invitation to Prayer

The importance and significance of this invitation are as follows. The priest has only a few moments, a few seconds — the time it takes for a sentence or two — to catch the people's attention and open their hearts to the Lord. It is the time when the priest tries, with the grace of God, to capture in each Mass the mystery lived by Lydia, the purple merchant from Thyatira, as recounted in the Acts of the Apostles: "The Lord touched her heart to give heed to what was being said by Paul."[30] Here at Mass, too, there are hearts to be opened so that they may heed the words of the prayer. Indeed, each community must find the right key for the unlocking of its heart — and the right door.

### 1) A GENERAL FORMULA

The proposed directives are usually rather comprehensive. Here is a sample of the first one, derived from 1 Tim. 2:4:

> Beloved brethern, let us turn our prayers toward
> God, the Father Almighty, *who wishes all men to
> be saved and to come to the knowledge of the truth.*[31]

Also prayers that are not so long may be used. They may even be nothing more than an expansion of *Oremus:*

> Let us pray for the intentions of the universal Church.

or even:

> Let us pray for the intentions given in the Word of God.

However, it would be good to observe the following rule: if there is nothing of great importance to say — then say nothing. The goal should be the utmost brevity.

### 2) A PARTICULAR FORMULA

The introduction can also vary according to each celebration, "taking into account the liturgical season, the theme of the feast, or the life of the saint to be celebrated and relating it to the prayer that follows."[32]

As soon as the formula is thus personalized, especially when it is inspired by the celebrated Word, it acquires a particularly striking force and captures, so to speak, the attention of the faithful. Here is an example for Christmas; it is drawn from Titus 3:4-5 and is found in the Epistle of the second Mass:

> *On this day,* my dear brethren, *when the goodness
> and kindness of God our Savior appears,* let us
> put our confidence *not in our good works but in
> mercy.* Let us humbly pray to God.[33]

Here is formula 11 for Passion Sunday derived from Heb. 5:7 —

> In this time of the Passion, *when Christ offered
> up prayer and supplication to his Father, with
> loud cries and tears,* let us implore God, in his
> goodness, to hear our prayers as he did then,
> because of his Son's piety.[34]

Formula 18, for the feast of Pentecost; its source is Rom. 8:15 —

> Because, my beloved brethren, *we have received a
> spirit of adoption as sons by virture of which we
> cry, "Abba! Father,"* let us direct our prayers
> with filial devotion to God, the Father Almighty.[35]

As you can see, we are no longer using a sometimes "empty" *Oremus.* It is now really a preface to prayer, drawn from the Word and dressed in its splendor.

### b. Intentions for Prayer

*1) FOUR CATEGORIES OF INTENTIONS*

The directives for the General Intercessions envision four regular categories of intentions.[36] As with the invitation to prayer, each intention can be incorporated into a general statement or can be presented in a more individual format.

The *first category* of intentions pertains to "the needs of the universal Church, the Pope, the Council, the pastors of the Church, the missions, Christian unity, priestly and religious vocations, etc."

Here is a general formula valid for any occasion:

> For the holy Church of God,
> that the Lord may preserve and sustain it,
> let us pray to the Lord.

Here is a formula specifically for the feast of Pentecost:

> For the Church of the living God,
> that, continually renewed by the Spirit,
> she may set the whole world aflame,
> let us pray to the Lord."[37]

The *second category* concerns "national or global problems, peace, governments, weather, harvest, elections, economic difficulties, etc."

Here is a general formula that can always be used:

> For the people of the whole world,
> that the Lord may keep them in peace,
> let us pray to the Lord.[38]

Here is a good one for the Christmas season, taken from the Gospel:

> For the people throughout the world,
> that the birth of Jesus in Bethlehem may
> *bring peace to men who love God,*
> let us pray to the Lord.

The *third category* applies to "those who are suffering and in difficulty, those who are lost, persecuted, the jobless, the sick and infirm, the dying, the prisoners, the exiled, etc."

Below is a formula especially suitable for Passiontide:

> For those suffering in soul and body who take up
> the sufferings of Christ, and who are crucified
> with him: so that the Lord may greet them one
> day in his Kingdom where he will dry all tears
> from their eyes, let us pray.

The *fourth category* of intentions is directed toward "the congregation itself and the people in the local community, for those in the parish who are to be baptized, confirmed, ordained; for those who are engaged, pastors, the next parish mission, first communion, etc."

Here is a general formula valid for any occasion:

> For ourselves and our congregation
> so that the Lord may receive us all as a pleasing sacrifice,
> let us pray to the Lord.[39]

The last category is not the least important. It is easy to understand that the congregation would be more immediately interested in the health of their friends and neighbors than in that of some bishop they do not know (first category); or that, in a nuptial Mass the people would prefer to pray for the newlyweds, for the joy and tranquility of their love, rather than for the well-being of the President (second category).

These four categories should provide a framework in which the congregation can express their own prayers with great freedom. Yet we can see that they could be so rigidly interpreted that the general intentions of the Church, as well as the private prayers of the faithful, would be smothered in prefabricated formulas. However, the framework they provide is to encourage initiative, not to make it sterile. In other words, communities which do not know how to compose or formulate the General Intercessions would do well to adhere to the suggested format of the four categories, but communities which, even before the Council, were already accustomed to such prayers, or which may have had the General Intercessions for many years,[40] should keep their traditional format and enrich it with new meaning according to the spirit of the framework provided. The directives rightly note:

> For common prayer to express the true prayer of the Church universal but adapted to each place and time, it should have the freedom to change the formulae and adapt them to the mentality of the region and the people.[41]

Such necessary freedom in prayer, joined with the wisdom of obedience, is particularly advantageous for votive Masses:

> If a votive Mass is celebrated, for marriage, funerals, etc., more space should be allotted to the votive intention than the others but the universal intentions should never be totally forsaken.[42]

In such a case it would be good to reverse the order of the four categories, i.e., begin with the fourth category which sets forth the intentions for which the community has gathered to celebrate the Mass.[43] In a funeral Mass, for instance, everyone would find it proper to pray first for the deceased and only afterwards for other intentions.

### 2) PERSONAL INTENTIONS

Most personal intentions cannot be presented in the presence of the community precisely because they are too personal. They are burdens that weigh heavily on the heart, or joys that cannot be shared, except through intimate dialogue with the Lord. Nevertheless, it is good to recommend them to the prayer of the congregation. This can be done in the following manner:

— After the announcement of the last "official" intention and the people's response, and before the concluding prayer, the following may be added: "Let us continue our prayer to the Lord," or "Let us now pray to the Lord for our personal intentions."

— Then should follow a moment or two of silence.

— Finally the concluding prayer should be said.

The brief time of silence, during which each one communes with the Lord in his own way, is of the greatest importance on the pastoral level.[44]

### 3) THE NUMBER OF INTENTIONS

How many intentions should be presented to the community? If a number must be given, let us say at least three or four but no more than eight or nine. One must take into consideration, however, how long the intentions are, how involved they are, how long the people's responses are, and how long the ensuing silence. All such elements enter into the formation of the General Intercessions and constitute its rhythmic structure, which itself must be incorporated into the general rhythm of the celebration. General Intercessions that are either too short or too long will interrupt this over-all rhythm, whereas prayers that are well-balanced will sustain it.

### 4) STRUCTURE

Finally, let us say a word about the structure of the intentions. The directives give three possible forms:[45]

— The *complete* form which states the intention first and then the special grace for which we pray. For example:

> Let us pray for the holy Church of the living God.
> May God grant it unity.

— The *partial* form which requests only the special grace:

> Let us pray that God may preserve the unity of his Church.

— An *alternative* to the partial form mentions only those for whom we pray. For example:

> Let us pray for the Church.

Yet these distinctions are not hard and fast, and they can be easily accommodated to the local needs for a universal prayer. A more important point, it seems, is that a certain literary perfection be achieved in the wording of the intentions. Beauty of form, which demands simplicity and nobility, is never a thing to be ignored when it concerns a text to be proclaimed to a congregation.

### c. The Congregation's Response

To each intention, the congregation responds with a supplication or an acclamation. This response of the people can be expressed in a general statement valid for all occasions. Here are a few examples:

O Lord, have mer - cy.

We pray to you, O Lord.

Re-mem-ber us, O Lord.

Ky-ri-e e-le-i-son.

Re-mem-ber us, O Lord, in your king - dom.

O Lord, hear us, we pray; O Lord, give us your love!

O Lord, give us your love!

It does not seem necessary that the community know and use many different formulas. They should simply avoid getting into a rut.

Their response can also be formulated in more individual expressions adapted to the liturgical occasion. Here are a few examples:

*Advent:*

Em-man-u-el! Come, save your peo-ple.

*or:*

Come, Je-sus Christ, come save your peo-ple.

*Christmas:*

Glo-ry to God on high!

*Lent:*

Have mer-cy, O Lord, have mer-cy on us.

*Easter:*

Christ, who is ris-en from the dead, have mer-cy on us.

*Pentecost:*

Come and pray in us, Spir-it of the Lord.

In order to arouse a certain spontaneity from the congregation, the response should be "called forth." This will be easy if the same phrase is used at the end of each intention; thus, too, the congregation will feel more secure because it will know exactly when to join in.

Such a useful phrase may be:

— *literary,* as, for example, the expression "Let us pray to the Lord," or "Let us implore the kindness of the Lord."

— or *literary* and *melodic* at the same time.

A few seconds of silence may be inserted between the people's response and the next intention to avoid distraction and help devotion. On the other hand, it is not advantageous to have such a silence before the people's response, for unity is our goal.

Like the response, the phrase used to call it forth can change when need be. During Advent, for example, one could say, "We beseech the Lord who comes." If "Glory to God in the highest" is used at Christmas, one could also use the following phrase: "We beseech the Lord and give him glory."

### d. The Concluding Prayer

In the concluding prayer, the priest asks God to look favorably upon our prayers. Yet it should not be an exact copy of the Collect of the Day. In votive celebrations, however, if most of our prayers emphasize a particular intention, the concluding prayer of the priest can include that same intention.[46]

When there is no particular reference to be made to the General Intercessions, the Collect from the Twenty-second Sunday after Pentecost can be used:

O God, our refuge and our strength,
source of all good,
hear the earnest prayers of your Church,
and grant us the requests we confidently make of you.
Through Jesus Christ.

Every one of the examples for prayers given in the directives ends with the brief conclusion: "Through Jesus Christ our Lord."[47]

## 4. SINGING

### a. The Invitation to Prayer

The introductory invitation does not necessarily require a musical setting. If it comes immediately after the priest's homily, it would seem to be better not to sing it. The connection between the presidential homily and the people's prayer will then be more natural.

### b. Intentions

"The intentions can be sung or read."[48] If they are sung, they are subject to the general laws for singing.

The directives do not hide their preference for singing the intentions: *optabile est* — "this is most desirable."[49] Yet singing is not always applicable; sometimes the literary composition of the text must be taken into account. It is only desirable to sing a text if the text is "singable." It should have musical "balance," a certain interior rhythm in the grouping of the words and phrases.

Moreover, everything depends upon the person singing. The directives note:

> When the intentions are sung, as should be the case, the minister or assistant (who sings them) should know how to sing well.[50]

Such directives show good sense. The singing should be of such perfection that it will bring a positive element into the celebration. It should make the intentions more meaningful, the prayer more pleasing; it should entice the faithful to sing. To sing or not to sing, that is *not* the question; the important thing is to enhance the prayer. When all the elements are united — intentions that are given in a beautiful literary style, recitative that is solemn and pleasing, and a voice that is harmonious and inviting — then singing serves the celebration by creating a favorable atmosphere for prayer.

There are countless melodic schemes for recitatives now being used successfully. Here are two that are particularly simple.[51] The first in the key of F is based upon the major third:

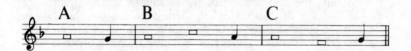

The second, in Gm, is constructed on the minor third:

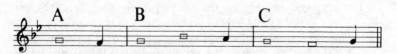

### c. The People's Response

Usually the invocations of the people are to be sung.[52] Why? As was stated earlier, one of the ministerial functions of singing is to assemble the voices to express the congregation's unity in the same prayer. A large congregation can express its unity only in song. Without the rhythm of song and the leadership of the melody, its response would lose all stability and quickly dissolve into a confused murmur.

A practical detail: at the outset, the congregation doesn't know the text and the melody of its response. It seems opportune, therefore, to give a few helpful directions after the invitation to prayer and before the first intention. This can easily be done in the following manner: a soloist, or the choir, or whoever is presenting the intentions, sings the response first; the congregation immediately repeats it; then the intentions are begun.

### d. The Concluding Prayer

The rules governing prayers apply equally well to the prayer which concludes the General Intercessions.

## 5. THE PARTICIPANTS

### a. The Introduction and Concluding Prayer

Both of these are the function of the priest:

> The celebrant should bring the faithful to the common prayer with a preliminary admonition about its great liturgical and pastoral importance.

> The conclusion of the General Intercessions is left to the presiding minister.[53]

### b. The Intentions

As a rule, the presentation of the intentions to the community is a function for the deacon. When there is no deacon, this duty is given to the commentator or to perhaps a member of the choir; it can also be assumed by the celebrant himself "in accordance with the old Roman practice," or by one of the concelebrants.[54]

### c. The Response

The response belongs to the congregation. The directives explicity note that the choir cannot take the place of the people:

> Since the Constitution on the Sacred Liturgy expressly calls for the participation of the people and since this participation is the principal part of the prayer of the faithful, it is not suitable for only the choir or ministers to respond to the intentions at public Masses.[55]

The choir, however, could support the congregation's response by adding harmony.

# C. The Agnus Dei

## 1. THE BIBLICAL SENSE

### a. The Lamb of God

The liturgical text of the Agnus Dei is taken from the acknowledgement given Jesus at his baptism by John the Baptist:

Seeing Jesus coming toward him, John said:
*"Behold the lamb of God,
who takes away the sin of the world."*                     *Jn. 1:29*

The next day, John was there with two of
his disciples and, looking at Jesus as he
passed, he said: *"Behold the lamb of God."*               *Jn. 1:36*

Even though, according to the Synoptics, the preaching of John the Baptist was threatening that "brood of vipers" who would not be able to flee the wrath to come unless they changed their ways (Mt. 3:7-8; Luke 3:7-8), the fourth Gospel gives us a peaceful look at the mystery of Christ the Redeemer. In the words of the Baptist, John the Evangelist wishes us to know that Jesus "takes away the sins of the world." To signify this mystery, he presents Jesus as "the lamb of God."

Various influences played a great part in the choice of this image.[56] The most important is found in the fourth song of the Servant of Yahweh, according to the book of Isaiah:

"The Lord laid upon him the guilt of us all.

Though he was harshly treated, he submitted,
and opened not his mouth;
*Like a lamb* led to the slaughter."

Because of his affliction
he shall see the light in fullness of days;
Through his suffering, my servant shall justify many,
and their guilt he shall bear.                          *Is. 53:6-7, 11*

The early community saw, in the suffering of the Servant of Yahweh and in his glorification, the prophecy concerning Jesus. Therefore, in the Acts of the Apostles, the deacon Philip preaches Jesus Christ to the eunuch of Queen Candace by beginning with the fourth song of the Servant of Yahweh:

He was led like a sheep to slaughter;
and just as a lamb dumb before its shearer,
so did he not open his mouth.
In humiliation his judgment was denied him;
Who shall declare his generation?
For his life is taken from the earth.   *Acts 8:32-33; Is. 53:7-8*

As we know, too, the early Christians liked to apply to Jesus the title of "Servant"[57] — a word which could be translated also as "child" or "son." For that title represents, in summation, the story of the Messiah: Jesus was "the holy servant" of God (Acts 4:27, 30), who was humiliated in his Passion, but "was foreordained Son of God . . . by resurrection from the dead." (Rom. 1:4)

Moreover, Isaiah compared his holy servant to a lamb by the use of the Aramaic word *talya,* which can mean "son" as well as "lamb." The early community was well aware of his superimposition of meanings. Besides, the humility of the title *servant* could be the cause for its replacement by the word *lamb.* Indeed, John the Baptist may have hailed Christ as:

> "Behold the Servant of God who takes away the sins of the world."

After the Resurrection, however, the early Christians preferred to say:

> "Behold the lamb of God who takes away the sins of the world."

In fact, this change is confirmed in the text of I Peter 1: 18-19:

> You were redeemed . . . with the precious blood of Christ, as of a lamb without blemish and without spot.

Of course, in each of the four texts we have quoted, Jn. 1:29 and 30; Acts 8:32; and I Peter 1:19, the analogy of Jesus as the "Lamb of God" is combined with the theme of the Servant of Yahweh. But another tradition guides us toward the theme of the paschal lamb. This comparison is implicit in the historical circumstances of the Lord's death — Jesus died at the time when the lamb of the Jewish *Pasch* was being sacrificed! Paul will clearly emphasize this connection when he writes, as early as 57 A.D.:

> Christ, our Passover, has been sacrificed.      *I Cor. 5: 7*

Moreover, John points up the connection in his account of the Passion. He shows that the Roman soldiers did not break Christ's legs as they did those of the two thieves crucified with him, so that "the Scripture may be fulfilled" (Jn. 19:36) when it quotes the prescription from Ex. 12:46 concerning the paschal lamb:

> "You shall not break any of its bones."

Thus, all of these texts, when taken together, emphasize the following realities:

— the humility and patience of Christ, suffering like a lamb being led to the slaughter.

— the expiatory character of his death, climaxing with the triumph of the resurrection. He is the servant crushed by suffering and the Son glorified by his Resurrection. He has cloaked himself with our sins and God has dressed him in light and glory.

— the memorial of the paschal mystery. Jesus is the Lamb of the Pasch of the New Covenant. Whereas the old Pasch was concerned with only the people of Israel, the new Pasch is offered for all mankind — the Lamb of God "takes away the sins of the world."

### b. The Lamb in the Visions of the Apocalypse

The texts from the Apocalypse are another source of reflection. The image of the Lamb is a particular favorite. Applied to Christ, the word is used twenty-eight times. But, curiously, John does not use the term *amnos,* as in the Gospels, but the diminutive *arnion,* which means literally "little lamb."[58]

For contrast, the image of the Lamb is sometimes seen by the light of Him whose eyes are as a flame of fire (Ap. 19:13), but at other times it represents the kindness of Him who welcomes his Spouse "to the marriage supper of the Lamb" (19:9). These contrasting images follow one after the other and complete the message. Thus, one of the Angels announces: "the lion of the tribe of Juda, the root of David" in the triumph of victory; and John immediately sees "a Lamb, standing as if slain," before the throne (5:5-6). It still bears evidence of the knife on its throat. In the blood that flows forth from the divine wounds, those "who have come out of the great tribulation" can wash their robes white (7:14). Therefore, throughout all eternity, the Resurrected One bears the marks of his martyrdom!

This Lamb who was sacrificed is the "Lord of Lords, and the King of kings" (17:14). He is the one acclaimed by the angelic hosts in the heavenly liturgy with a sevenfold doxology, which signifies the fullness of glory:

> Worthy is the Lamb who was slain to receive power and divinity and wisdom and strength and honor and glory and blessing. (5:12)

He is also the one who breaks the book of seven seals (5:9), who makes judgments, condemns those who worship the Beast, and makes them drink from the cup of wrath (14:10).

Alternating, however, with these fiery images is the more gentle image of the shepherd leading his flock:

> For the Lamb who is in the midst of the throne will shepherd them, and will guide them to the fountains of the waters of life, and God will wipe away every tear from their eyes. (7:17)

It is difficult to summarize all these images. Let us simply say that around 95 A.D., the date when John put the finishing touches on the Apocalypse, the title of Lamb became one of the privileged titles of Christ. It recalled his redemptive immolation and heavenly glorification. It was the symbol of the Paschal mystery.

## 2. THE LITURGICAL MEANING

The first examples we have of music for the Agnus Dei in the Roman liturgy date back to the seventh century. According to the *Liber Pontificalis,*[59] Pope Sergius I (687-701) ordered that "during the breaking of the Lord's body, the clergy and the people should sing: 'Lamb of God, who take away the sins of the world, have mercy on us.' " Even if the authenticity of this account were contested — the author was "most" generous to Sergius I — it is certain that this song came from the East (Sergius himself was from the East), although we do not know whether another such song had been in use in the Roman liturgy. In Rome, at that time, the entire *presbyterium* participated in the breaking of the bread. The Pope broke the bread on a paten, and the other priests put their pieces of bread into containers which the servers had given them.[60]

There is a two-fold meaning to this rite in Christian tradition.

### a. One Bread

The first significance is biblical. The Eucharist renews the Lord's example in accordance with his command: "Do this in memory of me." The four passages which tell us about the institution of the Eucharist at the Last Supper—Mt. 26:26; Mark 14:22; and I Cor. 11:24, to which Luke 22:19 is related — all mention the breaking of bread: Jesus took bread, gave thanks to his Father, broke it and said: "This is my Body." This is a typically Jewish rite and was unknown to the Greeks. The expression *breaking of bread* denotes the beginning of a meal,[61] when the father of the family breaks the bread into pieces and passes it to his guests.

In the early Church the ritual of breaking bread took on considerable significance. The Acts of the Apostles identify the breaking of the bread with the Eucharistic meal:

> And they continued steadfastly in the teaching of the apostles and in the communion of *the breaking of the bread* and in the prayers.
> *Acts 2:42*

> And continuing daily with one accord in the temple, and breaking bread in their houses, they took their food with gladness and simplicity of heart.
> *Acts 2:46*

The act of breaking bread signifies the unity of a single family around the same table, sharing the same bread. Around 57 A.D., Paul explains in his first letter to the Corinthians:

> The cup of blessing that we bless, is it not the sharing of the blood of Christ? And the bread that we break, is it not the partaking of the body of the Lord?

> Because the bread is one, we though many, are one body, all of us who partake of the one bread.
> *I Cor. 10:16-17*

However, the grace of unity signified by the ritual of breaking the bread would remain present at every Mass, even after the rite itself is finished. Today, the rite symbolizing this grace has happily been restored to the ritual of concelebration.[62]

### b. His Body Given for Us

Since the sixth century, the breaking of bread had been considered by the Eastern church as a remembrance of the Lord's suffering. The emphasis was not on the division of the bread as much as on the body *given* for us, the blood *shed* for us in the Passion.[63] In western Syria, the priest recites the following prayer:

> Truly, the Word of God suffered in the flesh, was sacrificed and broken upon the cross . . . His side was opened by a lance and blood and water flowed forth, propitiation for the whole world.[64]

Another prayer, from the same liturgy, evokes the theme of the lamb of God:

> You are Christ, you are God, you whose side was opened for us on Golgotha in Jerusalem, you are the Lamb of God who takes away the sins of the world. Forgive us our faults and remove our sins.[65]

Such an interpretation fulfills the prophecy of the Servant of Yahweh according to the book of Isaiah and the Passion according to John. It may seem secondary to the ritual of breaking bread, but it is deeply imbedded in the biblical context of the Agnus.

Even if you disregard the rite itself, the litany of the Agnus remains a Eucharistic song of great biblical and liturgical import. The Mass is, in fact, the memorial of the Passion and the Resurrection of the Lord. It is precisely this paschal theme which is signified by the image of the Lamb of God. Situated between the Eucharistic Prayer and the Communion, between the offering the Church makes of Christ to the Father and the offering the Father makes of Christ to the Church, the Agnus Dei song must reach the heights of great solemnity. It must echo the acclamations addressed by the heavenly liturgy to the immolated and triumphant Lamb. Yet the new Paschal Lamb, who is going to become our food, is the center of both the heavenly and the earthly liturgies. Therefore while the Church in heaven sings to the Lamb her hymns of victory, the Church on earth, which is still in her own Exodus, directs supplications to him for the forgiveness of sin, for deliverance from servitude, for peace of mind and soul: "Have mercy on us; grant us peace!"

### 3. MUSIC AND FORM

No music can fully express the various biblical and liturgical themes involved; it can simply suggest some different aspects. However, the musical formulas should be varied. Therefore, during penitential seasons, the Agnus Dei should be kept very simple so that the entire melodic intensity is concentrated in the entreaty "Have mercy on us." During Paschaltide, however, it would be good to have gay and lively melodies, eventually harmonized by the choir, to emphasize the triumph of the Paschal Lamb. It is difficult to be any more explicit. Variety is the keynote within simple but beautiful settings. Yet the pastoral importance of this hymn is not such that it bears the essential weight of our liturgical efforts.

For the form is, at least, partially determined by its function. The latter, as was said earlier, is to accompany the rite of the breaking of the bread. Yet it can be effective or imperfect.

### a. Function

Its function is effective when there are hosts to break, as in con-celebrated Masses, and Masses where large hosts are used for the Communion of the faithful. The Instruction on *Music in the Liturgy* sees the following possibility:

> The Agnus Dei may be repeated as often as necessary, espe-cially in concelebrations, where it accompanies the Fraction...[66]

The Agnus Dei can be sung an indefinite number of times. It is preferable, therefore, always to use the same melody for the refrain. This is true also for *Agnus XVIII,* found at the end of the litany of the saints.

It is necessary that such a litany melody have a solid "backbone" — an internal structure which assures its stability and autonomy. It must also be able to sustain repetition without provoking fatigue. This is true of the previously mentioned *Agnus XVIII.* It is a tiny masterpiece of architecture, resting on two major thirds F - A and G - B, like a bridge on two arches. Anchored in the granite of the key of G, it defies erosion; it can be used again and again, always with the same simple joy.

### b. Music

In the present state of the liturgy, two musical forms are possible.

The litany formula with its triple repetition of the same melody can be retained. Thus the litany character of the Agnus Dei would be high-lighted. However, there could also be three musical phrases constituting one musical entity. Carried by the text, such parallel phrases would be like an echo. Yet according to the norm, they must be connected logically in a melodic progression, as in all well-conceived works. The Agnus Dei treated in this way would resemble a short hymn with three stanzas in a melodic progression.

## 4. THE PARTICIPANTS

The General Instruction to the 1969 *Order of Mass,* no. 56e, states:

> During the breaking of the bread and the commingling the Lamb of God is ordinarily sung by the choir or cantor with the people responding.

By saying "ordinarily," the Church shows a way, but, nevertheless, permits flexibility and freedom.

The choir can perform many versions of the Agnus Dei which are of great musical value (by Palestrina, for example) and present them to the congregation. Ordinarily, however, it should not do so. Would it not be better, perhaps, to have the people sing a simple Agnus and reserve the polyphonic Agnus, or another piece, as a motet during communion, before or after the people's song?

The participation of the people could be structured in the following manner:

Soloist:          Lamb of God,

Choir:            You take away the sins of the world:

Congregation:   Have mercy on us.

This is a good format for the litany style. It permits both melodic and harmonic developments upon the text that the choir sings alone. For, indeed, nothing prevents the choir from providing a harmonic background for the people's supplication, "Have mercy on us." An Agnus Dei which is written like a hymn in three stanzas with melodic progression can be sung by the congregation from beginning to end without any alternation.

The formulas for the Agnus Dei should always be flexible in order to follow this rule: vary the beauty of the music without tiring the congregation.

# CHAPTER VIII
# HYMNS

The hymn is a poetic composition expressing the Christian mystery and designed to be sung in the liturgical celebration.[1]

## POETIC EXPRESSION OF THE CHRISTIAN MYSTERY

The Christian mystery is expressed throughout the celebration of the Mass in the readings, prayers, psalms, homily, anaphora, litanies, and even in the rites themselves. But here we are speaking of a poetic expression of this mystery. The biblical readings express the *kerygma* — which is the heart of the Christian message — by proclaiming: "Jesus was born in Bethlehem," or "Jesus is risen from the dead," yet the hymn has as its function the clothing of that *kerygma* in poetic beauty and human tenderness. With the splendor of art and the magic of words, it repeats the thousand sentiments of joy, thanksgiving, sadness, exultation, all those things which the *kerygma* arouses in the heart of the Church, which is the beloved spouse of Jesus Christ. It cannot simply say: "Christ is risen," but must sing in the *Victimae paschali laudes*:

*Surrexit Christus, spes mea.*
*Agnus redemit oves.*
*Tu nobis Victor Rex, miserere!*

Christ, my hope, has risen.
The Lamb redeemed the sheep.
Do you, conqueror and King, have mercy on us.

The *kerygma* also proclaims: "Jesus is born in Bethlehem." The hymn sings with joy:

*Tu Lumen et splendor Patris.*
*Natalis ob diem tui*
*Hymni tributum solvimus.*

You are the Father's light and radiance . . .
We . . . make this tribute of a hymn of praise
    on your birthday.[2]

The Patristic era and the Middle Ages, as we have already said, have transmitted to us some thirty thousand hymns, which are presently known and published. Each age has felt the need to sing Christ according to its own personal charisma, its own particular outlook toward the Christian message, and its own inner feelings awakened by the Holy Spirit. Obviously, then, the composition of hymns is the obligation of each age, a duty for all time to come. Indeed, in order to remain faithful to tradition, we must constantly create new traditions. A Christianity which, owing to laziness, has stopped inventing "new songs" for Christ is a miserable kind of Christianity, for it has renounced its most urgent duty of presenting Christ in the words, images, and rhythms of its own age. Christ is eternal; he is contemporary to every age. Yet, because they are frail and perishable, the forms we use to sing of him must be constantly renewed. In fact, their variety is necessitated by the constantly changing literary sensibilities and tastes of the public. Of course, the Church need make no pronouncements about such fluctuations in the world, for she is not the guardian of poetic art, nor does she possess the necessary qualifications to make statements about prosody. She should, rather, be ready to utilize all possible forms, so that each generation can place its "tribute of praise" at the feet of the Risen Christ. The words of Eusebius of Caesarea concerning the first Christians should apply to all generations: "So many psalms and canticles, written by the brothers in faith from the earliest days, sing Christ the Word of God, and proclaim him Lord."[3]

Hymns are especially necessary for feasts and celebrations when the biblical context is more succinct and therefore requires some "orchestration." Here are two examples:

Never in one account has Scripture presented all the titles of the Church. A sacerdotal and royal people, the Kingdom of God, the Body of Christ, his Spouse, a Holy Temple, the Vine planted by the Father, etc. — it is up to the hymn to assemble all these titles, to develop them according to the present needs of the community, and to embody their divine message in human beauty so as to nourish the faith.

Nowhere does Scripture say that Mary is the Mother of God. This belief is an assumption drawn from the fact that she is the mother of Christ the Lord, who is God.[4] Thus her maternal role is enlarged to encompass the entire Mystical Body. Once again, therefore, it is the role of the hymn to shed light upon the rich texts of Scripture.

> *Monstra te esse matrem . . .*
> *Ut videntes Jesum*
> *semper collaetemur!*
>
> Show yourself a mother . . .
> So that we may see Jesus
> and rejoice together for ever.[5]

The hymn clothes the Christian mystery in a garment of poetry. True, that mystery can be perfectly explained in a course in theology or in a homily, but neither the *Summa* of St. Thomas nor a homily can claim to be a hymn, a form which requires a certain literary perfection. Although such poetic perfection is of minor importance in relation to the essence of the message, it is essential from the point of view of form.

Let us simply state that poetic beauty, too, is a creation of God, who obviously has not judged it useless, since he has used it in order to give us His Word. Indeed, two thirds of the Bible itself is written in poetic form! This is true not only of the passages in which the rhythm of the words and the splendor of the images are acclaimed for their plastic beauty from the artistic point of view (as in parts of the *Canticle of Canticles*), but also — and even more often — is this true of passages where the message reaches its greatest intensity, where we may find the most essential revelations about God,[6] the sources of Christian knowledge about God, and the Christian outlook on the world. We should, moreover, remember that the last prayers of Christ on the cross were in poetic form — the "poetry" of Psalm 22(21): "My God, my God, why have you abandoned me?" and Psalm 31(30), verse 6: "Into your hands I commend my spirit."

## MUSICAL EXPRESSION OF THE CHRISTIAN MYSTERY

Music is as essential to the hymn as the text itself. Without it, the poetry of the hymn is like a body without a soul, for the text becomes a hymn only when it is sung by the community. This rule applies: a song is not a song unless it is sung. Thus the ministerial function of a song, as discussed in Chapter 1, is again seen to be of utmost importance.

Music is just as important for the least of the hymns as it is for the greatest of processionals. Indeed, all things being equal — i.e., the text of such a processional having the same pastoral value as the text of the hymn — the music of the hymn is even greater. A processional accompanies a rite; thus its text and music, because they are linked to this rite and are sung whenever the rite occurs, endow the liturgy with a certain stability. This fact, however, diminishes the autonomy of the processional, for it is sung only as an accompaniment of the rite. The hymn, on the other hand, can be sung by itself: when the *Gloria in excelsis* is sung, no other action occurs — a fact demonstrating its autonomy as a hymn. The same fact, however, also explains the fragility of its position in the liturgical celebration; it can be removed and replaced as easily as a statue may be removed from church without having the building collapse. In fact, it is, as we know, omitted from many Masses without any resultant damage to their basic structure.

Yet every hymn should not be removed from every celebration, just as all our statues and our stained-glass windows should not be removed from all our churches. Man does not live on concepts alone; he also needs a minimum of beauty, because his soul is nourished with poetry and music also.

The lyrical element contained in the singing of the hymn is necessary to the liturgical celebration to insure a balance among the various forms. A celebration in which the only songs are psalmodies with antiphons will soon deteriorate into boredom, just as a liturgy that contains nothing but hymns. An excess of lyricism will disrupt the necessary balance as surely as its absence.

The liturgy of the Mass contains three hymns:

the Gloria,
the hymn relevant to the biblical readings (sequence),
the hymn after communion (the closing hymn).

## A. Glory to God in the Highest

### 1. THE TRADITIONAL CONTEXT

The text of the hymn *Glory to God in the highest* was transmitted to us in three traditions:

— from the Syrian text in the Nestorian liturgy,

— from the Greek text in the *Apostolic Constitutions,*

— finally from the Greek text in the *Codex Alexandrinus,* which is practically the exact text found in the current Roman Missal.

Here is the Syrian text from the Nestorian liturgy.[7] It is undoubtedly the most lyrical of the three traditions, being enhanced with numerous Scriptural connotations:

> *Glory to God in the highest*
> *and peace on earth,*
> *among men of good will.*             *Luke 2:14*
>
> We adore you, we glorify you, we exalt you,
> You who are for all eternity,
> hidden and of an incomprehensible nature,
> Father, Son, and Holy Spirit,
> *the King of Kings and Lord of Lords;*
> *who dwells in light inaccessible,*
> *whom no man has seen or can see,*       *1 Tim. 6:16*
> who alone is holy,
> who alone is powerful,
> who alone is immortal.
>
> We confess you through the *Mediator* of our praises, *1 Tim. 2:5*
> *Jesus Christ, Savior of the World*           *Jn. 4:42*
> and Son of the Most High.

> *Lamb* of the living God,
> You *who take away the sins of the World,*       Jn. 1:29
> have mercy on us.
>
> *You who are seated at the right hand of God*       Col. 3:1
> receive our prayer,
> For you are our God and our Lord.
>
> You are our King and Savior,
> It is you who take away sins.
> *The eyes of all look hopefully to you,*       Ps. 145(144):15
> Jesus Christ.
> Glory to God, Your Father,
> to You and to the Holy Spirit forever, Amen.

Here is a synopsis of the version in the *Apostolic Constitutions*
and the *Codex Alexandrinus:*⁸

| *Apostolic Constitutions*<br>(around 380 A.D.) | *Codex Alexandrinus*<br>(around the fifth century) |
|---|---|
| *Glory to God in the highest*<br>and peace on earth<br>among men of good will.<br>  (of God)    Luke 2:14 | *Glory to God in the highest*<br>and peace on earth<br>among men of good will.<br>  (of God)    Luke 2:14 |
| We praise you,<br>We celebrate you,<br>We bless you, | We praise you,<br><br>We bless you,<br>We adore you, |
| We glorify you,<br>through the Great Priest,<br>You, the true God,<br>the only begotten,<br>the only inaccessible,<br>for your great glory! | We glorify you,<br>We give you thanks<br><br><br><br>for your great glory! |
| Lord, King of heaven,<br>God, the Father Almighty! | Lord, King of heaven,<br>God, the Father Almighty! |
| Lord God,<br>Father of Christ, | Lord, the only Son,<br>Jesus Christ,<br>and the Holy Spirit. |
| *Immaculate Lamb,* | Lord, God,<br>*Lamb of God,*<br>Son of the Father, |
| *You who take away the sins of<br>the world,*    (Jn. 1:29) | *You who take away the sins of<br>the world,*    (Jn. 1:29)<br>have mercy on us. |

receive our prayer
*From your throne upon the*
*cherubim.* [*Ps. 80(79):2*]

You alone are holy,
you alone
are Lord, Jesus Christ,
(the Anointed One) of God,
of all created things
our King.
Through him, glory to You
honor and adoration.

You who take away the sins of
the world,
receive our prayer.
*You who sit at the right hand*
*of the Father,*
have mercy on us.
For you alone are holy,
you alone
are Lord, Jesus Christ

to the glory of God the Father.

Note that the Syrian tradition and that of the *Apostolic Constitutions* stress, above all, the mediation of the Son, while the *Codex Alexandrinus* puts more emphasis upon the equality of the Son with the Father. In the former two, an Arian influence can be detected in its insistence upon the subordination of the Son to the Father. In the last, one suspects an anti-Arian reaction, emphasizing the equality of the two divine persons.[9] Note, too, that if we consider these hymns in the light of the Trinitarian controversy, we will find that none of the three in question give equal praise, theologically speaking, to the Holy Spirit. This fact should make it clear that the hymn is not a treatise on the Trinity. It might be added, too, that the addressing of supplication and praise to the Father through the Son is the general rule in the New Testament and in ancient prayers; consequently, hymn texts should not be critized for doing so.

As with the Kyrie or the Credo, the Gloria was not composed for the liturgy of the Mass. At the present time, it is not used in the Eastern liturgies. How was it, then, introduced into the Western liturgy?

Along with the old song *Joyous Light* and the *Te decet laus,* the Gloria is one of the ancient hymns that, in accordance with the tradition of the New Testament, Christian devotion had composed in honor of Jesus Christ.[10] According to the *Apostolic Constitutions* it was sung as a morning prayer, and Athanasius[11] considers it a morning hymn of praise and joins it with the Canticle of the Three Children (Dan. 3:57-88) and with Psalm 63(62), "O God, you are my God whom I seek." It was introduced into the Roman Mass through the liturgy of Christmas: a hymn which opened with the song of the Angels in Bethlehem could not have been more perfect for the Mass on the Lord's nativity. Then, according to the *Liber Pontificalis,* Pope Symmachus (498-514) extended its use to Masses celebrated by bishops on Sundays and on the feasts of martyrs.

Subsequently, because it was normal — and quite human — for the priests to have wished to imitate their bishops in this regard, they obtained, according to the *Ordo* of Saint-Amand, the right to sing the Gloria in their own Masses on the night of Easter Sunday and in their first Masses in their titular churches. Finally, toward the end of the eleventh century, the priests had obtained equality with the bishops and were permitted to recite the Gloria at each Mass having a festive nature.

## 2. BIBLICAL AND LITURGICAL SIGNIFICANCE

The beginning of the Gloria is taken from the hymn of the angels of Bethlehem.

> Glory to God in the highest,
> and peace to his people on earth.

"His people on earth" are those to whom God has extended his good will. The translation "to men whom God loves" renders perfectly the sense of the biblical text. Looking back, we find that the former translation "to men of good will," although venerable, did not really give the message of God's Word. Peace is a messianic good which, in its biblical perspective, is essentially the fruit of *divine* good will. Man can do nothing but welcome it and make it bear fruit.

Another translation is used by some Eastern liturgies. It is presented in an extremely powerful ternary rhythm:

> Glory to God in the highest
> and on earth, peace,
> good will (God's) to men.

This text evidently recalls the joyous acclamation with which the disciples addressed Jesus at his messianic entrance into Jerusalem:

> The whole company of the disciples began to rejoice and to praise God with a loud voice for all the miracles that they had seen, saying,
>
> > "Blessed is he who comes as King,
> > in the name of the Lord!
> > Peace in heaven,
> > and glory in the highest!"                          *Luke 19:37*

The final acclamations in the Gloria are found in the rites of communion in the Eastern liturgies. To the bishop who offers the people the body of the Lord, the congregation replies:

> You alone are holy, you alone are the Lord,
> Jesus Christ, who is blessed forever
> in the glory of God the Father! Amen.[12]

It has already been pointed out that the text of the Gloria collected, in a rather pleasant literary disorder, the most diverse elements of Christian prayer: God is adored, given thanks, his name blessed, his forgiveness of our sins sought, and, in a very general way, is asked to "receive our prayers." The dominant note of this symphony of acclamations and supplications remains, however, the glorification of God. On the one hand, the text begins with *"Glory to God* in the highest"; on the other hand, it ends with the inclusion of *"In the glory of God* the Father." All the other prayers in the hymn seem to bask in the radiance of God's glory being acclaimed. Hence, the Eastern liturgies call the Gloria, the "Great Doxology."[13]

Along with its doxology, the Gloria belongs to the highest form of Christian prayer. Faced with the transcendence of the Father who lives in unapproachable light, faced with the wonders of salvation that God works among his people, faced with the mystery of the Eucharist in which Jesus abides in the midst of human poverty, man can only repeat, "Glory to God!" Yet he surely knows that he can neither add nor subtract from the infinity of the divine glory. But he also remembers that his human grandeur consists precisely in recognizing and acclaiming the grandeur of God, in opening himself to the shining light of God's all-penetrating glory through the "amen" of his whole being.

Like an Entrance Song, the Gloria introduces, to some degree, the Preface and is a prelude to the great thanksgiving of the Eucharistic Prayer.

## 3. THE LITERARY FORM OF THE TEXT

The original text of the Gloria is in rhythmic prose; consequently the vernacular translation, forced to adhere to its literal meaning, could only recast the hymn as rhythmic prose. Its form is venerable, we might add, because it is filled with tradition; for nine centuries, priests and faithful alike have been praying and singing it as such. We can imagine, however, that the translation from the Greek to the Latin and then from the Latin to the English has not produced a work of art. It is necessary to keep telling the people, and also to remind ourselves, that its text is truly that of a hymn. It is not a mixture of the Preface and the Collect.

Therefore, it is not an outrage against the liturgy and its tradition, if we eventually abandon the form of free-rhythm prose — a rather vague "rhythm," at that — to create a piece in isosyllabic and isorhythmic verse.[14] The result would be a form which is truly a hymn but which is clearly more popular and abundantly more musical. The new form, keeping the "spirit" of the Gloria but not the "letter," would also establish a balance in the praise offered to the Father, Son, and Holy Spirit. The Third Person, formerly mentioned in a passing "with the Holy Spirit," is really treated like a forgotten member of the family. Yet we must remember that the Gloria is not a presentation of Trinitarian theology, but the singing of God as revealed in Scripture.

Moreover, in order not to slow down the action of the liturgy, a hymn such as the Gloria should be relatively brief — two or three stanzas at most, with three or four lines in each stanza.

But, so that we may achieve a Gloria that is a universally accepted masterpiece, we may not economize on experience. The result, here as with every other new liturgical creation, will be the fruit of long patience; therefore, many attempts should be made. Those which do not succeed, the blind alleys, have some positive value in that they will show us in which direction *not* to go. To be aware of such negative experiences is an enormous advantage to communities striving for progress.

The more the authorities encourage creativity, the sooner they will be able to make use of all the available talents in the service of the liturgy. As has been rightly said, "Creativity is not a quality which can long be kept in 'suspended animation' waiting for the right moment to bring it forth, powerful and intact. The denial of creativity is disastrous to faith and to Christian life as well."[15] We cannot delay the use of our talents until tomorrow or even a few years from now and then expect them to revive fresh and new upon command. Nor should our work be left to a few specialists working behind closed doors. It must be very broad in experience — a fact which really implies more than the notion of "experimentation" — because in the domain of the spirit, a certain exuberance is needed, so that the mind may be completely free to produce accomplishments of a rare high quality.

How many treasures of artistic creativity and authentic devotion the Church has left untouched for centuries by refusing to integrate the new popular hymns into the liturgical celebrations! Meanwhile, the official hymnals were weighted down with interminable hymns in perfectly aseptic Latin, hymns which still fill our breviaries and which very few priests can really appreciate in their full poetic sense.

## 4. MUSIC

As stated earlier, music is important in a hymn. In itself, every musical form is possible for use with the Gloria, from a simple or ornate melody to a polyphony of many voices. The melody, harmony, and rhythm should add to the festive atmosphere. We cannot forget the necessary connection between the rhythm and the melody. Sometimes we have pretty melodies but they are invertebrate due to lack of rhythm; at other times, there is a well-defined rhythm but the tune is banal, lacking the grace of a beautiful melody.

It seems to me that the Gloria in the Gregorian repertoire reached the summit of vocal art in its genre. Look, for example, at the tenderness and freshness of the Gloria from the Paschal Mass *Lux et origo,* the rapture of the Gloria of Mass II *Fons bonitatis,* the supplication of the Gloria in Mass IX *Cum jubilo,* or the power of the Gloria of Mass XV *Dominator Deus.* These are pinnacles which, once they are reached in the celebration, can no longer be forgotten.

Likewise the polyphonic Masses of the classical period. Not all of these Masses are masterpieces, but of those that are, what magnificence!

But today it is not a question of recasting from the Gregorian or the Palestrinian mold. Nor should the community of today be forced to submit to the esthetics of yesterday. Yet the same lyricism and festivity once bursting through yesterday's melodies, harmonies, and rhythms, should do likewise today. To achieve this goal, every musical resource should be put at the disposal of the congregation: the organ accompaniment, the polyphony of the choir, a drum if needed, various instruments for use in group Masses — in short, every imaginable possibility should be explored with an open mind and a bold prudence. In regard to the Gloria, we would like to see the best musical artistry serving the liturgy.

## 5. THE PARTICIPANTS

The text of the Gloria is not reserved for any one participant (unlike the Preface, which is said by the priest alone, or the Sanctus, which is sung by the whole congregation). The Gloria is not even essential to the Eucharistic liturgy, as is evident from the fact that a number of Masses do not have a Gloria. Therefore the question of the participants in the Gloria presents no particular problem. It can be sung by:

— the entire congregation,

— the choir alone,

— the choir and congregation, alternating.

The priest, however, should not recite the Gloria alone, for it is not a sacerdotal prayer.

## 6. FURTHER REFLECTIONS

Let us suppose that we have solved the rubrical question of the Gloria in this way: the congregation recites or sings the Gloria every time it is ordered in the rubrics. The question of rubrics answered, still other questions arise. Should the Gloria remain in the same place it now holds? Should it even be retained at all in the liturgy of the Mass? Here are a few thoughts in answer.

— The beauty of the Gloria has often been remarked. "This is a liturgical pearl," writes Dom Cabrol, "one of the most venerable prayers of early Christianity." [16] However, the splendor of a liturgical piece and its traditional value do not constitute sufficient reason to retain it in the present liturgy. A prayer or rite is retained only insofar as it fills a precise ministerial function. The goal of the liturgical celebration today is not to retain yesterday's prayers — no matter how beautiful they may be. The community does not assemble as if in a museum to admire rare works of art, but gathers, rather, to celebrate God in its own day.

When Dom Cabrol speaks of a "liturgical pearl," he is thinking of the early Greek text, or even of the Latin text, which has its own pulsating rhythm and incomparable brilliance. The English text is no pearl, not even an imitation pearl. Certainly, the translation is literally honest, but it will always be a translation of a "dead" language — the fruit of a "dead" culture. By trying to reconstruct a masterpiece with the relics of the past, one may produce an antique treasure, but not necessarily a living liturgy.

Let us state the problem in other terms: if the English text had been a modern creation, what community of today would have accepted it as a "pearl"? No great importance would have been attributed to its lyricism and poetry. Suspicion would have been cast on the orthodoxy of its theology on the Holy Spirit. Without rubrical coercion, we think it would never have been kept.

The Gloria repeats several themes that are already part of the other prayers in the Mass:

| *Gloria* | *Other Prayers* |
|---|---|
| Glory to God . . . | Cf. the doxology of the Introit. |
| We worship you, we give you thanks, | Cf. the themes of the Preface. |
| We praise you for your glory. | |
| *Lord,* Jesus Christ . . . | *Lord,* |
| *Have mercy* on us. | *Have mercy* (cf. the Kyrie). |
| *Lamb of God,* | *Lamb of God,* |
| *you take away the sin of the world:* | *Who take away the sins of the world,* |
| *have mercy on us;* | *have mercy on us* (cf. the Agnus Dei). |
| For you alone are the *Holy One,* You alone are the *Lord* . . . | Cf. the Sanctus. |

It is, of course, possible to pray the same prayer several times during a celebration. But we can hardly say that the Gloria provides the community with themes for prayer which are not present elsewhere. In fact, the only original theme of the Gloria is that of the angels' song at Bethlehem: kindness and love. In this respect, the hymn is linked to the Lord's Nativity.

We have already spoken about the importance of opening hymns. But we should avoid a preponderance of such hymns as the Entrance Song, the Penitential Rite with the Kyrie, and the Gloria. The last acclaims God's glory in its first part, seeks the Son's mercy in its second, and acclaims his holiness, "with the Holy Spirit, in the glory of God the Father," in its third. All this, coming before the presidential prayer, runs the risk of weighing too heavily upon the congregation by demanding their extreme attention. In contrast to the Entrance Song and the Penitential Rite, which have a well-defined ministerial function, the Gloria seems to be a useless splendor without a specific function.

This conclusion is confirmed also by the fact that the rubrics consign the Gloria only to Masses on feast days and Sundays outside the seasons of Advent and Lent. A song which is suitable for all feasts expresses no particular mystery for any of them! Actually, there is no really decisive reason to reserve the Gloria for only Sundays and feast days; what is more, there is no really decisive reason to retain it in festive Masses at all.

This is particularly true when the Gloria is not sung, but simply recited. It loses its function as a hymn. It no longer has the festive nature so necessary for a feast.

What change is desirable?

One should be at liberty to include or omit the Gloria. As a result, communities could, then, amplify the entrance rites on certain feast days or simplify them on others, according to their needs. A better balance for the celebration and the prayers alike could be provided.

The Gloria might be used as an Entrance Song during the Christmas season. Thus its significance as the "Song of the Angels" would be considerably enhanced.

It might also be used as a song after communion — a procedure which would emphasize its aspect of praise; in such usage the eastern liturgies call it "the Great Doxology."

## B. The Hymn Based Upon the Gospel
## (The Sequence)

### 1. TRADITIONAL CONTEXT

The Word proclaimed in the Liturgy must not fall on dead hearts; it must call to a congregation that is alive and arouse a response. This response, in liturgical tradition, is the Responsorial Psalm, as explained earlier. Yet we can think of another more popular form of response, perhaps a hymn in which the congregation repeats the message it has just heard. The sequences and prose forms used in the Middle Ages offer numerous examples.

Such a hymn, however, is not meant to encroach upon the Gospel or repeat it mechanically. It is meant to adorn the Gospel by means of a rich orchestration. It comments upon it by revealing its many riches for Christian life; it is a prelude which sings the melody of the Good News in order to denote its splendor and charge it with a more intense and affective power.

The pastoral importance of such a hymn based upon the Gospel can be very great indeed. It shapes the piety of the faithful and places its mark upon them. What actually "sticks" in their memories? Our homilies? Not necessarily. Nor do they remember the "truths" contained in the catechism they once had to memorize, or in the official discourses on this or that subject, or in our theological discussions. Rather, the texts which enter their hearts when they meet God on the road of life are often those of the popular songs and hymns in which they express their faith. One old grandmother, on her way to celebrate the mystery of the eternal Pasch with Jesus Christ, softly repeated as she lay dying:

> The Lord is my shepherd;
> I shall not want.
> Yea, though I walk through the valley of the shadow of death,
> I will fear no evil: for thou art with me.

A few early sequences which the faith has woven around the Gospels are pure masterpieces. We are thinking of *Victimae Paschali Laudes,* which explains so perfectly the Paschal mystery. Or take the sequence, *Veni Sancte Spiritus,* for the feast of Pentecost, which is one of our beautiful prayers to the Holy Spirit. Here, borrowed from the Eastern tradition of the fifth century, is a hymn for the Easter vigil:[17]

> O night clearer than the day,
> O night more resplendant than the sun,
> O night more glistening than snow,
> O night more luminous than torches!

> O night more gentle than paradise,
> O night delivered from darkness,
> O night that chases sleep away,
> O night that has us keep this vigil with the angels!

> O night terrible for demons,
> O night toward which the year's desire tends,
> O night which leads the betrothed Church to her Spouse,
> O night, mother of those who are enlightened!

> O night in which the devil
> Is conquered while we sleep,
> O night in which the Heir
> Introduces the heirs into their heritage!

Closer to our own time, certain Negro spirituals are witness to the immense possibility of people to think and write about the Gospel according to their own particular sensibilities. Isn't this Gospel Song an example of a real meditation upon the Passion?[18]

> Oh, they whipped him up the hill,
>     up the hill, up the hill;
> Oh, they whipped him up the hill,
>     and he never said a mumbalin' word.
> Oh, they whipped him up the hill,
>     and he never said a mumbalin' word.
> He just hung down his head, and he cried.
>
> Oh, they crowned him with those thorns,
>     with those thorns, with those thorns;
> Oh, they crowned him with those thorns,
>     and he never said a mumbalin' word.
> Oh, they crowned him with those thorns,
>     and he never said a mumbalin' word.
> He just hung down his head, and he cried.
>
> Oh, they nailed him to the cross,
>     to the cross, to the cross;
> Oh, they nailed him to the cross,
>     and he never said a mumbalin' word.
> Oh, they nailed him to the cross,
>     and he never said a mumbalin' word.
> He just hung down his head, and he cried.
>
> Oh, they pierced him in the side,
>     in the side, in the side;
> Oh, they pierced him in the side,
>     and he never said a mumbalin' word.
> Oh, they pierced him in the side,
>     and he never said a mumbalin' word.
> He just hung down his head, and he cried.
>
> Oh, the blood came twinklin' down,
>     twinklin' down, twinklin' down;
> Oh, the blood came twinklin' down,
>     and he never said a mumbalin' word.
> Oh, the blood came twinklin' down,
>     and he never said a mumbalin' word.
> He just hung down his head, and he died.

When the occasion arises today, new hymns for the Gospel can be composed. Here is a new hymn for Ash Wednesday in the style of an old sequence.[19]

Solo:     Thus speaks the Lord who created you:

All:       *Why do you not want to be converted?*
*My people fast, but live in discord;*
*Why do you not want to be converted?*
You are seated upon ashes and wear a sack,
but you destroy yourselves by forgetting my law.
Do you think your fasting is more important to me?
*Why do you not want to be converted?*

Thus speaks the Lord who knows all and who sees all:
*I dare not trust your fasting.*
If you do not open your doors to the homeless,
*I dare not trust your fasting.*
If you do not break bread with prisoners,
If you do not comfort the unfortunate,
no, I will not hear your prayers.
*I dare not trust your fasting.*

Jesus says: love also your enemy,
*And the word of Jesus will set you free.*
Forgive the wicked as does my Father,
*And the word of Jesus will set you free.*
For he too lives with the wretched,
He gives them bread and brings them light;
He also loves the unbeliever.
*And the word of Jesus will set you free.*

## 2. LITURGICAL PROBLEMS

We will not discuss here the literary form of possible texts, or their musical adornment, or the participating singers. Questions on these subjects are the same for all hymns and require identical answers. We will discuss here a problem unique to the hymn that is based upon the Gospel: Is it desirable to introduce such a hymn into the liturgy? Into the framework of the Mass? Into other celebrations?

### a. Into the Framework of the Mass

There are several possibilities, such as attaching this hymn to the Responsorial Psalm and to the Alleluia or employing it to replace them.

*RESPONSORIAL PSALM — ALLELUIA,* **and** *HYMN*

In the present state of the liturgy, the songs belonging to the celebration of the Word are the Responsorial Psalm, which responds to the Word, and the Alleluia (or similar acclamation) which is a Gospel processional. Both of these songs insure a proper ministerial function. Consequently, the hymn based upon the Gospel (or the sequence) risks duplicating the Responsorial Psalm or the Alleluia and thereby becoming useless without a precise ministerial function to perform. The liturgy does not like to be encumbered with useless, though beautiful, things that slow down the action. Nor does the man in the pew, whose devotion is so often governed by his wrist watch!

Moreover, if, instead of linking this hymn to the Responsorial Psalm and the Alleluia, one were to put it after the Gospel and the Homily, it would be in competition with the Credo and the General Intercessions. Or, at any rate, it would be too far away from the Gospel it claims to examine![20]

In conclusion, then, let us say that the present situation does not seem to warrant the inclusion of a hymn based upon the Gospel into the celebration of the Liturgy of the Word at Mass. If such a procedure is ever followed, however, it should be only to emphasize the exceptional nature of a particular feast. A relevant example would be a community which still uses Latin to sing the sequence *Victimae Paschali Laudes* at Easter or the sequence *Veni Sancte Spiritus* for the feast of Pentecost.

### RESPONSORIAL PSALM or HYMN?

We spoke earlier of the profound veneration which the liturgy has for the Responsorial Psalm. In it the authentic Word of God is venerated; in it the face of Christ is seen and adored. Despite this inestimable value, would it not be possible, in a few special cases, to have a hymn in place of the Responsorial Psalm? To be sure, a hymn composed by man can never replace the Word written by the Spirit of God, but it can assume its function, at least partially.

What is this function?

The goal of the liturgy in the Responsorial Psalm is certainly not merely to "sing a psalm." The psalm itself is only a means; along with all the other rites, its purpose is to allow us to celebrate Jesus Christ. Consequently, in the celebration of the Word, there is a seesaw-like movement between the reading and psalm. On the one hand, God is revealed in Jesus Christ through the proclaimed Word; on the other, the community responds to this Word through the psalm, which is again a revelation of Jesus Christ. Thus the image of Christ revealed in the psalm responds to the image of Christ revealed in the Word. Paul wonderfully underscores this aspect when he says that Christ is both the "Yes" by which the Father fulfilled all his promises to the people of the Covenant, and also the "Amen" which the community raises to the Father.[21] This, too, is the mystery realized by the Responsorial Psalm; it is the "Amen" of the celebrating community expressed in Jesus Christ.

Naturally, we can conceive of situations in which this "Amen," though ideal in itself, is difficult to evoke from certain communities

— either because the text of the psalm is difficult to understand or because the community has not yet fully matured on the biblical level and therefore cannot grasp the psalm in all its fullness. Such may be the case as regards children or catechumens. (Perhaps there are more of such groups than it would seem at first glance. Too many parishes in the Church are still biblically under-developed!) Consequently, a popular hymn that the community understands will express its faith more authentically than a psalm which, though perfect in itself, is incomprehensible to the community at that moment.

We are in no way disparaging the psalm, or trying to deprive the community of the Word, but rather we are pastorally adapting our procedures to its weakness. One does not give a student in the sixth grade a mathematics text used in college or, as St. Paul says, "stuff a child with solid food when he is still taking only milk."[22] However, there are some inconveniences which should be considered:

— In the psalm, the spirit of God guarantees that one will find, in the security of faith, the authentic picture of Jesus Christ, but there is no such guarantee for hymns.

— In the psalm, one is certain to find this picture in union with the entire Church, which seeks Christ in its tradition of both past ages and present times, yet in the hymn one no longer has such assurance and is forced to plunge into a river of personal lyricism.

Yet if, in some instances, such inconveniences do not outweigh pastoral usefulness, a hymn may replace the Responsorial Psalm as a temporary solution. The liturgy, however, has permitted such substitutions only on very rare occasions.[23]

### *ALLELUIA* or *HYMN?*

The text of the Alleluia, or the acclamation for the Gospel, does not have the same biblical intensity as that of the Responsorial Psalm. Nor does it have the same liturgical function. In fact, there seems to be no major obstacle to prevent the replacement of the Alleluia with a hymn. Therefore, it is all the more important for us to ask whether a hymn of a strophic nature can fill the role of a processional for the Gospel as well as an acclamation can.

### b. Outside the Mass

There are many other forms of celebration which have more free-dom of structure and which are not constrained by rubrics; for example, celebrations of the Word, vigils, and penitential celebrations. In such instances, a hymn about the Gospel can be particularly opportune. It could be especially valuable for mission congregations who may not have a priest for Sunday Mass but only a deacon or a catechist (with or without the distribution of communion). Such celebrations could assume the following format:

Entrance Song and Penitential Rite.

A. *Celebration of the Word*
First Reading
Responsorial Psalm
Second Reading
Alleluia
Gospel
Homily
General Intercessions
Hymn based on the Gospel

B. *Communion Rite*
The Lord's Prayer
Distribution of Communion
Thanksgiving

Even outside the structure of a formal liturgical celebration, we can envisage prayer groups in which the hymn based on the Gospel could be quite effective.

I personally can think of several such meetings in equatorial Africa. One Sunday evening, when twilight fell and the animals of the jungle began their nocturnal concert, the community of Christians and catechumens gathered around the catechist to pray. They were talking, laughing, singing, and praying. In the light of the moon and stars, the celestial candles for this celebration, the "soloist" presented an invocation to Christ, taken from the Gospel of the day. The entire community came alive like one unified heartbeat. A great improvisation poured forth: the soloist seemed to recreate the Gospel heard that morning at Mass, weaving it into a beautiful tapestry of notes, and then the community praised it unceasingly. The result was unquestionably beautiful because it was a song in which the community expressed itself in all its human authenticity. Sometimes, owing to his piety or his special inspiration, the soloist "added a bit more to the story" and completed the Gospel of Mark or Matthew in his own way. He continued his thoughts also in the homily. Undoubtedly, a panel of liturgists would be appalled at such a "liturgy," yet this song, literally "based upon the Gospel," showed a deep and receptive faith.

## C. Hymn of Thanksgiving and Closing Hymn

### 1. THE HYMN OF PRAISE AND THANKSGIVING AFTER COMMUNION

The hymn of praise and thanksgiving after communion is new to the Roman liturgy. Its origin is found in the Instruction of May 4, 1967:

At public masses, when it is judged opportune, before the prayer which follows communion, there can be either a short pause, a time for sacred silence, or a psalm or song of praise can be sung or recited.[24]

The structure proposed in the Instruction is quite well-balanced and of great interest pastorally. The rites surrounding communion are as follows:

The Lord's Prayer.
    *Singing of the Agnus Dei.*
Distribution of communion with
    *singing of the communion processional.*
A time of silence.
    *Song of Thanksgiving.*
Postcommunion.

The possibility of endowing our thanksgiving with its full meaning should be particularly appreciated inasmuch as:

— the time of silence favors *individual* thanksgiving;

— community singing expresses *collective* thanksgiving;

— the postcommunion represents *presidential* thanksgiving.

The introduction of a thanksgiving song is left to pastoral judgment: "when it is considered opportune." The "best" is sometimes the enemy of what is good. Every "best" suggestion cannot always be applied to every Mass; many songs in themselves are excellent, but one certainly cannot sing every one of them at one Mass. Therefore, the following suggestions are appropriate:

— At a parish Mass on Sunday, when the distribution of communion has been in progress for quite a while and when the processional song has been followed by or interlaced with moments of silence for individual prayer, an additional time for silence or song of thanksgiving should not be added.

— In a group Mass for a more limited community, when the Communion rite has been short and has not been accompanied by a communion processional, the moment of silence and a song of thanksgiving give an excellent balance to the celebration.

As for psalms or biblical canticles that might be sung after communion, the Instruction suggests the traditional Psalm 34(33), Psalm 150, the Canticle of Creation (Dn. 3:57-88), and the Canticle of the Three Children (Dn. 3:52-56). But we think that after communion a popular hymn would be more functional than psalmody, and, though we do not wish to discuss any particular musical form, such as the Responsorial Psalm or the processional, we feel that a strophic song, without alternation, will serve our purpose best.

## 2. CLOSING HYMN

Most parishes are in the habit of singing a closing hymn. When speaking of such a song, the Instruction of March 5, 1967, rightly requires that it not only be "Eucharistic" but that it also reflect the mystery of the feast being celebrated.[25] In other words, one cannot attach just any song to the end of a Mass, especially since it will be the last song the people will hear before leaving the Church for the world outside. Besides, it should be an integral part of the celebration, regardless of whether it expresses the gratitude and thanksgiving of the community or repeats, for the last time, the theme of the feast or the liturgical season.

Yet, some have doubted the timeliness of singing a final song. They say that since the deacon (or priest) has just told the congregation, "Go in the peace of Christ," it is a liturgical contradiction to remain to sing another song.

Their reasoning is a bit hasty and somewhat mechanical. True, the deacon does indicate that the celebration has ended, but his words are not a signal for everyone to break for the doors in a mad rush. Nothing should prevent the faithful, even when they are told, "Go in the peace of Christ," from remaining a few moments more to prolong their individual thanksgiving (in fact, it is highly recommended), or to enjoy the tumultuous sounds of the organ, or even to sing the joy of their faith one more time. Again, as always, a pastoral judgment will have to be made to decide the best method for concluding the celebration:

— in silence,[26]

— or by the playing of the organ (in parishes that have a good one),

— or by a song (which the organ could prolong in musical paraphrase).

In celebrations of greater solemnity, singing seems to be the best method. One can no more conceive of an important Mass in German-speaking countries without *Grosser Gott, wir loben Dich*,[27] or in English-speaking churches without *A Mighty Fortress Is Our God*,[28] than one can think of ending a festive office for Matins without the *Te Deum*.

Such a final song, however, will ordinarily be rather brief, in the form of an acclamation sung by the whole community or in strophic form. It should not duplicate the hymn of praise and thanksgiving after communion. It seems, therefore, that a choice must be made between the two following formulas:

| Communion | Communion |
|---|---|
| *Communion processional* | ——————————— |
| Thanksgiving | Thanksgiving |
| ——————————— | *Hymn of thanksgiving* |
| Benediction and dismissal | Benediction and dismissal |
| *Final song* | ——————————— |
| Exit (with organ) | Exit (with organ) |

Experience shows that each format has its own valid pastoral interest:

— The first, which has a song during the communion procession, is probably more popular and seems more suitable for parish communities. A silent procession runs the risk of diminishing the festive character of the rite, making it seem more like grief than joy.

— The second requires a certain asceticism to achieve a silence charged with prayer. It is better suited to homogeneous religious communities and, in general, to small groups.[29]

Never should both be used simultaneously, except in truly exceptional celebrations. Too much singing can be tiring. At any rate, it is better to be hungry for singing than to be sick of it; to have people say "just one more verse" rather than "not another one!"

# CHAPTER IX
# THE CREED

## A. Introduction

For a mind attuned to the liturgy of the Church before Vatican II, the singing of the Credo had great symbolic value. A community proclaiming its faith in the unison of thousands of voices in the great crowds of Rome, or even in a simple festive Sunday celebration, gave a vivid image of the unity of the Church. It was a jubilant and elating experience for all to unite in the same melody and in the "sacred" language of the Roman Church! Yet there was probably more romance here than anything else, in that many people mistook the Latin of the Roman Church as being *the* language of the Church, and, theologians excepted, would have been unable to explain the deep theological content of what they were singing!

However, now, within the context of post-Vatican II liturgy, the Credo presents a problem. The reason is not that the statements contained in this profession of faith seem any less adapted to present communities when recited in the vernacular, but, rather, that the pastoral usefulness of such a recitation is now in doubt. True, most of our Masses during the week do not have a Credo, and its absence in no way endangers the balance of the celebration; however, it is the balance of the Sunday Mass *with* the Credo that causes the trouble. In other words, if it is really necessary to proclaim our faith, couldn't it be done in other ways and with different rites?

Of course, an evolution in this regard will take shape only in time — perhaps a long time. One must consider not only what is desirable in the sphere of the liturgical rules for the celebration, but also the present mentality of the community, its evolution, and its sentimental and emotional attachment to the Credo.

## 1. HISTORICAL CONTEXT

The Roman liturgy contains three Creeds:

— The Apostles' Creed: This was a part of the preparatory ritual for baptism in the fifth century Church of Rome. It was centered upon the proclamation of the three divine Persons and upon the fulfillment of history by Jesus Christ, born of the Virgin Mary, suffering under Pontius Pilate, and rising on the third day.

— The Creed of St. Anthanasius, which combats especially the heresies of Nestorius, condemned by the Council of Ephesus in 431, and of Eutyches, condemned by the Council of Chalcedon in 451. It was introduced, around the eighth century, into the Romano-Benedictine office. It was recited at Prime on Sunday until removed from the office by the decree *De rubricis ad simpliciorem formam redigendis* of March 23, 1955.

— The creed of Nicea-Constantinople, which adds to the Apostles' Creed the statements of the Councils of Nicea (325) and of Constantinople (381). It is the text now used in the liturgy.

The insertion of the Credo into the Mass came about slowly and only after much resistance. In the sixth century, the patriarch Timothy of Constantinople (511-517) ordered the Creed to be recited at all solemn Masses, even though he knew it would stir up controversy.[1] In the West, an identical order was issued by the Third Council of Toledo (589) as a reaction against Arianism. The recitation of the Credo was then placed just before the *Lord's Prayer* as a preparation for communion. In 794, overcome with the fervor of orthodoxy, Charlemagne introduced its use into his court at Aix-la-Chapelle. Finally, in 1014, Emperor Henry II came to Rome and pressured Pope Benedict VIII to adopt the same custom there.

## 2. BIBLICAL AND LITURGICAL SIGNIFICANCE

Each celebration on Sunday is a memorial of the Lord's Pasch, recalling the death and resurrection of Jesus Christ for the benefit of the community. It is also the supreme baptismal feast, constituting for each Christian the anniversary of his own death and resurrection in Christ:

> Do you not know that all we who have been baptized into Christ Jesus have been baptized into his death? For we were buried with him by means of Baptism in order that, just as Christ has risen from the dead through the glory of the Father, so we also may walk in newness of life.          *Rom. 6:3-4*

It is good that, in his baptismal feast, the Christian should proclaim his faith in the Christ who died and is now risen. Of course, we know the importance in the fifth century of both the "transmission of the creed" *(traditio symboli)* when the catechumens preparing for baptism received, on the fifth Sunday in Lent, the proclamation of the Christian faith, and also of the "profession of the creed" *(redditio symboli)* in which they proclaimed their faith before the community at the Easter Vigil. Now the Credo in the Sunday Mass, if we may say so, is the *redditio symboli* of the entire community celebrating its own baptism.

Rather than dwell too long upon the anti-heretical statements in the Credo, we will now highlight the biblical elements which present the history of salvation, fulfilled in Jesus Christ. The Credo is, indeed, a profession of theological and polemic faith in which orthodoxy attacks past errors — errors which are completely unknown to Christians today. Its anti-heretical statements had the advantage of barring the road to heresy; hence its accumulation of images and statements concerning Christ:

> Light from Light,
> true God from true God,
> begotten not made,
> One in Being with the Father.

Such a litany of affirmations as this, which was collected in the Council of Nicea near Nicomedia on June 19, 325, was meant to nullify the arguments of the malcontent who refused to recognize the Son as *Homo-ousios,* "consubstantial" with the Father. The affirmations, which were all made with the authority of the Council of Nicea, are still studied in courses on patristic history and recall to the faithful their link with past tradition in the affirmation of one Lord, one faith, one baptism, one God and Father. But are they really appropriate for a parish celebration at Sunday Mass? They have the disadvantage of presenting the revelation of Jesus Christ in a way that is "anti-heretical" rather than "pro-Christian." The undefined truths of our faith are often more meaningful than those defined in opposition to the heretics. Therefore, if it is good to proclaim that Christ is consubstantial with the Father, is it not better — more existential, more alive, and more rich, theologically speaking — to know that God is a Father filled with tenderness, that his eternal mercy has come to us through his Son, and that his Spirit lives in our hearts?

Of course, we can see the relevancy of such formulas to the ages in which they were produced. Certainly, their truths remain unchanged, fixed in the divine eternity which gives them their strength and vitality. But the words which give them form are fragile and changing. They are whirled about by the winds of history; at times they even drift in the ebb and flow of changing fancy. In a word, their lives are filled with impermanence. The Church has no direct hold upon them; she uses them simply as conceptional material.

She can neither direct, restrain, nor accelerate the evolution of a vocabulary. For example, the word "substance" does not have the same meaning for the contemporary man that it once had for the Greek of the fourth century; the concepts of nature and person, too, must be considered in the same light. The only thing we can say, then, is that the correct act of faith is not necessarily conserved through the simple repetition of ancient formulas. Thus when we say in the Apostles' Creed that Christ "descended into hell," perhaps a large majority of the faithful incorrectly understand a statement which is basically correct, but whose meaning has now evolved. Hence, although the Church must adhere to tradition, she must also speak in the evolving language of today.

One last remark. An *act* of faith cannot be reduced to a musical formula, but must be treated precisely as an *act*. Christian faith is not recited nor sung; above all else, it is lived. The real Credo at Sunday Mass is realized by the Christian when he receives the Body and Blood of the Lord. Consequently, it would be normal for anyone who says the Credo to receive Communion as well. Although the sacred Liturgy is not greatly disturbed because most Masses do not have a Credo, as is presently the case, it is greatly disturbed when most of the faithful do not receive Communion. In the solemn peace of its celebration, the Liturgy hardly notices the tumultuous proclamation of orthodoxy. It prefers the memory of "the blessed passion of Christ, his Resurrection and Ascension into heavenly glory" — a memory which is ratified by the communicant's "Amen."

## 3. TEXT

To translate the official professions of our faith into the vernacular is the responsibility of competent authorities designated for the language in question.

Now we should not think that the Apostles' Creed, because it is short, is less venerable than the Creed of Nicea-Constantinople, which is noted for its Christological disputes. It is not the complexity of its statements which makes the text venerable, but rather its comprehensibility. In this respect, then, the Apostles' Creed is pastorally better than the Nicean one.

We should also note here that even the New Testament presents professions of faith that were once used in baptismal celebrations. These have the enormous advantage both of being simple and also of being able to lay claim to the incomparable dignity of the Word of God and the inspiration of the Spirit. They may be used as a Credo for ecumenical celebrations, or for other celebrations of the Word.

One of the oldest formulas comes to us from the Epistle to the Romans:

> For if thou confess with thy mouth that Jesus is the Lord,
> and believe in thy heart that God has raised him from the dead,
> thou shalt be saved. *Rom. 10:9*

An amazing statement! Salvation, the very fullness of salvation, simply depends upon faith in the lordship of Jesus, raised from the dead!

Another profession of faith is found in the Epistle to the Ephesians. It is a hymn of Christian unity.

> One Lord, one faith,
> one Baptism;
> one God and Father of all,
> who is above all,
> and throughout all,
> and in us all. *Eph. 4:46*

Finally, here is a text from the first Epistle to Timothy, a hymn about "the mystery of godliness," which was obviously great:

> Which was manifested in the flesh,
> was justified in the spirit,
> appeared to angels,
> was preached to Gentiles,
> believed in the world,
> taken up in glory." *1 Tim. 3:16*

We should not forget such ancient professions of faith, but give them the respect they deserve: they are the promise of eternity. "Though the grass withers and the flower wilts," as will every creed ever written by man, still "the word of our God stands forever." (Is. 40:8)

## 4. MUSIC

The Instruction on *Music in the Liturgy* of March 5, 1967, classifies the Credo, along with the Kyrie, the Gloria, the Agnus Dei, and the General Intercessions, among the songs belonging to the second degree of participation.[2] In doing so, the Instruction accords great honor to the Credo — perhaps even too much, musically speaking. Ostensibly, this move shows the influence of the solemn high Masses of old in which pieces from the ordinary were offered for the people's participation. We might wonder, however, whether the Credo, which does not appear in every Mass, really has the same importance for the liturgical structure of the Mass as the Sanctus and Agnus Dei, which are obligatory parts of every Mass, or as the General Intercessions, which should also be part of every Mass. A practical pastoral question might be: wouldn't it be better to recite the Credo and reserve our musical efforts for more important songs?

### a. Elements of the Problem

In favor of the simple recitation of the Credo — which is the norm for the Eastern liturgies — we must consider the following points.

The Credo is a profession of faith, a text which is not so lyrical that it requires singing. In fact, a simple recitation conforms more to the literary genre of the Credo. Incidentally, singing it would inflate the importance of the Credo to an exaggerated degree. It would be the longest song in the ordinary. Wouldn't this run the risk of implying that it was also the most important? Besides, it would be too lengthy an insert between the homily and the General Intercessions, separating what is integrally linked together and thus interrupting the people's train of thought from the first reading to the General Intercessions. In short, it would threaten to disrupt the harmonious structure of the celebration of the Word.

However, the following argument, which is not without weight, can be proposed in favor of singing the Credo: in more numerous communities, singing is the only way to present a unified text — a procedure which the dignity of the celebration deserves. A recitation in which each person proceeds at his own pace (thinking he has the correct rhythm) may sound like the murmur of leaves in the evening breeze, but not like a profession of faith.

Perhaps we should restate the ministerial function of song: it must be a unifying element. Obviously, then, that function plays an especially important role in regard to western languages which are not extremely rhythmic, as is true regarding English. Indeed, we can state, in general, that the more evolved and intellectual languages are at times musically deficient, whereas certain primitive languages are often melodically and rhythmically superior. Take, for example, the tonal languages of Equatorial Africa, which are so musical that any problem in regard to singing in unison rarely arises. Every word is sung and every song is rhythmic. I myself can remember such a congregation "singing" the common prayers and the Apostles' Creed with melodic, moving inflections and with a pulsating, grandiose rhythm in which the words resounded.

### b. Elements for Solution

For the pastor who does not live in the shade of a palm tree but, rather, amidst the bustling world of a city parish, the Credo will always present a problem. There is no ideal solution, but here are a few possibilities:

*SINGING*

— The Credo can be sung on special occasions, when the profession of faith is emphasized. One such occasion may be when large groups are assembled or when the celebrations center around the profession of faith.

— Simple recitatives should be chosen. The Gregorian *Credo I* and its variant, *Credo II,* present excellent examples.[3] The vernacular texts could use them as models. The very popular *Credo III* and *Credo IV* are perfect examples of beautiful melodies from the fifteenth century, but aren't they to be treasured as being beautiful Gregorian chants rather than as professions of faith?

— The Credo should not be sung out of habit, simply because it has always been sung. Such liturgical laziness would be the surest way to transform the profession of faith into an anemic ritual. This would indeed be a disgrace!

— Finally, practices of long standing should not be changed abruptly. What I mean is this: if communities are used to singing the Credo with joy as a mature profession of faith and experiences no problems in doing so, let them sing. We can, then, focus our pastoral attention upon liturgical matters which are more essential. However, when a problem does present itself — for it will surely do so — as the community moves closer toward ritual authenticity, there will be time enough to reflect upon it and search for new solutions.

## RECITATION

— The recitation of the Credo is always valid in small communities. It is even preferable.

— In larger communities, the confusion created by group recitation can be reduced by having the congregation alternate with a soloist or a small group.[4] The soloist can set the pace, proceeding more quickly or slowly, as the case may be. However, such a procedure would not be possible in a recitation which does not have alternation, for once the congregational locomotive gets on the wrong track, all one can do is wait for the final *Amen* and hope for the best!

It is sometimes possible to "get them back" to the correct pace through the use of a microphone, but to do so requires discretion and tactfulness. For the microphone is an "instrument" which must be artfully played. An excess of decibels is a case of the "cure being worse than the ill."

## 5. PARTICIPANTS

The Credo is the profession of faith of the entire baptized community. It is, therefore, proper that the entire congregation recite it together. The collective character of the Credo is expressed by the plural form "*We* believe."

There is no reason why the Credo cannot be alternated between two choirs. Even then, it remains the expression of the faith of the entire community, in the same way that a psalm alternated between two choirs is still the prayer of the entire congregation. It should not, however, be reserved for the exclusive use of a single group. This was once the procedure in polyphonic Masses of the classical period. The polyphony was so enticing that the choir could not always resist the temptation to keep the Credo for itself![5]

## 6. FURTHER REFLECTIONS

### a. The Text

Our first question concerns the text. It is a simple one and can be summed up as follows:

Does the Church think that the faith of Christians in the twentieth century — and of Christians from now until the parousia — must necessarily be expressed in statements formulated in the fourth century at Nicea (325) and at Constantinople (381)? Or, without denying the legacy of faith or scorning tradition, does she wish us to formulate a more suitable statement for our times, based directly on the Word of God? True, the councils of Nicea and Constantinople are like precious vases filled with the living water which flows directly from the rock of the Scriptures. Yet we must remember that the Scriptures are the true source. Hence the question here is: should twentieth century Christians necessarily draw this living water from the vase of tradition when they can go directly to the source?

We should add another consideration: the history of the Church teaches us that the creeds of faith were always formulated in reaction to errors threatening the faith at a particular time in history — a fact which is verified even in the first stutterings of theology. Faced with the Docetism of the first century, which denied the reality of the Incarnation, Ignatius of Antioch (110 A.D.) established the following Credo:

> Truly he is of the race of David according to the flesh,
> Son of God in accordance with divine will and power.
> Truly he was born of a Virgin,
> was baptized by John
> in order that justice might be fulfilled.
> Under Pontius Pilate and Herod the Tetrarch,
> he was truly nailed in his flesh for us.
> It is by his cross and holy resurrection
> that we should live.
> By his resurrection,
> he lifted the standard for the ages,
> in order to gather his saints and faithful, Jews and Pagans,
> into the unique body which is his Church.[6]

In the onslaught of the Gnostic heresies of his time, Irenaeus of Lyons, toward the end of the second century, asserts his belief in:

> One God, the Father Almighty,
> Maker of heaven and earth,
> and the sea, and all things that are in them;
> and in one Christ Jesus, the Son of God,
> who became incarnate for our salvation;
> and in the Holy Spirit,
> who proclaimed through the prophets
> the dispensations of God, and advents,
> and the birth from a virgin,
> and the passion and the resurrection from the dead,
> and the ascension into heaven in the flesh
> of the beloved Christ Jesus, our Lord,
> and His future manifestation from heaven
> in the glory of the Father.[7]

In accord with tradition,[8] the following question should be asked: what are the errors theatening the Church today? How can we formulate our faith when confronted with these errors? For example, in the presence of a world torn apart by war, divided by social and racial segregation, where so many people are dying from hunger, wouldn't it be wonderful to formulate a Credo about Christ whose incarnation brings us peace (cf. Luke 4:14), who came to unify the children of God scattered by sin (cf. Jn. 11:52), and who was sent to announce the Good News to the poor (cf. Luke 4:18)? Wouldn't such affirmations engender more faith than the simple fact of singing that Christ "descended into hell," a mystery which no one contests and which is not found to be directly threatened now by a heresy?

### b. In Every Mass?

Our second question concerns the expediency of including the Credo in every Sunday Mass.

Here are a few suggestions. Obviously, each prayer and rite is not included for its own sake, but rather to help the community in its celebration. Liturgical formulas are for the service of the community, just as the entire ecclesiastical institution is for the service of men, just as Christ himself came, as we state in the Credo, *propter nos homines, et propter nostram salutem* — "for us men and for our salvation." Wouldn't it be preferable to let the community itself, with the aid of local authority, judge the expediency of the Credo in Sunday Masses, in accordance with the "service" such a profession of faith would effectively afford the celebration? This immediately brings to mind children's Masses, but there are a number of "adult" Masses which reflect the same type of problem.

Nor should we forget that the Credo is only one of many possible expressions of faith. Our very celebration of the Eucharist is a *mysterium fidei,* "a mystery of faith." Our very celebration of the Word, in which Christ himself speaks to the community,[9] calls for a vision of faith. Therefore, it is not a matter of knowing whether or not we should proclaim our faith at the celebration of Sunday Mass, but whether our faith must be formally proclaimed within the affirmations of the Credo.

### c. The Limitations of the Problem

Although these are serious questions, they are still not insurmountable. Scholastic theology liked to assert the following principle, which dominates the whole debate about the statement of faith: the act of the believer goes beyond that which is stated in words and attains the very Person it affirms.[10] In other words, over and above the propositions of a Credo and beyond any conceptual material stated, it is the Subsistent Truth, God himself, the most personal Being imaginable — it is He who must be found and affirmed! Consequently the dynamism of our faith is not to be restrained by the difficult statements in the Credo, nor by the more or less fragmentary statements about the mysteries, but must tend, rather, with all the forcefulness of love, toward that God of kindness and mercy which we affirm: "He who believes in me has everlasting life."[11]

These limitations show that the statements in a Credo, even the most perfect Credo, are only crutches to help us, crippled as we are, to walk. The point is not only to perfect these crutches and use them to better advantage, but more especially to place our hands in the hands of God, who, without crutches, can guide us along the way to Him.

# CHAPTER X

# THE READINGS

## CHANTING THE READINGS

In this chapter we will discuss the chanting of biblical readings.[1] By chanting we mean the intoned recitative of the text. In the Roman liturgy, this chanting is — or was — used not only for the biblical readings but also for the dialogues, the presidential prayers, the Preface, the central part of the Eucharistic Prayer and its final doxology, and the Lord's Prayer and the Embolism. The rules that are applicable to them are the same as those that govern the chanting of the readings.

We are concerned here with the European languages. The others (the Oriental ones, for example) also pose a problem, but we shall not discuss it now. In fact, there is often no difficulty at all, as in the tonal African languages, for example. In these, the meaning of the words depends upon the relative pitch of each sound. Every word, therefore, is quite naturally "sung." Even in collective recitation, singing them can extend to a fifth on the musical scale. Of course, all singing should essentially accentuate the natural melody of the words in order to preserve the meaning of the sentence. It is an amplification of chant.

The main purpose of all rules for liturgical singing, in any language, should be the clarification of the Word of God. Whatever the method used, the presentation of the Word to the community is not to be reduced to a pious reading from the Bible, but merits a truly liturgical proclamation.

## THE PROBLEM OF CHANT

The proclamation of the Word of God to the Christian community is a *liturgical act*. As such, it is distinguished from a private reading because it requires at least a minimum of solemnization. "The liturgical reading," writes J. A. Jungmann, "can never be satisfied for any length of time by merely a prose declamation, motivated solely for practical reasons. The recitation is stylized . . . The reader should not interject his own feeling into the sacred text; he should present it in strict objectivity and with a sacred respect, as if it rested on a golden tray: for he recites the Word of God."[2]

When the Word of God was proclaimed only in Latin, there was practically no problem at all. The declamation was made according to the *toni communes missae.* The screen of the language and the official nature of Gregorian chant protected the priest from scandal and ridicule when he mistreated the sacred text. The worst possible errors could be made — misplaced accents, defective cadences, incomprehensible sense groups — without being noticed by the faithful and without damage to the liturgical celebration. Rather, it was a symbolic presentation of the Word of God. The community faithfully venerated it as such, even though it could not understand its meaning.

But now that the readings are in the vernacular, the proclamation must be made in such a way that it will be immediately understood, with careful preservation of the solemnity of the liturgical action. It will be received with the unlimited veneration of faith, but, at the same time, that faith will be aroused, sustained, and strengthened. The Word, then, is adored in its mystery, which no longer resides in the unintelligibility of the language but in the divinity of the Word itself. Chanting presents "the Word" (Jn. 1:1) to the community, and he who presents it is no longer a "cantor" but becomes a "prophet."[3] He does not primarily fulfill a rubric, but, rather, a prophetic ministry. He is a messenger from God.

In the Old Testament tradition, the reading of the sacred text without chant was inconceivable. Whoever recited Scripture without "chanting" it, according to the *Mishna,* was considered an idolator! In fact, the tradition of the sung reading was so profoundly instilled that the language of the time spoke indiscriminately of the *singing* and the *recitation* of a canticle.[4] The proclamation of the Word of God was thought of as divine music flooding the earth, such as the *announcement* of the angels in Bethlehem *singing* the glory of God. Clement of Alexandria enthusiastically declared: "The prophets are speaking: the sound of their *music* is everywhere."[5]

This biblical tradition of singing the reading is best explained by the desire to protect the divine Word from the banality of earthly prose and to grace it with the magic of rhythm and melody. It is also justified by the fact that ancient oriental languages, especially Hebrew, possess a verbal rhythm that is extremely fluid and musically rich.

"Chanting" in modern languages, however, presents awesome problems. The most important concern:

— the text to be proclaimed,
— the musical elements of the recitative,
— the festive nature of the liturgical celebration.

## A. The Text

We can start with the following principle: *the chanting of the Word of God is the solemnization of the proclamation of that Word.* If one accepts this principle, the first thing required of the biblical text is that the text itself should have a minimum of solemnity; it should belong to a literary genre which is of the same hieratic nature as chant.

It is clear that the entire Bible is inspired by the Holy Spirit and possesses the incomparable dignity of the Word of God. But that dignity, great as it is, does not automatically create a solemn or lyrical character. Thus the list of David's officers or the story of Suzanna, although inspired by the Holy Spirit, does not possess the lyricism required for it to be chanted.

Although the Bible is inspired in its entirety and in its parts, it is also evident that certain texts have a greater value for faith than others. (The entire Bible is inspired but is not necessarily an article of faith; an article of faith is only that which the author proposes as such.) Yet we do not mean to say that every article of faith is necessarily solemn and would, therefore, require some sort of "chanting." On the contrary, it is more likely that certain catechetical sections should be read.

Finally, it is obvious that some texts possess an innate rhythm and lyrical nature which are, above all others, suited for chanting. The hymn from the prologue of the Gospel of John[6] is not "read," nor is the Epistle to the Philippians,[7] or the wonderful poem of Isaiah 60,[8] or the text of the Beatitudes.[9] They were written to be chanted. To read them would be as bad as reciting a canticle or psalm *recto tono*.

Needless to say, the first step of approaching the biblical text to determine its literary genre should be taken in deep humility and serious study. Certain passages clearly demonstrate their musico-literary make-up. For example, the wonderful hymn from the First Epistle of St. Paul to Timothy (3:16) which, doubtless, represents one of the first professions of baptismal faith,[10] and the moving text from his Second Epistle to Timothy written just before Paul was martyred:

Remember that Jesus Christ
rose from the dead
and was descended from David.
This saying is true:

If we have died with him,
we shall also live with him;

If we endure,
we shall also reign with him.[11]                    *2 Tim. 2:8, 11*

These two examples, however, are exceptional cases. The musicality of other passages may not be so apparent. At any rate, an astute analysis is required to discover a Christological hymn in the Epistle from the Fourth Sunday of Easter.

Christ also has suffered for you,
Leaving you an example
that you may follow in his steps:

'Who did no sin,
neither was deceit found in his mouth.'

Who when he was reviled, did not revile,
when he suffered, did not threaten,
but yielded himself to him who judged him unjustly.

Who himself bore our sins in his body upon the tree,
that we, having died to sin, might live to justice;
and by his stripes you were healed.

For you were as sheep going astray,
but now you have returned to the shepherd
and guardian of your souls.[12]                    *I Peter 2:21-25*

Concerning the Gospels, it may be noted that, when a narrative is involved, chanting is not necessary. However, we should remember that the historical narratives of the Gospels are not on the same redactional level; certain ones have a hieratical form which more readily lends itself to chanting. In the pre-synoptic period these accounts were transmitted in a hieratical style, according to special mnemonic techniques.

Therefore, while Mark presents the account of Jesus' baptism in a very simple narrative, Matthew succeeds in condensing his text in a wonderful style of three stanzas consisting of three lines each:

When Jesus had been baptized,
he immediately came up from the water.
And behold, the heavens were opened,

And he saw the Spirit of God
descending as a dove
and coming upon him.

> And behold, a voice from the heavens said,
> "This is my beloved Son,
> in whom I am well pleased."[13]                *Mt. 3:16-17*

Here is the introduction to the Sermon on the Mount according to Matthew (three stanzas of two lines), whose literal pattern of the original Greek gives the following rhythm:

> And seeing the crowds,
> he went up on the mountain.

> And when he was seated,
> his disciples came to him.

> And opening his mouth
> he taught them, saying, . . .                *Mt. 5:1-2*

Obviously, the translations should faithfully convey the powerful rhythm of the original. Moreover, the recitative should not only sustain this rhythm, but also enhance and emphasize it. Thanks to "chanting," which is much more than ordinary reading, we should, therefore, rediscover the three stanzas of the account of the Temptation of Jesus, the five stanzas of the Sermon on the Mount based on the verb *agrafe* (to worry),[14] the eight Beatitudes of Matthew, etc.

These few remarks about the biblical text, although incomplete, lead to this first important conclusion: the choice of chanting does not reside primarily in the choice of the melody of the recitative, but rather in the text itself. The literary structure of the text should be adaptable to chant, which solemnizes and thus amplifies and underscores its message. Here, more than anywhere else, the music must fulfill its ministerial function.

## B. Musical Elements of the Recitative

Rhythm and melody comprise the musical elements of the recitative.

### 1. RHYTHM

Following the example of former chants, the rhythm of the recitative should fully incorporate the rhythm of the text it proclaims:

— a rhythm which is as subtle as a bird in flight and as alive as a child at play.

— a rhythm which is constantly renewed, never becoming "prefabricated." The recitative invents its own rhythm with each phrase, based on the rhythm of the text; it is uniquely concerned with the demands of a good declamation.

— a rhythm which is free, but not anarchic. For, if the recitative is the solemnization of the word, the rhythm of the recitative is the solemnization of the rhythm of the word.

At the same time, the rules which govern the execution of a musical work as well as those which regulate the proclamation of the Word apply also to rhythm. As a general rule, the larger and the greater the echo produced, the slower the rhythm must be.

## 2. THE MELODY

The main purpose of the recitative is not to develop a musical argument. The melody itself is not emphasized, but is simply the vehicle through which the Word of God is presented. The melodic elements present should serve merely as punctuation for the phrases, not as ornaments with any value in themselves. Of course, again the eternal problem of balance between the music and the text arises. To solve it is an awesome undertaking, because the melody must attempt to incarnate the transcendent Word of God in humble notes, formulated in accordance with human laws. If the recitative is too poorly sung, human weakness may perhaps cast a shadow upon the transcendent message. If the melody is too brilliant, however, the music may detract from the texts. Frail but seductive human beauty may veil the splendor of the message; musical ornamentation may hide the person of Jesus Christ, who is precisely the one to be honored.

The chanting of the Word of God should be a continual search for balance in the text-music relationship, the balance here consisting of the full and joyous submission of the music to the text. Here, more than anywhere else, music is a servant of the text, or, more exactly, of the inner message the text proclaims. "The sung word . . . is not an art in itself; it is not an ornament of worship, but a bridge between man and God." [15] Better still, it is a proclamation of God. It is an exterior sign of an inner message, just as a sacrament is a sign of an inner grace, just as the Eucharistic appearances of bread and wine indicate the presence of the real Body and Blood of Jesus Christ.

### a. Melodic Elements of the Recitative

The recitative necessarily calls for a *tenor* (recitation tone) and a *final cadence*. On occasion, it can even contain an *introduction formula*, one or several *modulations,* as well as *passing notes.* Here is an example of a recitative in the key of *A*.[16]

## b. Classification

An analysis of the musical elements in the recitative permits a classification of recitatives into several genres. This classification is as follows:

### 1) THE RECITATIVE OF PUNCTUATION

The entire phrase is sung on a single note (the *tenor*), except at the end, where a final cadence is introduced to "punctuate" the declamation. A most typical example is that of the Latin recitative for the proclamation of the Gospel[17]: the sacred text is proclaimed entirely on a single note, with the exception of the fourth syllable from the end, which goes down to a minor third:

Dixit Jesus discipulis    suis: Vos es-tis sal    - ræ.

A few Latin recitatives have a double punctuation, that of *metrum* and of *punctum*.

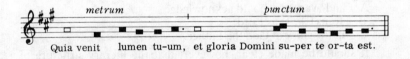

Quia venit    lumen tu-um, et gloria Domini su-per te or-ta est.

We can include here also the Latin psalmodies which have two punctuations: the *mediant*, which concludes the first half of each verse, and the *final*, which concludes the second. By adding a third element, the *flex*, to the two elements which comprise the *metrum* and the *punctum*, a recitative of three elements of punctuation is produced, A+B+C. This format is adopted in the following example:[18]

### 2) STROPHIC RECITATIVE

The biblical account can sometimes be proclaimed and divided into a certain number of "strophes" which are each given in the same melodic pattern. Here, for example, is the hymn from the

Epistle to the Philippians, which can be proclaimed according to the recitative cited above:[19]

A  Brothers,
   be of the same attitude
       as was Christ Jesus.

A  Although he was by nature God,
B  he did not cling to
C  equality with God

A  but laid it aside
B  to take on the nature of a slave,
C  and become like other men.

A  When he assumed human form,
B  he still further humbled himself,
       becoming obedient to death
C  even death upon the cross.

A  Therefore has God so greatly exalted him,
B  and given him the name
C  above all others,

A  so that at the name of Jesus
B  everyone should kneel
C  in heaven, on earth, and under the earth,

A  and everyone should acknowledge
B  Jesus Christ as Lord
C  in the glory of God the Father.

It should be made clear, however, that the literary structure of these stanzas is rather flexible, and the number of lines can vary. It is not always possible to apply such a melodic *schema* to all strophic divisions without at least a minimum of adaptation. The melodic *schema* should therefore be quite flexible. Adding a flex or possibly changing or eliminating one of the melodic elements will achieve the adaptation.

### 3) THE ORNATE RECITATIVE

The ornate recitative is one in which the text, according to H. Hucke,[20] is "durch-komponiert," i.e., composed syllable by syllable upon a melody. The recitatives of the Pater Noster in the *Missa cantata*, from the great Lamentation of Holy Saturday *(Incipit oratio Jeremiae prophetae)*, or from the *Exsultet*, are grandiose examples of this genre. Yet there are also a few masterpieces which somehow go beyond the framework of the recitative. They cannot be executed from memory and must be written down note for note.[21]

### c.  The Tessitura[22]

The melody of the recitatives should stay within a reasonable range, a range in which the voice retains both its timbre and fullness.

In the Latin recitatives, this limit does not exceed a fifth (the tones for the orations) or a sixth (the Preface and the Pater).

It appears that the old pentatone (C, D, E, G, A), which does not go beyond the limits of a sixth, no matter what the key, is fully adaptable to chanting:

— first of all, because the pentatone is the musical scale easiest to sing and the most pleasant to hear;

— secondly, because a nomal voice can easily attain these limits.

Obviously, each lector will choose whatever key is best for his particular voice. Therefore, there should be no hesitation to raise or lower the recitative. We should remember that there is a fundamental difference between the interpretation of a work of art, the first principle of which is fidelity to the work itself, and the performance of a liturgical recitative, in which the authenticity of the liturgical ministry is most important.

In observing the suggestion given above, the best tessitura, based on the limit of a sixth, is the following:

— for a bass voice: C-A or D-B;

— for a baritone voice: E-C or F-D;

— for a tenor voice: G-E.

Thanks to the microphone, it is easy to amplify voices which otherwise are not strong enough to be heard. Here, too, amplification renders an irreplaceable service to weak voices and to the hard of hearing. But it also gives rise to the temptation for normally good voices to use a low, almost confidential tone. The result is often visceral. Such emotional techniques should be left to popular singers who use the method for our entertainment. A liturgical celebration, however, needs a proclamation presented with a certain objectivity, in a normal and firm voice. Follow this simple rule: a voice which is not adequate in itself for a proclamation to a congregation, is not adequate even with a microphone. When sonorization amplifies a voice, it amplifies all of its faults as well.

### d. The Tone for Recitation or "tenor"

As a general rule, chanting should be introduced by a *single* tone for recitative or *tenor*. Yet one can intone the phrase itself, adorning it with passing notes and concluding with final cadences. Such variations should emphasize and enhance the *tenor* rather than harm it. This is easy to understand. Since the recitative serves the text it is proclaiming, it will focus attention upon the text rather than on the melody.

Naturally, there are *exceptions*. There are some who deliberately wish to destroy a too classical framework and attract attention. Take, for example, the *systematic rise* of the voice, as used in the eastern liturgies. In general, the ambitus of the melody hardly varies at all, but moves from low to high. At times this rise is almost imperceptible, changing by only a third or a quarter of a tone within the phrase. Thus these recitatives are part of the strange and mysterious world of Eastern music (untouched by our tempered scale). At other times, the systematic rise is made at the beginning of the phrases. Such a procedure communicates a brilliance and a life to the reading, which, as a result, surpasses the usual chant; it is the expression of a solemnity that never ceases to grow.

Although employed a bit more wisely and somewhat more subdued by Western discipline, the same procedure appears in the Roman liturgy:

— In the triple *Ave, sanctum chrisma* of the Mass of Chrism for Holy Thursday,

— in the triple *Ecce lignum crucis* of Good Friday,

— in the triple *Lumen Christi* of the Easter Vigil.

In addition, there is the very popular *Parce, Domine* which, in certain parishes, is sung three times, each on a higher tone.

Finally, let us say that even popular songs, whether old[23] or new, use the same procedure — a fact which proves that it is appreciated by the people.

#### e. The Ornaments or Passing Notes

According to S. Corbin,[24] the "ornaments of chant and their degree of concentration vary infinitely from one place to another and especially from one rite to another. There is a world of difference between the pure chant melodies in the Latin liturgy and those of the East." We can assume that Western communities prefer to use such adornments with moderation and that their liturgical singing reflects this reserve and modesty. It is not appropriate to extend the sacred text for the sake of the neumes, nor to inject one's own feelings into the sacred text. In our opinion, all musical embellishments should be used only to facilitate a more natural diction; they should help and enhance the text, not detract from it. At any rate, they should be omitted whenever there is danger of obscuring the verbal rhythm of the text.

## C. The Nature of the Liturgical Celebration

The following rule has already been stated above: *chanting is the solemnization of the proclamation of the Word of God.* From this, it naturally follows that chanting will be used whenever the liturgical celebration itself is one of a festive nature.

How can this festive nature be defined or stated?

We must say, first of all, that this festive nature is not uniquely a question of *rites* and *rubrics.* There can be a sung Mass with sacred ministers, a deacon and a sub-deacon, without the community being "miraculously" transported into a festive atmosphere. We have often seen Masses where the choir stalls are filled with clergy and the nave is filled with boredom! However, a solemn liturgy can effectively emphasize the festive nature of a celebration.

It is also true that a large number of participants does not thereby guarantee a festive atmosphere. True, every liturgical gathering of the faithful is an incarnation of the entire Church, celebrating Jesus present in her midst. But a congregation of twenty people can sometimes be more festive and solemn than a crowd of a thousand. We have often seen churches that were full, but were not communities. They seemed more like automats, where the people came just to hear the Word of God and receive Communion, as if they were at a cafeteria and not a common table, or were just a crowd of people and not a celebrating community.

However, the number of participants can greatly enhance the festive nature of a celebration; their chanting will greatly aid the proclamation of the Word of God:

— It gives the sacred text a certain objectivity and protects it from subjective interpretation. The intimate feelings of the reader, sincere though they may be, give way to the *actio liturgica* and the *service* of the Word.

— It sustains an objective atmosphere for the congregation. It is received, not as the word of "so and so," but as that Word which transcends every human category for all time and reaches the shores of eternity.

— In the final analysis, it is the *edification* — in the strongest sense of the word — of the Christian community, which is the goal of the proclamation of the Word. Indeed, it is this edification which regulates the proclamation of the Word and determines the appropriateness or inappropriateness of having a chanted proclamation of the Word of God.

# CHAPTER XI
# THE INSTRUMENTS

— What about guitars at Mass?

— And what about a "rock" group?

— Why is the Church against "pop" music?

We don't really intend to answer these questions here, for the ministerial function of instruments in liturgical celebrations seems easy to understand from what we have already explained. But, because these questions are constantly being raised by so many people, as often to condemn as to praise, we feel it necessary to speak of them briefly. We shall first discuss the organ and then the other instruments.

## A. The Pipe Organ

### 1. THE "KING OF INSTRUMENTS"[1]

The organ was allowed in churches only after a long time. Organ music was thought to be an intrusion that would disturb the devotion of the faithful. However, we should not be too quick to blame ecclesiastical authorities for such mistrust nor accuse them of being totally against anything new. Aside from the name, the ancient "organ" had little in common with the instrument we have today. It wasn't even a "mini-organ" but rather a portable midget-accordion that was slung over the shoulder, played with the right hand while the left hand worked the bellows. It took long periods of development and perfecting for this embryonic organ to reach the fullness and splendor of a Silbermann, a Clicquot, and a Dom Bedos in the eighteenth century.

History mentions the "great organs" of Bonn in 1230, of Prague in 1256, of Strasbourg in 1292, and of Bruges in 1299. In the fourteenth century, the first pedal keyboards appeared in Belgium, Italy, and Germany. However, organs were at first given only limited use in liturgical celebrations. In 1415, the great organ of Notre Dame in Paris was used in only twenty-three solemn feasts. Toward the fifteenth century, a repertoire for the organ began to grow, often drawing its inspiration from the vocal polyphony of the time. A manuscript found in Faenza, dating from about 1400, presents arrangements for madrigals and songs by the fourteenth century authors Jocopo da Bologna, Landini, and Machaut. Among the first composers of organ literature we should mention Konrad Paumann, the blind organist of Nuremberg (†1473 A.D.) who published the *Fundamentum organisandi* in 1452; the author of the *Buxheimer Orgelbuch;* the anonymous verses for the *Magnificat* and the *Te Deum;* and the famous Cabezon (†1566 A.D.) of Spain. Fifteenth century organ music had by no means attained the high artistic level of the *Orgelbüchlein* of J. S. Bach, the prince of organists, but even by this time its future worth was in evidence.

Until the beginning of this century, the position of Roman authority was rather restrictive. We must admit that organists of ages past have not always known how to make their instruments pray with the discretion and power prescribed. Unfortunately, in the history of music there was only one Bach, who said, "Music which does not have as its goal the glory of God and the re-creation of the soul is only a diabolic din."[2] The brilliant improvisations of certain eighteenth century masters of the organ made birds sing, bells ring, and people swoon in amazement, but they still were no more than pleasant trivia. They produced many notes, little music, and less prayer. There were even occasions when some pieces became merely buffoonery. What liturgical advantage did they have for the community?

But from the beginning of this century until Pius XII, official documents have shown a growing esteem for the king of instruments:

In *Tra le Sollecitudini* of November 22, 1903, St. Pius X allows only music that is accompanied by the organ, as well as preludes, interludes and other pieces, as long as they are brief and preserve "the proper character of this instrument."[3]

In *Divini Cultus* of December 20, 1928, Pius XI begins a panegyric on the organ:

> There is one instrument, however, which comes to us from the ancients and which properly belongs to the Church. It is called the organ. Its most wonderful amplitude and majesty have rendered it worthy of being associated with the liturgical rites, both to support the chant and also to elicit, during the periods when the choir is silent, sweet music that harmonizes with the prescribed rules.[4]

In *Musicae Sacrae Disciplina,* of December 25, 1955, Pius XII continues the discourse. But one wonders if his warm praise for the organ isn't really an attempt to discourage other less highly esteemed instruments from trying to scale the organ loft:

> Among the musical instruments that have a place in church the organ rightly holds the principal position, since it is especially fitted for the sacred chants and sacred rites. It adds a wonderful splendor and a special magnificence to the ceremonies of the Church. It moves the souls of the faithful by the grandeur and sweetness of its tones. It gives minds an almost heavenly joy and it lifts them up powerfully to God and to higher things.[5]

We have reached here the pinnacle of panegyric. However, it is fortunate that Vatican II has concluded that the Church's position of excluding all other instruments from her service was untenable and should be forsaken as soon as possible. It was feared that the Church of the Roman Rite, which uses the organ, was being confused with the entire Church in which the organ is not universally used. The *Constitution on the Sacred Liturgy* states:

> In the Latin Church the pipe organ is to be held in high esteem, for it is the traditional musical instrument, and one that adds a wonderful splendor to the Church's ceremonies and powerfully lifts up man's mind to God and to heavenly things.[6]

In practice, the reign of the king of instruments extends to the following liturgical and geographical limits:

— On the liturgical map, the organ is used in the Latin Church (and in the Protestant Churches); the Eastern Churches have *a cappella* choirs.

— On the geographic map, the organ is used particularly in Nordic countries and temperate climates; to build such an instrument with wooden pipes in tropical lands would be futile, for no wood can long withstand the onslaught of termites, nor undergo the two extremes of dryness and humidity.

However, the Constitution is correct in stating that the entire Latin Church should "highly esteem" the pipe organ. This means, for example, that the Christians in the Congo should be happy that Notre Dame in Paris has a beautiful organ. Yes, communities that have such a fine, well-balanced instrument are indeed fortunate, because they possess a treasure of joy, beauty, and prayer. But it certainly doesn't mean that the Christians in the Congo should go right out and start building organs for their churches. They have other riches that Notre Dame could never have.

## B. The "Other" Instruments

What are the possibilites of using other instruments in liturgical celebrations? In principle, there are a great many. Here is what the *Constitution on the Sacred Liturgy* of Vatican II has to say on the subject:

> But other instruments also may be admitted for use in divine worship, with the knowledge and consent of the competent territorial authority . . . . This may be done, however, only on condition that the instruments are suitable for sacred use, or can be made so, that they accord with the dignity of the temple, and truly contribute to the edification of the faithful.[7]

Vatican II thus recognizes the usefulness of every instrument. The organ is no longer offered as the *only* instrument suitable for church, as Pius XI once said, but simply is the one which should especially be esteemed in the Latin Church. *Every other instrument, without exception,* can be allowed to celebrate God with its melodies, harmonies, and rhythms.

In principle, the Church has always held this very liberal position; in practice, such liberalism was counterbalanced by a mistrust which was difficult to overcome. "Other" instruments were considered too secular. Did anyone ever think of "winning over" and "clericalizing" those same dance hall instruments, which preferred dance rhythms to the steps of a procession and a spotlight to the shadowy darkness of the sanctuary? Such mistrust and prohibitions resulted in paradoxical situations. On the one hand, the choir would loudly sing Psalm 150, "Praise God with timbrel and dance, praise him with sounding cymbals," yet, on the other, nothing happened — neither in the choir nor in the sanctuary. No one danced or played the tambourine (except the "spiritual" tambourine and "mystical" cymbals)!

This gap between practice and principle showed a lack of clear thinking and decisive conclusions. One had the impression that such reasoning was often built upon the shifting sands of religious sentiment, one instrument being judged "religious" while another was judged impious or immoral. Some of the resultant condemnations were even made on the spur of the moment. Of course, such failings are human and quite natural. Similarly, no bishop ever thinks of expressly praising an organist for playing his organ quietly, yet as soon as he plays with any kind of gusto, with too much harmony or rhythm (real or imagined), one sees the sudden waving of crosiers and shaking of mitres!

Such reactions, however, are not reserved for the authorities alone; the community, too, is often to blame, for the authorities only interpret the feelings of the people. Nor are they confined to Catholic circles. (J. S. Bach was once harshly critized for his too colorful harmonizations, which "confused" the Protestant community of Arnstadt.) Despite their negative character, they are the result of a positive pastoral attitude: they are to protect the community — clumsily, perhaps, but in good faith — from anything that may injure its sensibility and disturb the peace of its prayer. In this respect, they show a valid concern for the liturgical congregation, and any resultant restrictions, even those most open to criticism, are to be respected.[8]

We must, then, ask the following questions: what are the conditions that instruments must fulfill in order to be suitable for church service? Or, better yet, what are the criteria for deciding whether or not they may be permitted in church?

## 1. IMPERFECT CRITERIA

In the past, the criterion most often used was that of "religiosity," i.e., the instrument's potential to express "religious feelings." The basic reasoning behind this was that liturgical singing must express spiritual sentiments, and that, as *Divini Cultus* affirmed, "no instrument, however excellent and perfect, can surpass the human voice *in expressing emotions.*"[9] An instrument, then, is to be judged suitable for the liturgy only insofar as it furthers such expression by accompanying the human voice, or in an instrumental solo. This is the thought behind Pius XII's recommendation that string instruments be placed next in line of acceptability, for they "express the joyous and sad sentiments of the soul with an indescribable power."[10]

Yet this criterion seems to be imperfect, for it limits the role of the music to the simple expression of emotions only. Singing can and must do more. When the priest sings the account of the Institution of the Eucharist or the cantor proclaims the Responsorial Psalm, he does not express emotions primarily, but rather a message. The entire ministerial function of singing is to be considered here.

Subjectivity, too, began to play a major role in the criteria for musical instruments in the liturgy. Who is to judge what is best? Who is to say that a tom-tom is any less expressive than a guitar, or a guitar less than a violin, or a violin less than an organ? Everything depends upon the locality and the musical sensibility of the celebrating community.

Another criterion — just as incomplete as "religiosity" — is that of "solemnity." We sometimes think that the use of certain instruments is an indication of greater solemnity: for a very solemn and joyous feast such as Easter, many violins should be used; for an ordinary feast, a few or none at all should be used; for Good Friday, nothing at all should be played, not even to accompany the people's singing. True, solemnization is an important element in the ministerial function of music, but not the only one. Thus this criterion remains only partially valid—and therefore partially open to criticism. For we must also consider the fact that the true solemnity of a service is not to be judged merely by the number of musical instruments responsible for the massive chords emanating from the choir loft, but, rather, by the integrity with which each participant executes the function proper to his rank. A festive congregation is one in which everyone expresses joy in his own participation, in accordance with the role he plays in the celebration.

## 2. THE TRUE CRITERION

At the risk of "rehashing" the principles, we must return to the ministerial function of singing. The principle governing this question is really quite simple:

— Singing has a ministerial function to fulfill.

Therefore any instrument which allows the congregation to perfect its ministerial function may be used in the liturgy; any instrument which does not provide such a service to the community must be excluded.

The Instruction on *Music in the Liturgy* of March 5, 1967, proposes the following considerations:

> In permitting and using musical instruments, the culture and traditions of individual peoples must be taken into account. However, those instruments which are, by common opinion and use, suitable for secular music only, are to be altogether prohibited from every liturgical celebration and from popular devotions.
>
> Any musical instrument permitted in divine worship should be used in such a way that it meets the needs of the liturgical celebration, and is in the interests both of the beauty of worship and the edification of the faithful.[11]

The first rule says "the culture and traditions of individual peoples must be taken into account." It is difficult to define the musical temperament of a people, but quite easy to consider common sense and current practice. Therefore, if a traditionally oriented community finds joy in hearing an organ but is completely dumbfounded by the new rhythms, it is not necessary to submit them to a barrage of rhythmic beats in place of the organ. On the other hand, if a group of young people like the guitar and the rhythms of a rock group, there is no reason to deny them this preference. Most Sunday congregations are mixed, composed of a thousand different and complementary people who constitute the holy people of God, including staid grandmothers and lively young teen-agers, people who like classical music and those who yearn for "pop." The preference of one group should not be imposed upon the entire assembly. Singing should *edify* the congregation, not divide it. It is absolutely unacceptable that a community's charity, which is its prime richness and resource, be jeopardized by drum beats or trumpet blasts.

The second rule concerns the *manner* or the "style" of playing. "Any musical instrument . . . should be used in such a way that it meets the needs of the liturgical celebration, and is in the interests both of the beauty of worship and the edification of the faithful." The precision of this Instruction is fortunate and clarifies a point that is frequently confused. There are no "religious" instruments; there are no "secular" instruments. A guitar is no less pious than a violin; a percussion instrument is as Christian as a trumpet; cymbals have a fervor comparable to that of the great organs. The holiness of a thing comes from how it is used in the liturgy. A loaf of bread or a grain of incense is not inherently either sacred or secular. But when the bread becomes the Body of the Lord and when the incense burns at the altar, they acquire a particular holiness of their own. It is not the bread and the incense that make the liturgy sacred, but their *use* in the liturgy. Likewise, this is true in regard to guitars, trumpets, and cymbals. The liturgy does not choose its instruments, any more than it chooses its music or the language of its celebrations. It receives these from the people gathered together. The only condition placed on the use of its instruments is that they be played in a style which "meets the needs of the liturgical celebration, and is in the interests both of the beauty of worship and the edification of the faithful."

## C. The Role of the Instruments

### 1. ACCOMPANIMENT OF THE SINGING

When speaking of the ministerial function of instruments, the 1967 Instruction gives as their primary role the accompaniment of singing:

> The use of musical instruments to accompany the singing can act as a support to the voices, render participation easier, and achieve a deeper union in the assembly. However, their sound should not so overwhelm the voices that it is difficult to make out the text; and when some part is proclaimed aloud by the priest or a minister by reason of his role, they should be silent.

> In sung or said Masses the organ, or other instrument legitimately admitted, can be used to accompany the singing of the choir and the people; it can also be played "solo" at the beginning before the priest reaches the altar, at the Offertory, at the Communion, and at the end of Mass.[12]

These statements seem banal, but, historically, they are revolutionary and codify a recent practice in Catholic liturgy. In fact, until the nineteenth century, Gregorian chant was sung without accompaniment,[13] and the organ was played solo only. It was only after the Church banned orchestras — often as an economic measure — that the organ was asked to undertake the role of all instruments. It began to occupy a position of greater importance, and as an instrument of accompaniment, succeeded in invading the choir lofts of all the churches, a role for which it had not been intended.

Yet its ministerial function in this role is an extremely important one. Under the command of a master, this fine instrument will unify the community, while sustaining the melody, rhythm, and modality of the song. Thus, this king of instruments will be of true service to the community in its prayer.

Of course, the knowledge and ability of the organist and of the other musicians involved should be faultless. Mediocrity is unpardonable. The accompaniment of voices is a service which, if not done properly, should not be done at all.

## 2. THE SOLO

The organ and other instruments can play solos:

— to provide a setting for the liturgical songs by introducing them in preludes and prolonging them in postludes. (The chorales in the *Orgelbüchlein* show the heights that this art can reach.)

— to provide a setting for the celebration itself.

The 1967 Instruction speaks of solos being played before the celebration, at the Offertory, at the Communion, and as a recessional hymn.[14] The organist should not use his priviledge sparingly. Let him greet the people entering as one greets long-awaited friends; let his postlude accompany the departing congregation as one regretfully accompanies old friends to the door.

His playing, however, should be fully adapted to the celebration. Even though the temptation to play a concert repertoire is great, to do so for an unappreciative congregation is an injustice to the liturgy. What artist can boast such a docile and patient public every Sunday of the year, rain or shine? Yet to play "classics" on any and every occasion is the best way to make them meaningless. Certain toccatas, if they could speak, would cry in despair at being dragged into any and every cortege. The Christian organist must place the needs of the celebrating community and the liturgy before his desire for fame as a virtuoso.

The 1967 Instruction does not authorize solo organ playing during Advent, Lent, and Passiontide.[15] This decision is unfortunate, and has been influenced by the traditional concept of the organ as a joyous and festive instrument only. For the organ can also be of service to the community during times of penance and grief. Silbermann organs have *bourdons* that can cry, and certain chorales by J. S. Bach have notes that are actually tears in themselves. In other words, we must have confidence in our organists. Furthermore, an organist who does not know how to pray with the community in a time of penance will not know how to celebrate with them in times of joy.

# D. Further Reflections

What evolution of the role of the "other" instruments in the liturgy is to be desired? In principle, the answer is a simple one. It may be formulated as follows:

> No kind of sacred music is prohibited from liturgical actions by the Church as long as it corresponds to the spirit of the liturgical celebration itself and the nature of its individual parts, and does not hinder the active participation of the people.[16]

Yet there is a world of difference between this affirmation of principle, quietly formulated in the serenity of an official document, and its practical realizations, which are at times fervently embraced and at other times just as fervently rejected! This "world of difference" between principle and practice is the domain of the celebrating congregations, which are not nourished on liturgical principles, but rather on a living liturgy.

## 1. THE TEMPTATION OF EXTREMES

### a. The Traditionalist Position

The tenants of this position want to construct the present and the future by using only materials from the past. They prefer the organ and "classical" music over all other instruments to the same extent that they favor Latin over the vernacular. Their position is most at home in archeology: only what was once done in the past is valuable! In the guise of being faithful to tradition, these people are actually preserving only the *forms* in which the ever-living tradition was formerly expressed. They are thinking in the terms of St. Gregory, the Middle Ages, and the Council of Trent, while the Church is busy dealing with the "today" of God. They adhere to their past traditions at the cost of any new experiences, taking refuge in the term "obedience" rather than daring to try new ways. If an experiment of someone else fails, they claim this failure as their own personal "victory."

Such a position is the temptation of the traditionalist clergy and of a few laymen who are of the same mind. They show their resentment by retreating to Gregorian chant and taking refuge in classical music. They know nothing of popular music; they consider jazz as "musical slang" and the instruments which play it as worthless.

Of course, we are speaking here of the traditionalist position which emphasizes tradition but does not really represent the living tradition of the Church, which has always generously employed contemporary music. One cannot build a living, liturgical community by embalming mummies!

### b. The Modernist Position

The other temptation is to go overboard with "modernism." To the modernist, nothing that was used in the past has any value at all. For him only "modern" music is valid, and, instead of being a foundation, tradition becomes a millstone. From such a point of view, one might think that all that is needed for a living liturgy is that it be "popular," and that the inspiration of the moment be substituted for the study of both liturgical and musical laws.

This position of the "modernist" is just as false as that the of "traditionalist." The latter embraces corpses; the former cremates them! In either case, the community is sacrificed. Of course, the two positions described here are caricatures. No one with any sense would truly wish to support the one or the other. Still, it pays to be most careful, for we can all be tempted at times by both. We can be perhaps too conservative on one point and too liberal on another. There are some people who are avid traditionalists one day and just as avid modernists the next. To be well-balanced in every instance is not something which can be acquired once and for all; rather, we must check our equilibrium constantly so that a balance between fidelity to tradition and fidelity to a new life is ever maintained. Both are essential. A tree that wishes to flower and bear fruit and would cut its own roots would be a stupid tree; and a tree that keeps its roots, but refuses to produce new fruit would soon be a dead tree.

## 2. ELEMENTS FOR A SOLUTION

If the problem concerning liturgical music is presented in the form of a dilemma — i.e., ancient music or modern music? — it is insoluble, because it is poorly presented. Whether a Mass is one of Gregorian chant or a folk Mass with guitars matters little if the people only passively "attend" the Mass. The result will be exactly the same in both instances: the negation of the celebrating assembly. The solution is not to sprinkle a few Gregorian chants throughout an English Mass, nor to revive the Gregorian Mass and then spice it with a few rhythmic English hymns. The only true solution will always be based on the ministerial function of the music and the instruments. If a particular music and certain instruments, according to the terms set down in the Instruction, "are in accordance with liturgical action" and favor "the active participation of the people," they will be completely valid, because they will fulfill their ministerial function. In agreement with this principle, rhythmic music may be valid for one congregation but not for another; likewise, Gregorian and Palestrinian polyphony may enhance the celebration of one congregation but only subject another group to complete boredom. Obviously, then, there is no music or instrument that is good or bad in itself, but simply music that is well or poorly adapted to a particular congregation.

Up to now, liturgical music seldom left the church. When, in some instances, it did leave, it quickly scurried to the safety of a concert hall. Similarly, "pop" music never found its way into the church. In fact, a sort of racial segregation existed in regard to the two kinds of music. Moreover, this apartheid was upheld in official documents and was quite easily accepted by a great majority of the faithful. The Church had its own music, just as it had its own language, architecture, ornaments, and way of life. To the faithful, only "church songs" were apropriate in church; other songs, in which they honestly and fully expressed themselves, were appropriate only outside of church. But today, since the *Pastoral Constitution on the Church in the Modern World,* the church no longer wishes to confront the world, but, rather, chooses to put herself *into the world of today* (ecclesia *in* mundo hujus temporis). The Constitution states:

> Let the Church also acknowledge new forms of art which are adapted to our age and are in keeping with the characteristics of various nations and regions. Adjusted in their mode of expression and conformed to liturgical requirements, they may be introduced into the sanctuary when they raise the mind to God.[17]

The encounter between the music of "today's world" and the music of tradition should result in a new creation. Neither of these two kinds of music will remain exactly the same as it was before, but will be enriched by the other. Here is a comparison. When a culture — let's say, Western — meets another culture — let's say, African — the result will be a sort of hybrid. The emerging culture will be no longer uniquely Western, nor completely African; it will be something entirely different from either. In this way a new kind of music is emerging even now.

Our problem of church music can be considered from the point of view of "style," or musical language. Everyone knows that, after many centuries, the language used by the church became fixed in an ecclesiastical jargon that was quite foreign to everyday usage. It was thought that such rigidity of style and ecclesiastical format represented a rich traditional heritage, whereas it was really an impoverishment of our tradition. Church history shows us that our true tradition is represented by the use of Koine and the biblical Latin of the Vulgate. In the third and second centuries before Christ, when the Hebrew Bible was being translated into the modern language of the day for use in the liturgies of the synagogues of the Diaspora, it was not the Greek of Plato and Demosthenes that was chosen, but the Greek of the Koine, the popular language spoken throughout the Mediterranean basin. The New Testament also was written in the same kind of Greek. Later, when Latin began to outrank Greek, it was not the learned and ornate Latin of Cicero or Livy that was used in the liturgy, but the popular Latin. Thus was created the Latin of the Vulgate and of the Liturgy, which was at first "an eminently vulgar idiom."[18] Today also we must turn toward the popular language of our own day in the area of song and instruments; we must adopt a "vulgar" style exempt from all vulgarity — a style whose authentic nobility will be that of expressing fully the people it serves.

Undoubtedly, many excellent musicians have already taken great strides in this direction, even before the Council. For, without some renewal of classical or modern vocal polyphony, and of an organ repertoire, no choir would have been ready to assume its new role. Yet we have still a long way to go in order to achieve a new style. The road is long and filled with obstacles, and there will be many unhappy experiences. Such is the price of progress. A child learns to walk only after he has fallen on his "derrière" several times! Naturally, pastoral wisdom dictates that we try to make as few mistakes as possible, but a restriction cannot be imposed on new experiences, if new trails are to be blazed. False prudence sometimes hides real cowardice.

As the Instruction says so well, instruments which are suitable for sacred use or "which can be adapted to it"[19] are admissable. The implication, then, is that instruments are capable of "conversion"; hence they should be given time to adapt. Such common sense applies not only to the instruments themselves but, more importantly, to the artists who play them and to the audiences who listen to them. It is especially in the mentality of the celebrating congregation that a change must occur.

I remember a concelebrated Mass in the cathedral of Bangassou, in the Central African Republic. It was a poor church of red brick, covered with tiles that flapped in the wind, but it enjoyed a liturgy that was alive and joyful. The congregation's singing was accompanied by a large drum, about three feet high, played by a husky young man sitting like a king in the middle of the church. He played admirably, not slapping the drum like the "savages" in some Parisian nightclubs, but making it speak through his exceptionally rhythmic fingers. I still remember the people as they came from Communion, singing the praises of Jesus Christ, whom they had just received, and showing the joy of their faith in a seemingly unending rhythm. Here were people truly in celebration! At the end of the Mass, the drummer took the drum in his arms, as one would a baby,

with veneration and affection. I caught up to him outside the cathedral, and, after congratulating him, asked him to let me test the sound
of the instrument. He told me, "Father, don't touch the drum out
here! It is God's drum!" In his eyes, the drum used in the liturgy
had become a "sacred instrument" which was not to be played outside the church.

There is no instrument — whether drum, guitar, or trumpet —
which cannot become just as "sacred" by being used to sing Jesus
Christ.

# CHAPTER XII

# NOTES ON GREGORIAN CHANT

## A. The Problem of Gregorian Chant

Everyone is aware of the importance that the *Constitution on the Sacred Liturgy* accords Gregorian chant in the celebrations of the Latin rite:

> The Church acknowledges Gregorian chant as proper to the Roman liturgy: therefore, other things being equal, it should be given pride of place in liturgical services.[1]

In spite of this statement and the optimism of official documents, we must admit that there has been a considerable decrease in the use of Gregorian chant. In fact, one is given the impression that the communities still singing it do not care to enrich their repertoire further by learning new chants. They also are progressively moving toward the disappearance of the music that is "proper to the Roman liturgy." Indeed, just as old Elias trembled in his heart for fear that the Ark of God would fall into the hands of the Philistines, so certain people today fear that the treasure of sacred music, and especially Gregorian chant, will fall into the hands of the new Philistines. Anxiously they ask, "What will we sing tomorrow?" Honestly, we must admit that their fears are not altogether unfounded, for it is quite evident that the movement begun by the Council is not going in the direction of a revival of Gregorian chant.

We cannot solve the problem of Gregorian chant by preterition, leaving to history the task of evaluation, for in the preceding pages we have too often used Gregorian chant as a point of departure for our other thoughts. One can never solve a problem by avoiding it. The post-Conciliar Church must be able to face all problems, especially the most current and pressing ones.

## B. Two Remarks

By the way of introduction let us offer the following thoughts.

### 1. THE USE OF GREGORIAN CHANT BEFORE THE COUNCIL

Let us not exaggerate the importance of Gregorian chant in the Church. Only in the Roman rite is it the official chant, and, within this same rite, it is not universally used. Although employed extensively in France, Belgium, Switzerland, or Canada, it is much less in evidence in German and English speaking countries. How many parishes in Germany, in the United States, and even in Italy and Spain have ever heard a single piece of real Gregorian chant? It is a misconception, then, to believe that the entire Catholic world sang Gregorian chant before the Council and abandoned it only afterwards. It would be more accurate to say that actually the Council taught communities how to "sing" for the very first time.

How was Gregorian chant sung? We must say here that, if many parishes should lose the Gregorian chant provided by the cantor or the spinster-organist, they would not necessarily be losing a priceless treasure. To sing Gregorian well, one must be willing to pay the price — which is quite high. A soloist, despite his wonderful devotion, cannot exact it alone. Even a well-trained choir, which possesses an excellent "capital" of voices, can hardly meet the price. It goes without saying that we completely respect the results which have been achieved so far, including those of the elderly soloist who faces, alone, the waves of *arses* and *theses*. Those results reflect a storehouse of love and praise for God, the liturgy, and the community. Yet our concern now is to discover whether Gregorian chant achieves its ministerial function; whether the Introit, Gradual, Alleluia, Offertory, and Communion were, in the past, executed in such a way as to earn the admiration of the community, to uplift the emotions, to call forth the splendor of the New Jerusalem, and to create a unity among all the faithful. Gregorian does not seem to do this, even if one is not too demanding as to what constitutes ministerial function. We are discussing now those chants which the schola executed humbly and obediently, and to which the faithful listened in a spirit of complete resignation.

The fact that Gregorian chant is seldom used even in the Roman rite does not solve our problem. For anyone adhering strictly to the juridic texts, that fact itself is an important problem. Although the importance of Gregorian chant has been magnified by impassioned defenses, its use, in practice, affects only a small percentage in the universal Church.

## 2. THE CONNECTION BETWEEN LATIN
## AND GREGORIAN CHANT

It should be noted that the decline in the use of Gregorian chant does not stem from any bad will or disobedience, but is directly related to the decline in the use of Latin, upon which the very existence of the chant depends. Gregorian chant has a common cause with the Latin language. It is married to it, so to speak, in a unique and indissoluble union. Latin once gave Gregorian its strength and, at times, its pride; today it makes it weak and vulnerable. The transition from a Latin liturgy to a modern language liturgy may lead, as a consequence, to the eventual disappearance of Gregorian chant. This evolution is not a matter of principle, but merely a fact.

But wasn't the *Constitution on the Sacred Liturgy* firm in its stand on Latin? "Particular law remaining in force, the use of the Latin language is to be preserved in the Latin rites." Yes, but it immediately added: "But since the use of the mother tongue . . . may frequently be of great advantage to the people, the limits of its employment may be extended . . . to the readings and directives, and to some of the prayers and chants . . . . "[2] Vatican II, therefore, removed the barrier placed in the path of the modern languages by the Council of Trent. Under the "pressure of circumstances" the barrier gave way and became the royal portal through which the people could enter into the liturgical celebration. This "pressure of circumstances" was due to the requests of the bishops and the wishes of the people. But we should remember that even circumstances issue from the mind of God and are inspired by him. That is why, just a few years after the end of the Council, we are placed in a rather paradoxical situation. We have, on the one hand, a Constitution which officially states that the language of the Roman liturgy is Latin, and, on the other, a Roman liturgy in which the Mass is in the vernacular. It is obvious, then, that the communities who have chosen to celebrate in the vernacular have bid farewell to Gregorian chant which, by definition, is married to Latin!

Yet, as we have said above, this fact in no way solves the problem of Gregorian chant, but it does show its relativity. For the problem is not an isolated one, which can be detached from the whole Constitution and solved by considering the esthetic qualities of the neumes alone. It necessarily refers to the entire group of principles that are affirmed in the Constitution. It is in the peaceful coexistence of these principles that a valid liturgical solution will be found.

— The first principle is that of the active participation of the faithful: "Mother Church earnestly desires that all the faithful be led to that full, conscious, and active participation in liturgical celebrations — which is demanded by the very nature of the liturgy. Such participation by the Christian people as 'a chosen race, a royal priesthood, a holy nation, a purchased people' is their right and duty by reason of their baptism."[3]

— To promote this participation, the Council permits the use of the "popular" language, which can "frequently be of great advantage to the people" and to which a "suitable place may be allotted"[4] in Masses which are celebrated with the people.

— It is left to episcopal meetings "to decide whether and to what extent the vernacular language is to be used."[5]

— It is the privilege of each pastor, after careful study of the different possibilities offered him by the present legislation, to select those which more profoundly favor the "full, conscious, and active" participation in his community. If such participation can be attained in Latin, he may gladly keep Gregorian chant; otherwise, a liturgy in the vernacular without Gregorian chant will have to be adopted.

## C. The Future of Gregorian Chant

We must now face our problem head on and ask the following question: what is the future of Gregorian chant?

If one lives in the serene world of principle, the answer is very simple: Gregorian chant will remain in the liturgy as long as it fulfills the ministerial function of liturgical song. An example taken from another art, architecture, will clarify our answer. Our ancestors in the faith built wonderful Romanesque and Gothic cathedrals, wonders of architecture and of faith, which give witness to particular periods in history. Today it is quite possible that these cathedrals, built in accordance with each period's conception of the liturgy, are no longer suited for our liturgy. Yet, just because we now use reinforced concrete for our modern buildings, must we ignore these cathedrals or even, heaven forbid, destroy them? On the contrary, we should use them insofar as they can furnish our present-day congregations with a place to celebrate. In other words, we should use them as long as they can still fulfill their ministerial function today. An analogy can be drawn in regard to Gregorian chant, which, like every other art, is at the service of the liturgy. It should live, then, as long as it performs a service; in other words, as long as its beauty and availability for today's liturgy allow it to fulfill its ministerial function. Otherwise, it will continue to be admired but only with the same awe and respect felt toward a cathedral; listened to, but only with the same kind of attention given a phonograph record; and studied, but only with the same kind of interest shown a museum piece.

However, we return to the same question: doesn't the *Constitution on the Sacred Liturgy* prefer Gregorian chant over other musical forms?

The Church acknowledges Gregorian chant as proper to the Roman liturgy: therefore, other things being equal, it should be given pride of place in liturgical services.[6]

This insistence is fortunate because it allows us to define our resolution more precisely. The Instruction of March 5, 1967, presents the authentic interpretation of the Constitution when it states:

In sung liturgical services *celebrated in Latin:*

Gregorian chant, as proper to the Roman liturgy, should be given pride of place, *other things being equal.* Its melodies, contained in the "typical" editions, should be used, to the extent that this is possible.[7]

It would be good to mention these two points:

— The Instruction does not say that Gregorian chant must always and everywhere occupy the first place. Nor does it say that liturgical actions celebrated in Latin are to be preferred to those held in the vernacular. It simply says that when, in a pastoral judgment formulated by a competent authority, it is decided *to celebrate in Latin,* then, in this particular instance, Gregorian chant should be accorded first place even in preference to the music of Palestrina and Victoria.

— The Instruction imposed a second condition by adding, "other things being equal." The statement can be paraphrased in this way: Gregorian chant is preferred only if it fulfills its ministerial function to the same extent as would an equivalent song in a modern language.

Again the ministerial function of music must be defined in relation both to the liturgy itself and also to the celebrating community.

Gregorian chant should be accorded the first place:

*1. If it fulfills the ministerial function assigned by the liturgy in accordance with tradition and present-day laws.*

Its function is not automatically fulfilled just because the notes are square! We must concede that not every piece of Gregorian chant is a "masterpiece." As everything human, it shows the imprint of human weakness. Although good technique is usually evident, inspiration has sometimes been "on vacation." And, even when the melodic line is perfect, one must still take into account the text, which can be weak, inadequate, and unsuitable for the liturgy of Vatican II. Such an example is the wonderful and solemn *Ecce advenit,* in the second mode, which comprises the Introit of the feast of the Epiphany. When the schola intones the verse of the psalm:

*Deus, judicium tuum regi da,*
*et justitiam tuam filio regis.*

what community, upon hearing this first verse of Psalm 72(71), remembers that tradition chose this psalm because of verses 10 and 11, which are perfectly suited to the feast of the Epiphany of Christ:

The kings of Tharsis and the Isles shall offer gifts;
The kings of Arabia and Saba shall bring tribute.
All kings shall pay him homage,
All nations shall serve him.

Fortunate indeed is the community that knows this psalm so well! But, quite frankly, isn't that a bit too much to expect of any parish community?

The Instruction of March 5, 1967, recognizes that there are two sides to every coin. Some music "corresponds to the needs of the renewed liturgy"; other music "does not correspond to the nature of the liturgy or cannot be harmonized with the pastoral celebration of the liturgy."[8] If the latter alternative is true, that music must be eliminated from Eucharistic celebrations, although it should be retained in the Church's musical "treasury" and not be entirely excluded from its repertoire. In fact, it can even be used in the celebration of the Word of God.

It almost breaks the heart of a musician, who can appreciate the wonderful development of neumatic art in the Gregorian chant of the Gradual psalms, to have the liturgy now decide that such chant is the least suitable for the new reforms. In its veneration for the Word of God, as evident in the Gradual psalm, Gregorian chant attempted to make that Word so beautiful that it embraced and caressed it with lines of neumes which almost suffocated it and practically imprisoned it within its beauty. However, what the Responsorial Psalm of today does not possess by way of musical splendor, it gains in the magnificence of the Word of God. Why, then, should we be sad? The Christian should rejoice.

Gregorian chant should be accorded first place:

*2. If it fulfills its ministerial function in relation to the celebrating community.*

— It should be an effective element of solemnization, in the sense that each participant effectively sings his own part.

For example, a Gregorian Introit should be preferred over any other song provided the community can sing both equally well.

— It should give the text a greater effectiveness.

For example, a Gregorian piece is preferable to a hymn in the vernacular, when the community can understand, speak, and sing Latin as easily as English. Such a situation is not altogether impossible in a parish community when very short pieces like the Sanctus are sung. But the Proper would probably be sung only by religious and monastic communities who completely understand and truly love Latin, expressing themselves in it as joyfully and as easily as in their mother tongue. This requires monks who are vituosos in Latin and Gregorian chant.[9]

— It should enhance the liturgy with beauty.

There must be a beautiful technique, not a mere solfeggio.

— It should be a unifying element.

It must effectively achieve a unity of the liturgical community through the unity of their voices — which expresses the unity of their hearts.

The 1967 Instruction foresees a particularly interesting use of Latin in the liturgy. In parishes in which the faithful do not all speak the same language, "it may be opportune to preserve one or more Masses celebrated in Latin . . . . "[10] This statement does not mean that foreigners who do not understand English will magically understand Latin. A homily in English, German, Spanish, or French will allow *only a part* of the congregation to understand, but there are certain Latin hymns which would permit the *entire* community to express musically its unity in the celebration.[11]

The phrase "other things being equal" places great demands on Gregorian chant in regard to comprehension of the text and execution of the music. Vatican II and the Instruction of March 5, 1967, in no way intend to deny Latin scholars and Gregorian masters their own musical preferences. On the contrary, the Church welcomes and encourages them to continue their work. It is simply a matter of common sense not to force someone who does not know Gregorian chant to sing it anyway. In fact, Vatican II has, on numerous occasions, shown itself to be a Council with common sense.

## D. Further Reflections: The Question of Principle

We will now examine more closely the preference the Church accords Gregorian chant. Obviously, no Christian wishes to act or speak against the teachings of the Council, yet we must consider the problems it has raised.

The affirmation of Gregorian chant by the Constitution is perfectly explained if seen in its historial context. In fact, it comes directly from St. Pius X, who stated in the Motu Proprio *Tra le Sollecitudini* of November 22, 1903:

> These qualities are found most perfectly in Gregorian Chant, which is therefore the proper chant of the Roman Church, the only chant which she has inherited from the ancient Fathers, which she has jealously guarded for so many centuries in her liturgical books, which she directly proposes to the faithful as her own music, which she prescribes exclusively for some parts of her liturgy, and which recent studies have so happily restored to its original integrity.[12]

This *Motu proprio* has been the basis of sacred music reform since the beginning of this century. Its teachings on Gregorian chant have been reiterated again and again without question. Furthermore, identical terminology was used in every official document to follow: the Apostolic Constitution *Divini Cultus* of Pius XI, December 20, 1928; the Encyclicals *Mediator Dei,* November 20, 1947, and *Musicae Sacrae Disciplina,* December 25, 1955, of Pius XII; and finally the Instruction on *Sacred Music and the Sacred Liturgy,* September 3, 1958.[13] By reaffirming the statements of Pius X, the Council, then, is simply repeating the traditional position of the Church.

Moreover, Pius X's own affirmation of the primacy of Gregorian chant is very easily explained in the historical context of 1903. From the very beginning of his pontificate, he had engaged in a struggle against what he called "direct abuses" that he "deplored" in the realm of liturgical music. These abuses, he explained, came from "the successive alterations in taste and custom during the lapse of time; . . . from the disastrous influence of secular and theatrical music on that of the Church. . . ." Church music was under the influence of the music of the theater, and the so-called religious melodies often received their inspiration from bad operettas. Confronted with such music, then, Pius X declared the superiority of Gregorian chant, which, at the time, was in the process of complete restoration. Consequently, his glorification of the Gregorian is to be considered as the natural offspring of the period in which it was written; it would be an anachronism to interpret it as an absolute. For it is scarcely certain that he himself would have preferred a schola singing faultless Gregorian chant (thereby overwhelming the liturgical congregation with its art) to a community singing songs in the vernacular with a dignity of heart and soul. Obviously, though, the scola's singing was much better than the warbling of some solosists of the time!

Considered thus, the teaching of Pius X becomes somewhat relative to his time, and Gregorian chant, like any human creation, has suffered the ravages of time. If the message of the Church is eternal — as, indeed, it is — the artistic forms in which that message is expressed are provisional and fleeting. Indeed, the Church has never even desired to link her message to any one particular artistic form. What was expressive of the faith in a bygone era is not necessarily expressive in ours. What would we say if a Pope were to state that the only architecture the Church will recognize is the Romanesque of the eleventh century, or the Gothic of Chartres? Or that the only painting good for the Church is that of Raphael? The statements that St. Pius X made about Gregorian chant and the classical polyphony of Palestrina are similar in kind.

There are eternal values expressed in Gregorian chant which dominate the ages: faith, adoration, and spirituality. On the other hand, there are also certain values in it which are subject to the ages: the concrete expression of these eternal values, for example. The Church will always safeguard the former, but give only secondary importance to the latter. The Church is not the curator of a museum. She has no other treasures to guard except faith and charity.[14]

The Church requires that we favorably judge Gregorian chant *a priori* and without dispute. But *a posteriori,* any modern community formed by Vatican II will state:

— Gregorian chant is linked with Latin — a fact which limits its use to Latin-speaking communities.

— It proposes texts which do not always fully respond to liturgical reform.

— Its structure completely lacks the rhythmic beat of today's music. It is no one's fault that the musical rhythms of today are not the same as those of the fifth and sixth centuries.

— Finally, its ascetic monody reserves it for a musical and intellectual elite and prevents it from becoming very popular with the general public.

Popular singing is no longer monodic; everything is garnished with a vocal or instrumental accompaniment. Just turn on the radio for a few minutes and you'll see what we mean. Yet the faithful who overcome the inconveniences of Gregorian chant will continue to sing it. The rest have the right to search elsewhere for any solutions which are suitable for them.

A final question: after consideration of these objections, why did the *Constitution on the Sacred Liturgy* of Vatican II reaffirm the text of St. Pius X concerning the special place of Latin and Gregorian chant?

Here we must consider the historical context of the first two sessions of Vatican II, which elaborated and voted upon the Constitution. Liturgical reform was, in fact, the primary problem considered by the Council. That consideration, however, was characterized by both a defiant reserve on the part of the minority and a circumspect enthusiasm on the part of the majority. The editors of the Constitution prudently estimated that, in order to attain new goals and to open up new perspectives, it was diplomatically wise to make some concessions in regard to the use of Latin and Gregorian chant. Consequently, the Fathers voted on the texts of Latin and the Gregorian without even a second thought. It was also without a second thought that they affirmed *article 116* in the Constitution:

> The Church acknowledges Gregorian chant as proper to the Roman liturgy *(cantum gregorianum ut proprium);*

and *article 123* of the same Constitution:

> The Church has not adopted any particular style of art as her very own *(nullum stilum veluti proprium).*

Both articles express a stage of liturgical reform. From the first to the last session, there was a noteworthy evolution in the attitudes of the Fathers. "It is apparent that if one had been able to expand the schema of the liturgy after the discussion of the outline of *The Church in the Modern World,* it would have had a completely different look, a completely different perspective."[15] Yet the Constitution on *The Church in the Modern World* is open to the future and claims complete freedom in its relationship to the past:

> But at the same time, the Church, sent to all peoples of every time and place, is not bound exclusively and indissolubly to any race or nation, nor to any particular way of life or any customary pattern of living, ancient or recent.[16]

Thus Vatican II, which is the result of the past, represents a point of departure for the future. It is destined to be surpassed, just as were all the previous Councils. This is good. Continually to surpass earlier efforts is to remain within a most authentic tradition. For it is in such perpetual adaptation to each generation that the liturgy remains true to its mission: to be the servant of the Church in prayer.

# FOOTNOTES

## Foreword

1. *Pastoral Constitution on the Church in the Modern World,* art. 44.

## Chapter I

1. *Constitution on the Sacred Liturgy,* art. 112.

2. Instruction on *Music in the Liturgy,* art. 1.

3. *Ibid.,* art. 2. Cf. *Doc. Cath.,* vol. 64, col. 495-496.

4. Council of Trent, Session VII, March 3, 1547, Canon 13 (our translation). Cf. Denzinger-Schönmetzer, *Enchiridion Symbolorum,* 32 ed., n. 1613.

5. P. Jounel. *Les Rites de la Messe en 1965,* Desclée, p. 13: "The *Ritus servandus* has had no major change in its successive editions of the Roman Missal from 1750 to 1962." (our translation)

6. *Constitution on the Sacred Liturgy,* art. 112.

7. The Rev. Joseph Connelly, M.A., *Hymns of the Roman Liturgy,* The Newman Press, Westminster, Maryland, 1957, p. 252.

8. Cf. Is:13; Joel 4:9-14; Amos 5:18-20; 2:13-16; 5:18-20; etc.

9. Cf. 2 Peter 1:19.

10. On the importance that Jewish and Christian antiquity placed upon the Sibyl and the writings attributed to her, see J. B. Frey, *Apocryphes de l'Ancien Testament,* and A. Amann, *Apocryphes du Nouveau Testament,* in the *Dictionnaire de la Bible Supplement,* vol. 1, pp. 423-428 and 530-533.

11. *Constitution on the Sacred Liturgy,* art. 7. In *Mediator Dei* (Nov. 20, 1947), Pius XII defined the liturgy thus: "The holy liturgy is the public cult our Redeemer gives to the Father as Head of the Church; it is also the cult given by the society of the faithful to its Founder and, through him, to the eternal Father; it is, in a word, the integral public cult of the Mystical Body of Christ, that is the Head and its members." (our translation) Cf. *La Liturgie,* col. "Les enseignements pontificaux," Ed. Desclée, p. 328.

12. *Ibid.*, art. 22. In *Mediator Dei*, "the right and duty of the bishops" is limited principally "to the diligent adherence to the exact observance of the precepts of the holy canons on the divine cult." (our translation) Cf. *La Liturgie, op. cit.*, p. 347.

13. H. Schmidt, *Constitution sur la Sainte liturgie,* Ed. Lumen vitae, 1966 (Coll. "Tradition et renouveau," 3), p. 200 (our translation).

14. Instruction on *Music in the Liturgy,* art. 33-34. Cf. *Doc. Cath.,* vol. 64 (1967), col. 503.

15. *Ibid.,* art. 6. Cf. *Doc. Cath., ibid.,* col. 497-498.

16. I Cor. 11:23-26.

17. Pius XI, Constitution, *Divini Cultus,* December 20, 1928. Cf. *La Liturgie, op. cit.,* p. 253.

18. Instruction on *Music in the Liturgy,* art. 51. Cf. *Doc. Cath.,* vol. 64 (1967), col. 507.

19. *Ibid.,* art. 59. Cf. *Doc. Cath., ibid.,* col. 509.

20. *Constitution on the Sacred Liturgy,* art. 30. See also articles 28 and 114.

21. Instruction on *Music in the Liturgy,* art. 9.

22. *Ibid.,* art. 10.

23. *Ibid.,* art. 15.

24. *Ibid.,* art. 16.

25. *Ibid.,* art. 18.

26. *Ibid.,* art. 51.

27. *Ibid.,* art. 5. Cf. *Doc. Cath.,* vol. 64 (1967), col. 497.

28. *Motu Proprio,* par. 1. Cf. *Lettres Apostoliques de S. S. Pie X,* vol. 1, pp. 49-50. Cf. *La Liturgie, op. cit.,* p. 176.

29. *Musicae Sacrae Disciplina,* par. 31 (our translation). Cf. *Doc. Cath.,* vol. 53 (1956), col. 75.

30. *Constitution on the Sacred Liturgy,* art. 112.

31. Instruction on *Music in the Liturgy,* art. 5.

32. *Ibid.,* art. 11. Cf. *Doc. Cath.,* vol. 64 (1967), col. 497.

33. *Sacred Music and the Sacred Liturgy,* art. 3. Cf. *Doc. Cath.,* vol. 55, col. 1429-1430.

34. *Motu Proprio,* par. 1. Cf. *Lettres Apostoliques de S. S. Pie X,* Paris (Bonne Presse), vol. 1, p. 50. Cf. *La Liturgie, op. cit.,* p. 176.

35. *Constitution on the Sacred Liturgy,* art. 112.

36. "Oratio suavius exprimitur — prayer is expressed in a more attractive way." art. 5. Cf. *Doc. Cath.,* vol. 64 (1967), col. 497.

37. A.A.S., vol. 48 (1956), p. 22-23. Cf. *Doc. Cath.,* vol. 53, col. 84.

38. Cf. *Lettres Apostoliques de S. S. Pie X, op. cit.,* vol. 1, p. 50. Cf. also *La Liturgie, op. cit.,* p. 176.

39. A.A.S., vol. 21 (1928), p. 37. Cf. *La Liturgie, op. cit.,* p. 251.

40. *Ibid.,* vol. 48 (1956), pp. 12-13. Cf. *Doc. Cath.,* vol. 53 (1956), col. 75-76.

41. Instruction on *Music in the Liturgy,* art. 5. Cf. *Doc. Cath.,* vol. 64 (1967), col. 497.

42. Wisdom 13:3-5.

43. Instruction on *Music in the Liturgy,* art. 21. Cf. *Doc. Cath.,* vol. 55 (1958), col. 1433.

44. *Constitution on the Sacred Liturgy,* art. 112. Tradition liked to note the unifying role of music. See on this topic the beautiful book of Fr. J. Basurco, *El Canto cristiano en la tradicion primitiva,* col. Christus Pastor, 17, Ed. Marova, Madrid, 1966, especially chapter IV, "El canto communitario como expresion eclesial," p. 93-115.

45. Instruction on *Music in the Liturgy,* art. 5. Cf. *Doc. Cath.,* vol. 64 (1967), col. 497.

46. *Ibid.,* art. 25. Cf. *Doc. Cath.,* vol. 55 (1958), col. 1435-1436.

47. Encyclical *Musicae Sacrae Disciplina,* Dec. 25, 1955, art. 45 (our translation). Cf. *Doc. Cath.,* vol. 53 (1956), col. 78-79.

48. *Pastoral Constitution on the Church in the Modern World,* art. 42. Cf. also the decree on missionary activity in the church *Ad Gentes,* art. 8.

49. *Ibid.,* art. 58.

# Chapter II

1. Instruction on *Music in the Liturgy,* March 5, 1967, art. 13. Cf. *Doc. Cath.,* vol. 64 (1967), col. 499. In the Encyclical *Musicae Sacrae Disciplina,* Dec. 25, 1955, art. 34, Pius XII wrote: "There can be nothing more exalted or sublime than its function of accompanying with beautiful sound *the voice of the priest* offering up the Divine Victim, answering him joyfully with the people who are present and enhancing the whole liturgical ceremony with its noble art." (our translation) Cf. *Doc. Cath.,* vol. 53 (1956), col. 76.

2. We once again discover the distinction found in the Instruction on *Music in the Liturgy,* art. 13: "The priest and his ministers, because of the sacred order they have received, hold a special place in these celebrations, as do also — by reason of the ministry they perform — the readers, commentators, and choir. Cf. *Doc. Cath.,* vol. 64 (1967), col. 499.

Yet, the distinction imposed by the Instruction between those who have received a sacred order and those who exercise a ministry lacks clarity, because those who have received a sacred order also exercise a ministry; that is precisely why they received a sacred order.

3. In *Divini Cultus,* Pius XI distinguished "the voice of the clergy, the voice of the singers, and the voice of the people." Cf. *La Liturgie, op. cit.,* p. 253.

4. See J. Lecuyer, *Le Célébrant* in *La Maison-Dieu*, 61, pp. 5-29.

5. *Constitution on the Sacred Liturgy*, art. 33.

6. See F. E. Brightman, *Liturgies, Eastern and Western*, Oxford, 1896 (Clarendon Press, 1965), p. 232.

7. *Ibid.*, pp. 176-177.

8. *Ibid.*, p. 178.

9. *Apologie*, I, 67.

10. Instruction on *Sacred Music and the Sacred Liturgy*, Sept. 3, 1955, art. 27: "After the Consecration, unless the *Benedictus* is still to be sung, devout silence is advised until the time of the Pater Noster." Cf. *Doc. Cath.*, 55 (1958), col. 1437.

11. Motu Proprio *Tra le Sollecitudini*, Nov. 22, 1903. Cf. *Lettres Apostoliques de S. S. Pie X, op. cit.*, p. 51; *La Liturgie, op. cit.*, p. 179.

12. The Council quotes this text in the *Dogmatic Constitution on the Church*, art. 9; in the *Constitution on the Sacred Liturgy*, art. 14; in the *Decree on the Apostolate of the Laity*, art. 3; and in the *Decree on the Church's Missionary Activity*, art. 15. Cf. also the *Decree on the Ministry and Life of Priests*, art. 2.

13. The *epiklesis* (Greek, invocation) is the prayer invoking the descent of the Holy Spirit upon the offerings.

The *anamnesis* (Greek, remembrance) is the prayer recalling the mysteries of salvation, based upon the Lord's words, "Do this *in memory* of me."

14. The 1030 orations, with two exceptions, contained in the Leonine Sacramentary (VI century) end with rhythmic clauses. The three most often used were:

the *cursus planus,* which carries the accent on the fifth and second syllables before the end ("nostris infunde");

the *cursus tardus,* which carries the accent on the sixth syllable and on the antepenult ("incarnationem cognovimus");

the *cursus velox,* which carries the accent on the seventh syllable and the second syllable before the end ("gloriam perducamur").

15. See in the same context the statement of G. Lercaro concerning the translation of the Canon: "A new translation must be carefully prepared. This translation must be both literal and integral . . . . It is not necessary to disrupt the stages. When the time comes to create, no one will have to fear a literal translation." (letter to the presidents of episcopal conferences, June 21, 1967 — our translation) Cf. *Doc. Cath.*, vol. 64 (1967), col. 1561-1562.

16. *The English-Latin Sacramentary,* Catholic Book Publishing Co., New York, 1966, p. 445.

17. Instruction on *Music in the Liturgy*, art. 8. Cf. *Doc. Cath.*, vol. 64 (1967), col. 498.

18. *Ibid.*

19. *Constitution on the Sacred Liturgy,* art. 14, with reference to I Peter 2:9.

20. Instruction on *Music in the Liturgy,* March 5, 1967, art. 15. Cf. *Doc. Cath.,* vol. 64 (1967), col. 499.

21. *Constitution on the Sacred Liturgy,* art. 11. Cf. Instruction of March 5, 1967, art. 15a. Cf. *Doc. Cath., ibid.*

22. Instruction on *Music in the Liturgy,* March 5, 1967.

23. *Lettres Apostoliques de S. S. Pie X, op. cit.,* p. 49. Cf. *La Liturgie, op. cit.,* p. 175.

24. *Ibid.,* p. 50.

25. *Ibid.,* p. 52.

26. Instruction on *Music in the Liturgy,* art. 16. Cf. *Doc. Cath.,* vol. 64 (1967), col. 500.

27. *Ibid.,* art. 9. Cf. *Doc. Cath., ibid.,* col. 498.

28. Instruction on *Sacred Music in the Sacred Liturgy,* Sept. 3, 1958, art. 3. Cf. *Doc. Cath.,* vol. 55, col. 1429-1430.

29. It is evident today that a priest will prefer, all things being equal, to concelebrate the Mass with the presiding priest (even while performing the essential services of a deacon) rather than simply performing those functions in the limited role of deacon.

30. Instruction on *Sacred Music in the Sacred Liturgy,* Sept. 3, 1958, art. 14a & 13b. Cf. *Doc. Cath.,* vol. 55, col. 1431.

31. Instruction on *Music in the Liturgy,* art. 7. Cf. *Doc. Cath.,* vol. 64 (1967), col. 498.

32. *Ibid.,* art. 6. Cf. *Doc. Cath., ibid.*

33. *Ibid.,* art. 7. Cf. *Doc. Cath., ibid.*

34. *Ibid.,* art. 28-31. Cf. *Doc. Cath., ibid.,* col. 502-503.

35. Romans 15:6.

36. Motu Proprio *Tra le Sollecitudini,* Nov. 22, 1903, *Lettres Apostoliques de S. S. Pie X, op. cit.,* p. 53. Cf. *La Liturgie, op. cit.,* p. 181.

37. *Ibid.* Cf. *La Liturgie, op. cit.,* p. 182.

38. Instruction on *Music in the Liturgy,* March 5, 1967, art. 22. Cf. Instruction of Sept. 3, 1958, art. 100. Cf. *Doc. Cath.,* vol. 55 (1958), col. 1451-1452.

39. *Ibid.,* art. 20.

40. *Ibid.,* art. 19b.

41. *Ibid.,* art. 21.

42. *Ibid.,* art. 19.

43. *Ibid.*

44. *Constitution on the Sacred Liturgy,* art. 115.

45. Instruction on *Music in the Liturgy,* March 5, 1967, art. 24.

46. Cf. P. Salmon, *La Prière des Pères,* in A. G. Martimort, *L'Eglise en prière: Introduction à la Liturgie,* Desclée et Cie, 1965, 3rd edition, p. 848.

47. It was limited to the last two stanzas of the *Pange Lingua* (viz. the *Tantum ergo* and *Genitori*), the first and last stanza of the *Veni Creator* and perhaps the *Ave Maria Stella:* these were, more or less, all that the people knew.

48. Instruction on *Music in the Liturgy,* March 5, 1967, art. 46 and 53. Cf. *Doc. Cath.,* vol. 64 (1967), col. 507-508. *Pia or sacra exercitia* are certain devotions, such as the Stations of the Cross or the rosary, which do not meet the requirements proper to a liturgical action according to ecclesiastical legislation. Cf. Instruction of Sept. 3, 1958, art. 1. Cf. *Doc. Cath.,* vol. 55 (1958), col. 1429.

49. *Ibid.,* art. 23. Cf. *Doc. Cath.,* vol. 64 (1967), col. 501. Cf. also the Instruction *Inter oecumenici,* Nov. 26, 1964, art. 97, which said: "The Schola and organ should be so situated as to be clearly seen by all to be a part of the congregation, at the same time fulfilling their liturgical function." (our translation) Cf. *Doc. Cath.,* vol. 61 (1964), col. 1375.

We see that the aforesaid Instruction of March 5, 1967, added this to article 23: "Whenever the choir also includes women, it should be placed outside the sanctuary (presbyterium)." In principle, the sanctuary does not include the space occupied by the choir; more precisely it is where the priests are when they celebrate or concelebrate the Mass.

## Chapter III

1. Instruction on *Sacred Music and the Sacred Liturgy,* September 3, 1958, art. 96. Cf. *Doc. Cath.,* vol. 55 (1958), col. 1450.

2. Instruction on *Music in the Liturgy,* March 5, 1967, art. 21. Cf. *Doc. Cath.,* vol. 64 (1967), col. 501.

3. *Ibid.* Cf. *Doc. Cath., ibid.*

4. Instruction on *Sacred Music and the Sacred Liturgy,* September 3, 1958, art. 96. Cf. *Doc. Cath.,* vol. 55 (1958), col. 1450. This Instruction is not particularly in favor of women's participation in the liturgy, since it forbids them from being commentators.

5. Letter from the Concilium dated January 5, 1968, to Msgr. Boudon. Cf. *Doc. Cath.,* vol. 65 (1968), col. 437-438.

6. "It is proper that the members of the choir, when singing in Church, wear the cassock and surplice." *Lettres Apostoliques,* S. S. Pius X, *op. cit.,* p. 53 (our translation). Cf. *La Liturgie, op. cit.,* p. 182.

7. *Constitution on the Sacred Liturgy,* art. 7. The altar and the pulpit are the two "tables" on which are celebrated "the two parts which, in a certain sense, go to make up the Mass, namely, the liturgy of the word and the Eucharistic liturgy . . . . " (art. 56).

8. Instruction on *Music in the Liturgy,* March 5, 1967, art. 9. Cf. *Doc. Cath.,* vol. 64 (1967), col. 498.

9. D. Julien, *Direction du chant d'assemblée* in *Eglise qui chante*, 81 (1967), p. 15 (our translation).

10. L. Deiss, *Biblical Hymns and Psalms,* World Library Publications, Inc., Cincinnati, Ohio, 1965, vol. 1, no. 15, p. 38.

11. *Ibid.,* no. 11, p. 28.

12. The *tessitura* of a *voice* is the range of sounds within which it can most comfortably sing. The *tessitura* of a *melody* is the average range of it.

13. The reverse is often the case in religious communities. One wonders why it is that religious congregations of women will so often intone their psalms on a note that is almost inhumanly high, making them sound like little girls in pain. On the other hand, as soon as priests gather together to sing the office, they descend to the very depth of sound and seem to be grumbling. An easy *tenor* for an ordinary psalmody would be *A, G,* or *F.*

14. L. Deiss, *Biblical Hymns and Psalms, op. cit.,* no. 29, p. 66.

15. *Ibid.,* no. 40, p. 86.

16. *Ibid.,* no. 38, p. 82.

17. Clement of Alexandria, *Protreptique,* I, 5, 3-4 (our translation).

## Chapter IV

1. Instruction on *Music in the Liturgy,* March 5, 1967, art. 29. Cf. *Doc. Cath.,* vol. 64 (1967), col. 502-503.

2. Cf. Gn. 26:3 and 46:3. For a detailed biblical analysis of the formula "The Lord be with you," see L. Deiss, *Marie, Fille de Sion,* col. "Thèmes Bibliques," Desclée de Brouwer, 1959, p. 91-101.

3. Cf. Dt. 20:1-4. Cf. Ps. 46:8 and 12.

4. Cf. Is. 41:8-14; 43:1-5.

5. Cf. Is. 7:14; 8:10. Mt. 1:23.

6. See L. Deiss, *Marie, Fille de Sion, op. cit.,* p. 71-114.

7. Cf. Ap. 21:3.

8. To the Philippians (4:23), Paul will write: "The grace of our Lord Jesus Christ be with your spirit."

9. Cf. *The Apostolic Tradition,* 4.

10. Instruction on *Music in the Liturgy,* March 5, 1967, art. 5. Cf. *Doc. Cath.,* vol. 64, col. 497.

11. An account of these benedictions and doxologies of the New Testament can be found in L. Deiss, *Hymnes et Prières,* col. "Vivant Tradition," 2, p. 15-29.

12. This benediction was once used in the liturgy of the Mass as the blessing of the faithful before Communion. Cf. J. A. Jungmann, *Missarum Solemnia,* col. "Theologie," 21, vol. 3, p. 221.

13. Cf. J. A. Jungmann, *op. cit.,* p. 381.

14. Matthew mentions it thirty-one times, Mark thirteen times, Luke six (by translating it as "truly") and John twenty-five times (doubling it in a quasi-liturgical manner).

15. We can also compare the ending of the Apocalypse with the *Maranatha* (O Lord, come) of 1 Cor. 16:22 and that of the prayer in the Didache (10): "Let grace come and the world pass away! Amen . . . Maranatha! Amen." See L. Deiss, *Les Pères Apostoliques,* col. "Vivante Tradition," 1, p. 18.

16. The doxology is a formula by which one praises the glory (in Greek *doxa*) of God. The Psalter ends each of the first four books with an Amen at the end of the doxology—Ps. 41(40):14; 72(71):19; 89(88): 53; 106(105):48. These doxologies seem to derive from the liturgy of the Temple and of the synagogues.

17. Cf Rm. 1:25; 9:5.

18. See also the three solemn doxologies of Rom. 11:33-36; 16:25-27; Gal. 1:5.

19. Cf Ap. 7:11-12, 19:4.

20. *Oeuvres oratoires,* Ed. Lebarcq, vol. 4, Paris, 1930, p. 291-292, cited by Dom Botte in *L'Ordinaire de la Messe,* col. *"Etudes liturgiques,"* no. 2, Paris, 1953, p. 103-104.

21. As a side note, consider the Amen in the final chorus of the Mass in B minor by J. S. Bach. It is repeated fifteen times by the sopranos alone, with powerful melodies continuing for eighty-nine measures! In this particular case, Bach uses the Latin words to "make music" and attain the grandiose style he desires. Elsewhere, he shows that he is quite capable of treating these words with the utmost respect. But here we are no longer speaking of a liturgical acclamation, but simply of musical splendor.

22. Fr. Th. Camelot, "Un Texte de Tertullien sur l'Amen de la Communion" in *La Maison-Dieu,* vol. 79 (1964), p. 113 (our translation).

23. Sermon 272. PL. 38,1247.

24. *In Gal. Comm.,* 1,2. PL. 26,355.

25. *Apologie I,* 65 and 67 (our translation).

26. Other musical settings of the triple Amen can be found in the *People's Mass Book,* 1970 edition, World Library Publications, Inc., Cincinnati, Ohio, no. 108, p. 122.

27. The triple repetition of "holy" has no particular symbolism. It is simply a question of literary procedure which is expressed today with the superlative. See Ph. Béguerie, "La Vocation d'Isaie" in *Etudes sur les prophètes d'Israël,* col. "Lectio Divina," 14, p. 21-22.

28. Judges 5:20.

29. On his return to Canaan, Jacob encountered angels. His first words were: "This is the encampment of God." (Gn. 32:3)

30. Job 38:7. The "sons of God" are the angels.

31. Gn. 2:1.

32. Cf. Ex. 24:16; Lv. 9:23 and Nb. 14:10; 1 Kg. 8:10-13.

33. The Latin tradition has shown us how difficult it was to translate the original Hebrew word (*kabod*) and even the Greek translation (*doxa*). It gives not only *gloria*, but in some texts you also find *maiestas* or *honor*. There are even a few cases where the terms are coupled as if the two together would better convey the full meaning of the original. This is the case in the translation for the Te Deum: Pleni sunt coeli et terra *maiestatis gloriae* tuae.

34. The Trisagion (from the Greek *tris* — three times, and *hagios* — holy) represents the triple repetition of the Sanctus like the prayer "Holy God, Holy Mighty One, Holy Immortal God" in the Eastern liturgies (a prayer the Roman liturgy retains in the Good Friday celebration).

35. Mt. 21:9 and Mk. 11:10. Concerning the meaning of Hosanna in the time of Christ, see Strack-Billerbeck, *Kommentar zum Neuen Testament aus Talmud und Midrasch*, vol. 1, p. 845-850.

36. Cf. Mt. 21:9, Mk. 11:9, Lk. 19:38.

37. Cf. Mt. 23:39 and Lk. 13:35.

38. The Gospels contain a series of sentences "I have come" and "I have been sent." See L. Deiss, *Synopse*, Desclée de Brouwer, vol. 1, p. 183.

39. Ap. 22:20.

40. 1 Cor. 11:26.

41. *Constitutions Apostoliques*, VIII, 13,13 (our translation).

42. St. Cesarius, *Sermo* 73:2; *Corpus christianorum* (Brepols), vol. 103, p. 307 (PL 39,2277).

43. Instruction on *Music in the Liturgy*, March 5, 1967, art. 34. Cf. *Doc. Cath.*, vol. 64 (1967), col. 503.

44. *Ibid.*, art. 26. Cf. *Doc. Cath.*, *ibid.*, col. 52.

45. Letter to the Corinthians, 34. Cf. L. Deiss, *Les Pères Apostoliques*, col. "Vivante Tradition," p. 26-27.

46. In other words, the text of Isaiah 6:2 was enriched by Daniel 7:10.

47. *Euchologe*, 13 (our translation).

48. *Constitutions Apostoliques*, VIII, 12:27 (our translation).

49. Instruction on *Sacred Music and the Sacred Liturgy*, September 3, 1958, art. 25b. Cf. *Doc. Cath.*, vol. 55 (1958), col. 1435.

50. Nevertheless, the Sanctus remains a venerable item in the history of the liturgy because it has appeared in the Mass ever since the 4th century (in the anaphora of Serapion); before this it was perhaps included in the matins of the office, as in the Jewish tradition. But a good

question is whether today's liturgy ought to incorporate every ancient piece simply because it is venerable.

51. Cf. the anamnesis of *l'Anaphore d'Addée et de Mari*, p. 154, also the one in the *Constitutions Apostoliques*, p. 189, and the one in the *Euchologe du Dêr Balyzeh*, p. 208.

52. L. Deiss, *Biblical Hymns and Psalms, op. cit.*, no. 55, p. 114.

## Chapter V

1. Instruction on *Music in the Liturgy*, March 5, 1967, art. 33. Cf. *Doc. Cath.*, vol. 64 (1967), col. 503.

2. Cf. Ap. 21:3.

3. Cf. Dt. 27:15-26. We are using here points from our study, *Le Psaume Graduel*, published in *Notitiae (Consilium ad exsequendam Constitutionem de Sacra Liturgia)*, 24 (1966), p. 365-372. This study appeared in German in *Musik und Altar*, Freiburg, 19, 1967, 2: "*Der Antwortpsalm*," p. 75-78, and in Italian in *Rivista liturgica*, Torino-Leumann, 1967, 3: "Il salmo graduale," p. 213-219.

4. This is assuredly the case with the canticles of Moses, Anna, Ezechias, Ananias, Misael and Azarias.

5. Cf. S. Corbin, *L'Eglise à la conquête de sa musique*, Gallimard, 1960, p. 182.

6. H. J. Kraus, *Psalmen*, vol. 1, 1960, col. "Biblischer Kommentar, Altes Testament," Neukirchener Verlag, p. xviii.

7. St. Pius X, *Tra le Sollecitudini*. Cf. *Lettres Apostoliques de S. S. Pie X, op. cit.*, p. 50. Cf. *La Liturgie, op. cit.*, p. 176.

8. *In Psalmum 40 Enarratio, Sermo ad plebem*, 1. *Corpus christianorum*, vol. 38, p. 447. PL 36, 453.

9. *Expositio in Psalmum 41:5 and 7*. PG 55, 163, 166-167 (our translation).

10. Instruction on *Music in the Liturgy*, March 5, 1967, art. 33. Cf. *Doc. Cath.*, vol. 64 (1967), col. 503.

11. The Instruction *Tres abhinc annos*, May 4, 1967, art. 15, suggests a short silence before the postcommunion (see *Doc. Cath.*, vol. 64 (1967), col. 891) and the Instruction *Eucharisticum mysterium*, May 25, 1967, art. 38, recommends "to those who have been nourished by holy communion to remain a few moments to pray" after Mass. (See *Doc. Cath., ibid.*, col. 1112).

12. Encyclical *Mediator Dei* (our translation).

13. Several fragments of the Book of Psalms, such as Psalms 18(17) and 68(67) can be found before the time of David and even in the 11th and 12th centuries B.C. Cf. H. J. Kraus, *Die Psalmen*, col. "Biblischer Kommentar," vol. 1, Neukirchener Verlag, 1960, p. lviii.

14. The definitive works on literary genres were those of H. Gunkel, *Einleitung in die Psalmen* and *Die Gattungen der religiosen Lyrik Israels*

(Gottingen, 2nd ed., 1966), completed by those of S. Mowinckel, *The Psalms in Israel's Workshop* (Oxford, 1962). For the classification of the psalms see L. Sabourin, *Un classement littéraire des Psaumes* in *Sciences ecclésiastiques*, Desclée de Brouwer, 1964, p. 23-58, and also P. Drijvers, *Les Psaumes: Genres littéraires et thèmes doctrinaux*, col. "Lectio divina," 21.

15. In most instances, it concerns liturgical psalms, i.e., those having their origin or utilization in the worship in the Temple. This question of dialogues in liturgical psalms has been treated by A. Szörenyi in *Psalmen und Kult im Alten Testament*, Budapest, 1961, p. 358-386.

# Chapter VI

1. *Constitution on the Sacred Liturgy*, art. 7: "Christ is always present in His Church, especially in her liturgical celebrations. He is present in the sacrifice of the Mass, not only in the person of His minister, 'the same one now offering, through the ministry of priests, who formerly offered himself on the cross,' (Council of Trent) but especially under the Eucharistic species . . . . He is present in His word, since it is He Himself who speaks when the holy Scriptures are read in the church. He is present, finally, when the Church prays and sings, for He promised: 'Where two or three are gathered together for my sake, there am I in the midst of them' (Mt. 18:20)."

2. Instruction *Eucharisticum Mysterium*, art. 9. Cf. *Doc. Cath.*, vol. 64 (1967), col. 1099, quoting Paul VI, Encyclical *Mysterium Fidei* (our translation).

3. *Constitution on the Sacred Liturgy*, art. 33.

4. *Ibid.*

5. *Ibid.*

6. A procession is considered "true" only if it is liturgically useful, i.e., if the community must change from one place to another. Such is the case in the celebration of the Paschal Vigil; the congregation first gathers outside the Church for the blessing of the new fire; then in the procession they proceed inside, following Christ, symbolized by the light of the Paschal Candle.

7. *Homilia V, De Studio Praesentium*, 2; PG 63, 486-487 (our translation).

8. C. Rozier, *Eglise qui chante*, 79-80 (1967), p. 27 (our translation).

9. Here is the text of the psalm: "If I were to count your thoughts (Lord), they would outnumber the sands! *Were I to reach the end of them, I should still be with you.*"

10. See J. A. Jungmann, *op. cit.*, 20, vol. 2, p. 84.

11. *Ibid.*, p. 74-75.

12. This is the main criticism against the *Graduale simplex in usum minorum ecclesiarum* (Vatican, 1967), which is of some help to "small"

churches but which equalizes every chant in the Mass. If you look at the ancient liturgies, you will see that tradition did not accord such an importance to the verses of the psalm in the Entrance Song. Cf. *Eglise qui chante*, p. 71-72; *Les chants processionnaux*, p. 16-18.

13. P. Salmon, *La Prière des heures* in A. G. Martimort, *L'Eglise en prière* (3rd edition), p. 848.

14. "To glorify your birth we offer you this tribute of praise." Hymn *Jesu Redemptor omnium*, Vespers for Christmas Day.

15. Cf. I Cor. 3:1-2.

16. Conservatories of music, throughout the world, use the same musical literature. A masterpiece of classical music no longer belongs to a particular ethnic background but is a part of the musical heritage of all mankind.

17. *Constitution on the Sacred Liturgy*, art. 40.

18. I Th. 5:19-21.

19. Instruction on *Music in the Liturgy*, art. 33. Cf. *Doc. Cath.*, vol. 64, col. 503.

20. Concerning this subject, see B. Huijbers, *Valeur et limite du Lied dans la Liturgie*, in *le Chant liturgique après Vatican II*, Collection "Kinnor," 6, p. 133-149.

21. D. Rimaud, *Le genre littéraire du tropaire* in *Eglise qui chante*, 71-72, p. 49 (our translation).

22. *Ibid.*, p. 46.

23. Lucien Deiss, *Biblical Hymns and Psalms*, vol. II, World Library Publications, Inc., Cincinnati, Ohio, 1970, p. 32.

24. "Die Last der drei Eroffnunsgesange," J. Wagner, in *Liturgisches Jahrbuch*, 1967, p. 44.

25. Instruction on *Music in the Liturgy*, art. 6. Cf. *Doc. Cath.*, vol. 64 (1967), col. 498.

26. Mt. 6: 7-8.

27. Chorale *Jesus Christus, unser Heiland*, text by M. Luther.

28. *Constitution on the Sacred Liturgy*, art. 7.

29. *Ritus servandus*, n. 42: "The deacon carries the book of Gospels to the altar and places it in the middle." P. Jounel notes "that it is preferable to foresee the use of two separate books for the Epistle and Gospel. In this case, conforming to the rubrics in the *Ordo*, the book of Gospels is placed on the altar at the end of the entrance procession and stays there until the deacon goes up to take it for the proclamation of the Gospel." In *Les Rites de la messe en 1965*, Desclée, 1965, p. 76-77 (our translation). Also, the General Instruction to the 1969 *Order of Mass* states: "The gospel book, distinct from the other book of readings, may be placed on the altar . . . . "

30. Instruction *De cultu Mysterii Eucharistici*, art. 24. *Doc. Cath.*, vol. 64, col. 1105.

31. *Constitution on the Sacred Liturgy*, art. 33.

32. Missals of Bobbio (10th and 11th centuries). Quoted by J. A. Jungmann, *Missarum Solemnia*, vol. 2, col. "Théologie," n. 20, p. 225.

33. The *Ritus servandus* of 1965, n. 42, says: "The deacon takes the book on the altar and, preceded by the thurifer and two acolytes carrying lighted candles, moves over to the pulpit." Usually, the congregation is standing throughout this procession. See also the General Instruction to the 1969 *Order of Mass*, no. 131: "If the Gospel book is on the altar, he (the deacon) takes it and goes to the lectern . . . ."

34. Cf. P. Evdokimus, *La Prière de l'Eglise d'Orient*, Ed. Salvator, 1966, p. 113.

35. After describing the procession from the altar to the pulpit, as is done in Solemn Masses (n. 42), the *Ritus servandus* of 1965, n. 45, foresees the proclamation of the Gospel at a Mass with the people and writes: "While the Alleluia is sung or read with its verse, or toward the end of any other songs that may follow the epistle, the celebrant will bow deeply toward the altar and say: *"Munda cor meum, Iube Domine* and *Dominus sit in corde meo;* and then turn to the pulpit or lectern to sing or read the Gospel." (our translation)

36. Tob. 13:17.

37. *Epistola* 77. PL 22,697.

38. An atmosphere of folklore completely encompassed the period from Shrove Tuesday to Holy Saturday. In the Middle Ages, on the Saturday before Septuagesima Sunday, the Alleluia was buried amidst great pomp, candles, incense, holy water, and lamentations around a catafalque (according to the *Ordo* from the church in Toul, in the fifteenth century; cf. J. Brinktrine, *Die Heilige Messe*, 1950, 3rd edition, p. 103-104). These were pious and inoffensive, yet futile actions which, if not edifying, were at least enjoyable to our ancestors in the faith, but for which modern man has neither the time nor inclination.

Another example of rubrical chicanery involves the replacement of the Alleluia by some equivalent formula and is found in the Roman breviary in the antiphon for matins on Sunday: from the second Sunday after Pentecost until September 30th the following antiphon is to be said: "The Lord who made us, Come, let us adore" but from October 1st to November 26th is said: "Let us adore the Lord for it is He who made us." Have you ever heard of a man asking his children to say, "Father, good morning" up to October 1st, and afterwards, until November 26th, to say, "Good morning, Father"?

39. *Ennarratio in Ps. 32:8*. PL 36,283 (our translation).

40. "Sonus quidam est laetitiae sine verbis." *Ennarratio in Ps. 99:4.* PL 37,1272.

41. P. Jounel, *Les rites de la messe, op. cit.,* p. 92 (our translation).

42. Lucien Deiss, *Biblical Hymns and Psalms, op. cit.,* vol. I, p. 98.

43. *Ibid.*, p. 96.

44. Here are a few other possibilities: "Wisdom Has Built Herself a House," *Biblical Hymns and Psalms, op. cit.*, vol. II, p. 14; use antiphon, verse 1, and antiphon. "Lord, in Your Tenderness," *Biblical Hymns and Psalms, op. cit.*, vol. II, p. 58; use antiphon, verse 1, and antiphon.

45. G. Khouri-Sarkis, *Le propre de la messe syrienne*, in *l'Orient chrétien*, 1956, p. 453-454. Quoted by G. Stephani in *Eglise qui chante*, 71-72, p. 26-27 (our translation).

46. *Constitutions Apostoliques*, VIII, 13 (our translation).

47. Cf. J. A. Jungmann, *op. cit.*, vol. 3, p. 306.

48. In *Kirchenlied* (Christophorus-Verlag, 1948), p. 64. Here is the translation of the canticle: At the Last Supper, the night before he died, Jesus took bread and wine, and giving thanks he said, "Take, drink, for this is my body and blood . . . . Never forget what my love has done."

49. A paraphrase of Psalm 46, based upon the *Eine feste Burg ist unser Gott*, of Martin Luther.

50. *Catéchèses mystagogiques*, V. 20. See *Cyrille de Jérusalem, Catéchèses mystagogiques*, col. "Sources chrétiennes," 126, p. 168-170.

51. Cf. Brightmann, *Liturgies, Eastern and Western, op. cit.*, vol. 1, p. 449-450.

52. *Des Mystères*, 58. Cf. Ambroise de Milan, *Des Sacraments et Des Mystères*, col. "Sources chrétiennes," 25, p. 191.

53. *Sermon 225*, 4. PL 38,1098.

54. *Commentaire d'Isaie*, II, 5, 20. PL 24,86D.

55. *Commentaire du Psaume* 144, 1. PG 55, 464.

56. For example, verses 6a-8 of Psalm 149 should not be used under any circumstances; they are in no way Christ-oriented.

57. Cf. A. Chavasse, in A. G. Martimort, *L'Eglise en Prière*, 3rd edition, p. 724.

58. Sometimes it is an exact resume of the Gospel. Thus, the antiphon for the second Sunday after the Epihany is given as follows: "The Lord said, 'Fill the jars with water and take them to the chief steward.' When the chief steward had tasted the water after it had become wine, he said to the bridegroom, 'You have kept the good wine until now.' This first miracle Jesus worked in the presence of his disciples." Cf. M. Ph. Schuermans, *Parole de Dieu et Rite Sacramentel*, col. "Tradition et Renouveau," 1, Lumen Vitale, 1963.

59. *Constitution on the Sacred Liturgy*, art. 56.

60. Mt. 26:28; Mark 14:24; Luke 22:20; 1 Cor. 11:25.

# Chapter VII

1. There is a brief historical account of the General Intercessions in *De oratione communi seu fidelium (Consilium ad exsequendam Constitutionem de S. Liturgia)*, Vatican, 1966, p. 163-169.

2. Lucien Deiss, *Early Sources of the Liturgy*, Alba House, Staten Island, New York, 1967, p. 14-15.

3. *Lettre aux Corinthiens*, 59 (our translation). Cf. L. Deiss, *Les Pères Apostoliques*, col. "Vivante Tradition," 1, p. 32.

4. *Apologie I*, 67.

5. H. Pétré, *Ethérie, Journal de voyage*, col. "Sources chrétiennes," n. 21, Paris, 1948, p. 191-192.

6. *Constitutions Apostoliques*, VIII, 6, 3-9.

7. See, for example, Pope Felix III (483-492), Letter 7: PL 58, 925.

8. Ex. 34:6. In these quotations, *hesed* is usually translated as *mercy*.

9. Cf. Jr. 31:3.

10. 1 John 4:8 and 16.

11. God justifies us not from our works, but according to his mercy, manifested in Jesus Christ — Titus 3:5.

12. Mt. 9:27.

13. Mark 10:47-48, Mt. 20:31, Luke 18:39.

14. Mt. 15:22.

15. Luke 1:58.

16. 1 Cor. 11:26 and 2 Tim. 1:18.

17. Eph. 2:4 and 1 Peter 2:10.

18. Eph. 1:12.

19. Jan Vermulst, in the *People's Mass Book*, World Library Publications, Inc., Cincinnati, Ohio, 1970, p. 77.

20. See G. Stefani, *L'acclamation de tout un peuple*, coll. "Kinnor," Paris, 1967, p. 68.

21. *Constitution on the Sacred Liturgy*, art. 53.

22. Instruction *Inter Oecumenici*, art. 56. Cf. *Doc. Cath.*, vol. 61 (1965), col. 1369.

23. *De oratione communi seu fidelium, Consilium ad exsequendam Constitutionem de Sacra Liturgia*, Vatican City, new edition dated April 17, 1966. The council proposes practical directives (Chapter I), fifty-four examples of common prayer (Chapter II), an appendix, and a brief historical analysis. The *Doc. Cath.*, vol. 62 (1965), col. 593-602, gives the translation of these practical directives and historical notes, according to the first edition, published January 13, 1965.

24. Ne. 8:8.

25. Luke 4:21-22.

26. Cf. Strack-Billerbeck, *Kommentar zum Neuen Testament aus Talmud und Midrasch*, ed. Beck, vol. 4, Munich, 1961, p. 173.

27. *De oratione communi seu fidelium*, art. 2, *op. cit.*, p. 7. Cf. *Doc. Cath.*, vol. 62 (1965), col. 593.

28. *Ibid.*, art. 12b, p. 10. Cf. *Doc. Cath., ibid*, col. 595.

29. C. Ferrière, *La Prière universelle* in *Eglise qui chante*, 65 (1965), p. 15 (our translation).

30. Acts 16:14.

31. *Op. cit.*, p. 17.

32. *Op. cit.*, p. 9. Cf. *Doc. Cath.*, vol. 62 (1965), col. 594.

33. *Op. cit.*, p. 33.

34. *Op. cit.*, p. 47.

35. *Op. cit.*, p. 63.

36. *Op. cit.*, p. 9-10. Cf. *Doc. Cath.*, vol. 62 (1965), col. 595.

37. *Op. cit.*, formula 1 and 18, p. 17 and p. 63.

38. *Op. cit.*, formula 1, p. 17.

39. *Op. cit.*, p. 19.

40. We can think of certain German dioceses which have their "Furbitten" for Masses and "Andachten." Some of these formularies are very rich. Among the most recent, we quote J. Gulden, W. Muschik, F. Kolbe, *Furbitten, Gebetseinladung,* Christophorus Verlag (3rd edition, 1965). Without corresponding to the schema of the four categories, these prayers are of great pastoral value.

Let us mention further the *Formules de prière universelle* (1966) whose text is approved by the bishops of France, Luxembourg, R.C.A., Senegal; *Oracion de les fieles* (1968), official text of the Spanish episcopate; and *Das Gebet der Glaubigen,* edited in Switzerland by G. Holzherr. These editions are witness to the present interest in the General Intercessions. They will be of the greatest interest for communities in that they do not exhaust their sources of inspiration, but promote research and creativity. They can also help communities who are unable to undertake the creative effort.

41. *De oratione communi seu fidelium,* art. 15, *op. cit.,* p. 11. Cf. *Doc. Cath.*, vol. 62 (1965), col. 596.

42. *Op. cit.*, art. 10, p. 10. Cf. *Doc. Cath., ibid.,* col. 595.

43. *Op. cit.*, p. 13.

44. The directive speaks of a "participation under the form of silent prayer, by observing a suitable pause"; it also mentions the pastoral value: "This participation has been proven in the venerable and old Roman practice of solemn prayers. While they may seem dormant, it can offer an extraordinary opportunity for prayer," art. 12, *op. cit.,* p. 10. Cf. *Doc. Cath.*, vol. 62 (1965), col. 596.

45. *Op. cit.*, art. 11, p. 10. Cf. *Doc. Cath., ibid.,* col. 595.

46. *Op. cit.*, art. 14, p. 11.

47. Instruction *Inter Oecumenici,* art. 56. Cf. *Doc Cath.*, vol. 61 (1964), col. 1369.

48. *Directives pratiques de la Commission Episcopale de la Liturgie* (Paris, 1964), art. 73 (our translation). Cf. *La réforme liturgique* (Ed. du Centurion, Paris, 1964), p. 116.

49. *De oratione communi seu fidelium,* art. 8, *op. cit.,* p. 9. Cf. *Doc. Cath.,* vol. 62 (1965), col. 594.

50. *Ibid.*

51. In these recitatives, formula A is repeated as many times as necessary (it is omitted when the intention has only two phrases); formulas B and C are used for the next-to-last and last phrase of the intention.

52. *Directives pratiques de la Commission Episcopale de la Liturgie, op. cit.,* art. 73.

53. *De oratione communi seu fidelium,* art. 7 and 14, *op. cit.,* p. 9-10. Cf. *Doc. Cath.,* vol. 62 (1965), col. 594 and 596.

54. Instruction *Inter Oecumenici,* art. 56. Cf. *Doc. Cath.,* vol. 61 (1964), col. 1369. *De oratione communi seu fidelium,* art. 8, *op. cit.,* p. 9. Cf. *Doc. Cath., ibid.,* col. 594.

55. *De oratione communi seu fidelium,* art. 13, *op. cit.,* p. 13. Cf. *Doc. Cath., ibid.,* col. 594 and 596.

56. See the articles of J. Jeremias in *Theologisches Wörterbuch zum Neuen Testament,* "amnos," vol. 1, p. 343-344, and "pais theou," vol. 5, p. 698-713, and the complimentary remarks of F. M. Braun in *Jean le Théologien,* Coll. "Etudes Bibliques," vol. 2 (1964), p. 69-86 and vol. 3 (1966), p. 160-165. The exegetes are not unanimous in the interpretation of the image.

57. See L. Deiss, *Synopse,* Desclée de Brouwer, vol. 1, p. 181-182.

58. As a rule, however, in the bibical language of the Septuagint, the difference between *amnos* and *arnion* was hardly noticed. See J. Jeremias, *Theologisches Wörterbuch zum Neuen Testament,* art. "arnion," vol. 1, p. 344.

59. *Liber Pontificalis,* Ed. Duchesne, vol. 1, p. 376.

60. Cf. M. Andrieu, *Les Ordines romani du haut moyen âge,* vol. 2 (Louvain, 1948), p. 100.

61. Cf. Jer. 16:7; Lam. 4:4.

62. Art. 45. Cf. P. Jounel, *La concélébration,* Desclée et Cie, 1966, p. 141.

63. "This is my body given for you" — Luke 22:19 and 1 Cor. 11:24; "The blood shed for many" — Mt. 26:28 and Mark 14:24; "shed for you" — Luke 22:20.

64. Cf. F. E. Brightman, *Liturgies, Eastern and Western, op. cit.,* vol. 1, p. 97.

65. *Ibid.,* p. 99.

66. Instruction on *Music in the Liturgy*, March 5, 1967, art. 34. Cf. *Doc. Cath.*, vol. 64 (1967), col. 504.

## Chapter VIII

1. We are using here the points developed in *Célébrer l'Office divin,* col. "Kinnor," 1967, p. 169-183.

On the first Christian hymns, see J. Quasten, *Initiation aux Pères de l'Eglise,* vol. 1, 1955, pp. 178-182. On their history in the liturgy, see S. Coubin, *L'Eglise à la conquête de sa musique,* Gallimard, 1960, p. 126-149. The texts of early Christian hymns will be found in L. Deiss, *Hymnes et Prières des premiers siècles,* col. "Vivante Tradition," vol. 2.

2. *The Hours of the Divine Office in English and Latin,* vol. 1, The Liturgical Press, Collegeville, Minnesota, 1963, p. 1186.

3. *Histoire Ecclésiastique,* V, 28, 5 (our translation). Cf. G. Brady, *Eusèbe de Césarée, Histoire Ecclésiastique,* col. "Sources chrétiennes," vol. 41, p. 75.

4. Through the words of Elizabeth, Scripture calls Mary "Mother of the Lord" in Luke 1:43: "Why is it that the mother of my Lord should come to me?"

5. *The Hours of the Divine Office,* vol. I, *op. cit.,* p. 975.

6. In the Bible, poetry is a superior form for expressing history. See G. Von Rad, *Théologie de l'Ancien Testament,* vol. 1, Labor et fides, Geneva, p. 101-102.

7. J. A. Jungmann, *Missarum Solemnia,* vol. 2, *op. cit.,* p. 104-105 (our translation).

8. Greek text in F. X. Funk, *Didascalia et Constitutiones Apostolorum,* vol. 1, p. 454-456.

9. On the considerable influence of the Arian and anti-Arian struggles inside the liturgy, see J. A. Jungmann, *Tradition liturgique et problèmes actuels de pastorale,* LePuy, 1962, p. 15-86.

10. An inventory of early biblical and patristic hymns will be found in L. Deiss, *Hymnes et Prières des premiers siècles,* col. "Vivante Tradition," 2, Paris, 1963.

11. *De Virginitate,* 20; PG 28, 276.

12. Translated from *Constitutions Apostoliques,* VIII, 12, 12-13.

13. As opposed to the small doxology ("Glory to the Father . . .") which is said at the end of the psalms.

14. In isosyllabism, each verse, from one stanza to the next, has the same number of syllables. In isorhythm, the word accents of the text are always in the same place for each verse in every stanza. Thanks to isosyllabism, the same melody is valid for each stanza; thanks to isorhythm, the strong beats of the melody can regularly coincide with the accents of the text. The melodic rhythm will then be perfectly matched to the verbal rhythm.

15. T. Leonard, *L'Eucharistie en français* in *Etudes,* 1968, p. 137-138 (our translation).

16. F. Cabrol, *Le Livre de la prière antique,* Paris, 1900, p. 150 and 156.

17. D'Asterios (410 A.D.) bishop of Amassée dans le Pont, *Homélie 19, sur le Psaume 5;* PG 40,436 C. See L. Deiss, *Hymnes et Prières des premières siècles,* col. "Vivante Tradition," vol. 2, p. 132-133.

18. "He Never Said a Mumbalin' Word," *People's Mass Book,* loose-leaf edition, World Library Publications, Inc., Cincinnati, Ohio, 1968, No. D-8.

19. Hymn taken from *Liturgische gezangen in het Nederlands,* cited in *Musique sacrée et langues modernes,* col. "Kinnor," 4, p. 101.

20. We noted earlier that the Syrian rites introduce a song "after the Gospel" between the Liturgy of the Word and the Eucharistic liturgy. Psychologically, this song is closer to the Eucharistic rite than the Gospel.

21. 2 Cor. 1:20.

22. Cf. 1 Cor. 3:2. "I fed you with milk, not with solid food, for you were not yet ready for it."

23. For example, the Mass *Salve Sancta Parens.*

24. Art. 15. Cf. *Doc. Cath.,* vol. 64 (1967), col. 891.

25. Instruction on *Music in the Liturgy,* art. 36. Cf. *Doc. Cath.,* vol. 64 (1967), col. 504.

26. Such silence would be more suitable for penitential services.

27. A broad paraphrase of the *Te Deum* ("Great God, we praise you").

28. Paraphrase of Psalm 46(45) according to Martin Luther ("Eine feste Burg ist unser Gott").

29. Our preference would be to use the first formula for Sunday Masses and the second for Masses during the week.

## Chapter IX

1. Timothy himself had monophysitic leanings. Jungmann (*op. cit.,* vol. 2, p. 240) writes concerning the subject: "He would have acted thus to blame his Catholic predecessor and to display his own zeal for orthodoxy." (our translation)

2. Instruction on *Music in the Liturgy,* art. 30. Cf. *Doc. Cath.,* vol. 64 (1967), col. 503.

3. H. Hucke (*Eglise qui chante,* 62-63, p. 51) states that the melody of the Credo in the Vatican edition is without doubt closely akin to an ancient melody from the popular ballad "Chevalier Barbe Bleue" once sung throughout Europe. This shows that the Church likes to utilize popular melodies for the people's singing.

4. During a celebration in the cathedral of Chartres, attended by some 8000 students, the bishop who presided at the concelebrated Mass alternated the recitation of the Credo with the entire congregation. This "face to face" proclamation of faith was of incomparably greater impact than if it had been sung.

5. In the tenth century, the Credo was sometimes sung by the clergy alone, which seemed — so they thought — all the more natural to take the place of the sermon. Cf. J. A. Jungmann, *Missarum Solemnia, op. cit.,* vol. 2, p. 246.

6. *Lettre aux Symriotes,* 1. Cf. L. Deiss, *Les Pères Apostoliques,* col. "Vivante Tradition," 1, p. 68-69.

7. *Contre les hérésies,* III, 4, 1-2. Cf. L. Deiss, *Printemps de la théologie,* col. "Vivante Tradition," vol. 4, p. 143.

8. Tradition contains a number of ancient creeds such as those of Eusebeus of Cesarea (circa 325; cf. Denzinger-Schönmerzer, *Enchiridion Symbolorum,* 32nd edition, quoted in the abridged version: D.S. 40), those of Cyril of Jerusalem (circa 348; D.S. 41), those of Epiphanus (D.S. 42-43), of Pseudo-Athanasius (D.S. 46-47), of the Armenian Church (D.S. 48-49), the baptismal creed of Antioch (D.S. 50), that of Theodore de Mapsueste (D.S. 51), and of Macarius the Great (D.S. 55), which does not include the creeds contained in the liturgical books such as the *Gelasian Sacramentarium* (D.S. 36), the *Apostolic Constitutions* (D.S. 60), the Testament of Our Lord, Jesus Christ (D.S. 61), the Constitutions of the Egyptian Church (D.S. 62-63), the Canons of Hippolytus (D.S. 64). There is, then, an abundance of professions of faith. A few others are also noteworthy and should not be forgotten.

9. "It is He Himself who speaks while the holy Scriptures are read in the Church." *Constitution on the Sacred Liturgy,* art. 7.

10. St. Thomas, *Summa Theologica,* IIa-IIae, I, 2, 2m: "Actus credentis non terminatur ad enuntiabile, sed ad rem."

11. John 6:47.

# Chapter X

1. We are using here some points developed in *Recitatifs pour la Proclamation de la Parole de Dieu et Psalmodies,* Edition du Levain, Paris, 1964. Spanish translation: *Recitativos, Salmodias,* Ed. Berit, 1965.

2. J. A. Jungmann, *Missarum Solemnia, op. cit.,* vol. 2, p. 174 (our translation).

3. See E. Gerson-Kiwi, art. "Musique" in *Dictionnaire de la Bible Supplément,* vol. 5, col. 1436.

4. Strack-Billerbeck, *Kommentar zum Neuen Testament aus Talmud und Mishna,* vol. 4, part I, 1961, p. 394 and 398. R. Aquiva taught: "sing, constantly sing," in the sense of "*constantly study* by singing the text of the Bible."

5. *Le Protreptique*, XII, 119. Cf. Mondesert, *Clément d'Alexandrie, Le Protreptique*, col. "Sources Chrétiennes," 2, p. 189 (our translation).

6. Gospel from the Mass of Christmas Day.

7. Epistle from Palm Sunday.

8. Epistle from the Epiphany.

9. Gospel from the Feast of All Saints.

10. See "Glory and Praise to You," L. Deiss, *Biblical Hymns and Psalms, op. cit.,* vol. I, p. 66.

11. See "Keep in Mind," *Biblical Hymns and Psalms, ibid.,* p. 28.

12. This hymn takes its inspiration from the song of the Servant of Yahweh according to Isaiah 53 (see especially verses 4, 5, 9 and 11-12) and contemplates Jesus as the model of the faithful servant persecuted unjustly. See M. E. Boismard, *Quatre hymnes baptismales dans la première Epître de Pierre*, col. "Lectro divina," 30, p. 111-132.

13. See L. Deiss, *Synopse*, Desclée de Brouwer, vol. 2, 1963, p. 34.

14. Mt. 6:25-34. See Luke 12:22-31.

15. S. Corbin, *L'Eglise á la conquête de sa musique, op. cit.,* p. 61.

16. Recitatif 1 in *Recitatifs pour la proclamation de la Parole de Dieu, op. cit.,* p. 20.

17. *Liber Usualis*, no. 780, p. 106.

18. Recitatif II in *Recitatifs pour la proclamation de la Parole de Dieu, op. cit.,* p. 22.

19. Phil. 2:5-11. In *Recitatifs pour la proclamation de la Parole de Dieu, op. cit.,* p. 22-25.

20. *Le Recitatif liturgique en langue moderne* in *Musique et langue moderne,* col. "Kinnor," 4, p. 61.

21. A prime example of an ornate recitative is "A Child Is Born," L. Deiss, *Biblical Hymns and Psalms, op. cit.,* vol. I, p. 14; and "We Give You Thanks, We Worship You," vol. II, p. 38.

22. "Tessitura" is: 1) the range of notes forming the texture of the melody; 2) the group of notes best suited for the voice.

23. An example of an old song using this method of singing each stanza on a higher tone is "Un soir me promenant dans mon jardin à l'ombre," found in H. Davenson, *Le Livre des chansons ou Introduction à la connaissance de la chanson populaire française,* Edition de la Baconnière, Neuchatel, 1946, p. 384-386.

24. *Revue de musicologie,* 47 (1961), p. 11 (our translation).

## Chapter XI

1. For the history of the organ in France, see N. Drefourcq, *Esquisse d'une histoire de l'orgue en France,* Paris, 1935. On the organ in Catholic liturgy, see G. Nassoy, *Le guide liturgique de l'organiste,* col. "Kinnor," Paris, 1965.

2. Cf. A. Schweitzer, *J. S. Bach*, p. 152-153 (our translation).

3. Art. 15 and 18. Cf. *La Liturgie, op. cit.*, p. 182.

4. Art. 8.

5. Art. 58. Along with the organ, Pius XII mentions the violin and other such stringed instruments for which he had a predilection.

6. *Constitution on the Sacred Liturgy*, art. 120.

7. *Ibid.*

8. The true criticism that can be leveled here is this: the authorities are not always perfectly aware of the community's feelings because of a lack of serious communication and real contact. Therefore, they run the risk of confusing their own feelings and personal reactions with the feelings and reactions of the congregation and, under the pretext of protecting the peace of liturgical prayer, they protect the tranquility of their own habits. Such inconveniences can be avoided, or at least substantially reduced, by establishing meaningful dialogue from top to bottom.

9. Pius XI in *Divini Cultus*, art. 7, December 20, 1928.

10. Pius XII in *Musicae Sacrae Disciplina*, art. 59, December 25, 1955. Cf. *Doc. Cath.*, vol. 53 (1956), col. 82.

11. Instruction on *Music in the Liturgy*, art. 63, March 5, 1967. Cf. *Doc. Cath.*, vol. 64 (1967), col. 510.

12. *Ibid.*, art. 64-65. Cf. *Doc. Cath.*, vol. 64 (1967), col. 510.

13. See J. Bonfils, *Note Historique sur le rôle de l'orgue dans la liturgie catholique* in *Eglise qui chante*, 16 (1959), p. 7-8.

14. Instruction on *Music in the Liturgy*, art. 65.

15. *Ibid.*, art. 66. Cf. *Doc. Cath.*, vol. 64 (1967), col. 510.

16. *Ibid.*, art. 9. Cf. *Doc. Cath., ibid.*, col. 498.

17. *Pastoral Constitution on the Church in the Modern World*, art. 62.

18. C. Mohrmann, *Le latin liturgique* in *L'Ordinaire de la messe*, col. "Etudes Liturgiques," 1953, p. 29.

19. Instruction on *Music in the Liturgy*, art. 62, reaffirming the *Constitution on the Sacred Liturgy*, art. 120.

## Chapter XII

1. *Constitution on the Sacred Liturgy*, art. 116. Cf. Instruction of March 5, 1967, art. 50: "Gregorian chant, as proper to the Roman liturgy, should be given pride of place, other things being equal."

2. *Ibid.*, art. 36.

3. *Ibid.*, art. 14.

4. *Ibid.*, art. 36 and 54.

5. *Ibid.*, art. 36.

6. *Ibid.*, art. 116.

7. Instruction on *Music in the Liturgy,* art. 50. Cf. *Doc. Cath.,* vol. 64 (1967), col. 507.

8. *Ibid.,* art. 53.

9. It is such virtuosity that Leo XIII speaks when he writes, "Gregorian melodies were composed with perfect taste and ability to clarify the meaning of the words. When artfully executed, it can easily inspire the souls of those who hear it." Letter *Nos Quidem* of May 17, 1901. Cf. *La Liturgie, op. cit.,* p. 151.

10. Instruction on *Music in the Liturgy,* art. 48.

11. We should not forget that singing is not the only way to unify the community, and that communion, i.e., the Eucharistic Bread, is the sign *par excellence* of that unity.

12. Art. 3.

13. Here are the texts:

The Encylical *Divini Cultus* of Pius XI, art. IV, December 20, 1928: " . . . all those who have the obligation of choir ought at least to know Gregorian chant well. And by Gregorian chant, whose usage is prescribed in all the churches of whatever order, We mean that form which, restored from ancient manuscripts, has been put forth by the Church in an authentic edition published by the Vatican Press."

The Encyclical *Mediator Dei* of Pius XII, art. 191, December 20, 1947: "Gregorian chant, which the Roman Church considers her own as handed down from antiquity and kept under her close tutelage, is proposed to the faithful as belonging to them also. In certain parts of the Liturgy the Church definitely prescribes it . . . ."

The Encyclical *Musicae Sacrae Disciplina* of Pius XII, art. 42 and 45, December 25, 1955: "The Gregorian chant which has been used in the Church over the course of so many centuries, and which may be called, as it were, its patrimony, is gloriously outstanding for this holiness. . . . And if in Catholic churches throughout the entire world Gregorian chant sounds forth without corruption or diminution, the chant itself, like the sacred Roman liturgy, will have a characteristic of universality, so that the faithful, wherever they may be, will hear music that is familiar to them and a part of their own home."

The Instruction on *Sacred Music and the Sacred Liturgy,* art. 16, September 3, 1958: "*Gregorian chant* is the sacred chant, proper and principal of the Roman Church. Therefore, not only can it be used in all liturgical actions, but unless there are mitigating circumstances, it is preferable to use it instead of other kinds of sacred music."

14. It is in reference to spiritual values and their preservation that the *Constitution on the Sacred Liturgy,* art. 114, can state: "The treasure of sacred music is to be preserved and fostered with very great care."

15. D. Vanbergen, *"La crise de la liturgie: vers un diagnostic,"* in *Paroisse et Liturgie,* 1967, p. 470.

16. *Constitution on the Church in the Modern World,* art. 58.

# INDEX

Date